Fan V[...]

A Study of Form, Technology, and Meaning

Walter C. Leedy, Jr.

Arts + Architecture Press
Santa Monica, California

Published in the United States by
Arts + Architecture Press
1119 Colorado Avenue
Santa Monica, California 90401

Published in England by
Scolar Press
90/91 Great Russell Street
London, WC1B 3PY

Library of Congress Catalogue Card Number 79-56250
ISBN 0-931228-03-4

Cataloging in Publication Data
Leedy, Walter C. Jr.
Fan vaulting: a study of form, technology, and meaning
Includes index and bibliography
1. Architecture–Medieval
2. Architecture–English Gothic
I. Title

Designed by Joe Molloy, Los Angeles, California.
Illustrations printed by Scott & Scott, Santa Monica, California.
Text printed by Publishers Press, Salt Lake City, Utah.
Bound by Mountain States Bindery, Salt Lake City, Utah.

To my
mother
and
father

Acknowledgements

I wish to acknowledge my indebtedness to all the individuals who facilitated my inspection of the monuments, and to the following architects or engineers who shared with me their technical knowledge of vault construction: the late G. G. Pace, B. J. Ashwell, C. Calladine, S. E. Dykes Bower, Dr. John Harvey, and Professor J. Heyman. L. S. Colchester of Wells Cathedral and the late J. Saltmarsh of King's College, Cambridge, generously shared their knowledge. Dr. Peter Kidson of the University of London made critical judgements of my work as presented for a Ph.D. thesis in 1972. Professor Stephen Murray commented on the manuscript in its present form. The Fellows of Peterhouse, Cambridge University, invited me to spend summers of 1974, 1975, and 1977 there, thus affording me time for research and thought. Mr. Colchester, along with my friends, Robert H. Anthony, Professor Alfred Moir, Esther McCoy, Paul Masson, Neil and Nancy Johnson, gave freely of their time to drive me to inspect many of the monuments.

The following institutions, among others, were generous in putting their collections at my disposal: the Public Records Office, the National Monuments Record, the British Museum, the Cambridge University Library, Archives of St. George's Chapel, Windsor and King's College, Cambridge, the Gloucester Public Library, the Taunton Public Library, The Corinium Museum, Cirencester, and especially the library of the Society of Antiquaries, London.

Finally, it is a pleasure to acknowledge the support for the work that has been provided through grants from the Samuel H. Kress Foundation and the Graduate College of the Cleveland State University. These grants enabled me to inspect ninety-nine percent of the fan vaults known to me.

Contents

1

Introduction

Throughout the continent of Europe, the Late Gothic period witnessed the development of elaborate stone vaulted ceilings. English masons abandoned quadripartite rib vaulting and developed new solutions to the structural and visual problems of how to span and articulate interior space. By the end of the fourteenth century, a new type of vaulting–known today as fan vaulting –appeared in England but not on the Continent.

Although technical terms were codified for individual components of a vault, a nomenclature did not evolve in medieval England that distinguished one type of vaulting from another.[1] However, fan vaulting was differentiated from other types of vaulting in the minds of the men who designed and commissioned them. Evidence for this can be found in an early sixteenth century contract for the construction of vaulting in King's College Chapel, Cambridge. There, a tierceron vault compared to a fan vault was ". . . to be made of more course work as apperith by a platte . . ." The difference between these vaults was based on visual appearance rather than on structural quality, for all the vaults were to be ". . . wele and workmanly wrought made and sett up after the best handelyng and fourme of good workmanship . . ."[2]

As seen by modern academic investigators and critics, fan vaults have the following specific interrelated visual and structural characteristics: (1) vaulting conoids of regular geometric form, (2) vertical ribs, each of consistent curvature and placement, (3) a distinct central spandrel panel, (4) ribs perpendicular to the vaulting surface, and (5) applied surface patterning.[3] While this definition helps to conceptualize and define what a fan vault is, the medieval mason was more interested in the image as a totality than in any of its specific parts. On occasion, he altered certain elements to accommodate the form for **2** use in specific contexts. For example, in the vaulting of King's College Chapel, Cambridge, the ribs are not spaced at equal angles apart, and in the Morton **3** Chapel at Bosbury, the ribs are not even of consistent curvature. Yet, the created image in both of these cases reads "fan vault." There can be no more precise definition for a fan vault.

If fan vaulting were solely a technological phenomenon, it would be possible to define it as a way of building. Most fan vaults are built of stone, but the manner in which the material is handled can vary. Some fan vaults are constructed totally of jointed masonry, some of ribs and panels, and others are a combination of ribs, panels, and jointed masonry. A few smaller fan vaults are suspended structures. Because there was no one way of building a fan vault, it was the final visual image of the fan vault that was of overriding importance and concern to the designer and patron, not its specific technical characteristics.

The aim of this study is to clarify the emergence and subsequent development of the new mode of building, and to ask what meaning, if any, fan vaults had to the men who commissioned and created them. Thereby, this study constitutes an inquiry into an important aspect of English architectural innovation in the Late Gothic period.

---

1. William Worcestre (circa 1480), however, used the term "fretted vault" with reference to the vaulting of St. Mary Redcliffe, Bristol. "Fretted" may refer to the foliated panels only and not the shape or kind of vault, for Worcestre also says "the west dore fretted yn the hede." See Robert Willis, *Architectural Nomenclature of the Middle Ages* (Cambridge: At the University Press, 1844), 42-43; James Dallaway, *Antiquities of Bristow* (Bristol: Mirror Office, 1834), 154, 157.
2. King's College Muniments, Printed in Robert Willis and John Clark, *The Architectural History of the University of Cambridge* (4 vols.; Cambridge: At the University Press, 1886), I, 608.
3. The term fan vault evolved in the nineteenth century, see the *Oxford English Dictionary.* By the mid-nineteenth century a precise definition was codified see Robert Willis, "On the Construction of the Vaults of the Middle Ages," *Transactions of the Royal Institute of British Architects,* I (1842). For an early twentieth century understanding of the fan vault see F. E. Howard, "Fan Vaults," *AJ,* LXVIII (1911), 2ff.

2

The Origins of Fan Vaulting

The most distinctive feature of the fan vault is its geometry. Francis Bond, and later F. E. Howard, noted that the monument to Hugh Lord Despencer in Tewkesbury Abbey, built shortly after 1350, has a canopy that is composed of conoidal forms.[1] Traces of color on the conoids indicate that a pattern of ribs had been painted on it. The idea of a regular stereometric form for a vault to which ribs were attached as surface ornament was not invented with fan vaulting, for this concept was employed in the Lady Chapel at Wells (ca. 1319),[2] and later in the chancel at Ottery St. Mary (ca. 1337).[3] However, the idea that a vaulting conoid was a ruled surface of rotation about a vertical axis, which was then articulated by ribs, was new to late medieval architecture. This differed from the traditional Gothic ribbed vault–a series of supports, or ribs, between which were placed small vaults with warped surfaces, or webs. Horizontal sections taken of most ribbed vaults are irregular in shape. Some even progress from triangular shapes at the bottom through trapezoids, to rectangles near the crown. Horizontal sections of tierceron and lierne vaults take on more complex shapes but still retain this distinct line-surface, rib-web, relationship. In contrast, all horizontal sections in a fan vault are always segments of circles, or a circular segment can be inscribed within them.

All the vertical ribs applied to a conoid that is a ruled surface of rotation will have the same curvature. By contrast, the wall and the transverse and diagonal ribs have different curvatures in a traditional pointed rib vault. Furthermore, in a French Gothic vault, the wall ribs were stilted to concentrate the vaulting thrusts on a narrow strip of wall.[4] When building a structure of great height, this solution had the advantage of transmitting and concentrating the vaulting thrusts as efficiently as possible at one point: the point at which the flying buttress could be placed to transfer it to the ground. This solution emphasized the vaulting ribs as a series of frames with infilling between them. Where great height and openness of the wall were not important design considerations, it was not structurally necessary to stilt the wall ribs, for the walls themselves could be thicker and used to absorb the thrusts. Therefore, when building a low, "heavy" structure, the curvature of the wall ribs was not as important a consideration as when building a high, "light" one. Consequently, in England where there was not the same striving for height and lightness as in France, all the ribs could approach the same curvature without endangering the stability of the structure. In doing so, the line of thrust would be dropped to such a level that flying buttresses were not a structural necessity, as in the nave of Sherborne Abbey. When wall ribs approach the same curvature as the others, the wall area above the vault inside the pockets increases. Since vaulting pockets usually contain rubble fill, the outward thrust of the vault is transferred in part from the shell through the rubble to the wall. In this English solution, vaulting thrusts are distributed across a greater section of wall.

Although the high vaults of Lincoln, Westminster Abbey, and Exeter follow French precedents, the tendency to make the wall ribs of the same curvature as the other ribs can be seen in the chapter house at Wells (1306),[5] the apse vault at Tewkesbury (ca. 1340),[6] and the north transept vault at **7** Gloucester (before 1377).[7] The West Country tendency to make all the ribs of the same curvature partly explains why conoids composed of ruled surfaces of rotation came into being, but the whole developmental process was more complex.

By the early fourteenth century the technique of laying a Gothic vault in England differed from that used in France and from general Continental **8** practices.[8] In most of France the stone coursing of the vault webs runs parallel to the vaulting ridges, forming right angles to the sides of the bay and acute angles with the diagonal ribs. Thus, the webs take on warped shapes which emphasize the conceptual difference between web and rib. In contrast, the **9** stone coursing joints in England form right angles with the diagonal ribs and acute angles with the ridge, transverse, and wall ribs. In plan, the coursing of an English quadripartite vault with ridge ribs can be conceptualized as a series of squares turned at forty-five degree angles to the main vaulting module. With the addition of tierceron ribs in the English vault, the plan of the stone jointing pattern approaches the form of concentric circular segments radiating out from the corners of the vaulting module. This way of coursing the stone must have led, in part, to the concept of the vault as being formed of a ruled surface of rotation. It is interesting to note that the keystone of the **10** Gloucester cloister fan vault–a huge square stone, eight-eight centimeters on a side–is placed at forty-five degree angles to the vaulting module, and it fits into the traditional English concept of stone jointing patterns. But the English method of coursing does not in itself account for the development of the fan vault.

1
5 The next major visual characteristic of the fan vault is the distinction made between the vaulting conoids and the flat central spandrel panel between them. This distinction, which is visually emphasized by a horizontal bounding rib at the top of the vaulting conoid, results from the fact that the conoids in fan vaults are ruled surfaces of rotation. Transverse and longitudinal ridges that are horizontal, or parallel to the ground, are easiest to build over a square

11 vaulting module, as in the Aerary porch, Windsor (1353).[9] Since the vertical ribs are not all of the same curvature, a flat central spandrel distinct from the vaulting conoids was not developed. The concept of a flat central spandrel panel may have evolved from a conjunction of the ideas that the vertical vault ribs should be of the same curvature, and that the ridges in both directions should be horizontal. Because a flat central spandrel panel can be most easily built over a square bay, it is plausible to hypothesize that the first fan vault was constructed over a square vaulting module. Vaulting conoids that are ruled surfaces of rotation about a vertical axis were combined with flat central

4 spandrel panels in the tomb canopy of Hugh Lord Despener. However, this canopy is non-structural. The problem of building a large vault in which intrados follows extrados raises a totally different set of technical considerations. Therefore, the tomb canopy should be understood as only a solution to the aesthetic problems.

The vaulting conoids and flat central spandrel panel in a fan vault are
12 distinctly structural, as well as visual elements.[10] If a fan vault conoid is to be in equilibrium, a compressive load must be present along its entire upper edge. When a relatively flat spandrel panel is wanted, this load is most easily provided by constructing the spandrel out of jointed masonry where the ribs and panels are carved together from the same piece of stone. The central spandrel panels of the cloister fan vault at Gloucester are cut from one piece of stone, and the same constructive pattern can be seen in the north porch

13 of St. John's, Cirencester. This technical solution diminishes the problem of buckling, and at the same time eliminates the complex jointing pattern that would have been necessary if the spandrel panels were constructed completely out of separate ribs and panels. It also efficiently provides the continual support necessary at the upper edge of the vaulting conoids, and the resulting vault is extremely stable. The employment of jointed masonry led to the use of the flat central spandrel panel–a crucial step for the development of the fan vault. In addition to the structural reasons, there was a more practical and pragmatic reason why jointed masonry was employed. This choice resulted from the decision to articulate the vaulting surface with cusped panels. It was easier to carve a panel with cusps out of one piece of stone than to construct it from several. Therefore, the desire for a high level of surface articulation probably influenced the development of technology: jointed masonry was a necessary precondition for the development of the fan vault.

Jointed masonry had earlier been used in canopies for niches and tombs,
14 as in the tomb of Bishop William de Marchia (d. 1302) at Wells.[11] Here again it would be an oversimplification to state that fan vaulting developed directly from this building practice.

15 The English practice of joining rib and web differed from the technique used in France, where it was common practice to lay the web courses right on top of the ribs.[12] In England, channels were cut into the upper edges of the ribs; the ribs were rebated, to receive the web panels.[13] Even in late Gothic vaults on the Continent, ribs sometimes were not rebated.[14] This practice in England led not only to the English technique of web coursing as described above, but more importantly, to the conceptual unification of rib and panel. Also, the panels became flat slabs of stone between rebated ribs in early lierne and tierceron vaults of short span.[15] From this point only one more step had to be taken: to cut the rib and adjoining panel from the same piece of stone. This happened in early fourteenth century vaults of long span in the West Country, such as in the vaults of the chancel and north transept of Gloucester. The new technique greatly increased vaulting rigidity and led to reduced panel thickness, which resulted in lighter vaults. Naturally enough, the technique was dependent on the availability of larger and better-worked stones from the quarry.[16] The tendency to make vaults lighter is also apparent in the construction of late Gothic continental vaults. Economic factors demanded that both materials and labor be used more efficiently.

16   Another notable feature of the fan vault is the relationship of the rib to the surface of the vault: the main axes of the ribs are always perpendicular to the surface of the vault, not to the floor.[17] The employment of more ribs in lierne and net vaults resulted in the multiplication of rib intersections on the surface of the vault. Perfect joints at rib intersections could only be obtained if the axes of all the intersecting ribs were perpendicular to the vaulting surface. This point is crucial because bosses–which could have masked imperfect intersections–were generally not employed. The first known fan vaults were built of jointed masonry, so it follows that the technique itself led to making the ribs square to the vaulting surface since they were carved directly out of it. This innovative rib-surface relationship, which emphasizes the form of the vaulting conoids instead of their linear patterning, had one major aesthetic consequence: it imparted to the fan vault conoids the quality of volumes in space.

   It is impossible to say with certainty where this rib-surface relationship first evolved in England. Extant archaeological evidence supports the theory that the use of ribs with axes perpendicular to the vaulting surface–at least in structural vaults–was an innovation which originated in the West Country of England. In fact, it may be an innovation of the so-called "Bristol School"; for it was used in the choir of St. Augustine's (the cathedral), Bristol, and in

17 the chancel of Wells Cathedral in the early years of the fourteenth century.[18]

   The ribs of the choir vault of St. Augustine's, Bristol, though still having bosses at their intersections, followed the main vaulting surface. This, along with the presence of a series of foiled figures and irregular lozenges instead of a longitudinal ridge rib, anticipated the spatial effects of the fan vault insofar as distinct bay divisions were broken down. The continuous handling of the vaulting surface creates a new feeling of spatial unity. The breakdown of bay divisions and consequently, the new stress of total spatial unity, can be seen in the chancel at Wells, and is further developed in the apse of Tewkesbury Abbey and in the choir and north transept at Gloucester. In contrast, the only important extant vaulting from the period which can be associated with the "London School" is that of the choir of Lichfield Cathedral, where William

Ramsey is known to have been employed in the late 1330s.[19] There, the vault is an advanced version of the Lincoln presbytery vault in which the ribs rise to a ridge rib. The striving toward unity of interior space, which negated bay divisions at the vaulting level and put emphasis instead on the total space, was primarily a West Country development, and it was only later accepted in the East. The addition of the horizontal, circular, bounding rib at the top of the vaulting conoid in a fan vault only underlined this contemporary West Country tendency by placing even more concentrated emphasis on the conoids; and since the conoids link one bay to the next, spatial unification was achieved.

The last and one of the most important features of the fan vault is its applied surface patterning, which is characterized by regularity, rectilinearity, and repetition of pattern. These applied patterns were not innovative in themselves, but were derived directly from contemporary window tracery. The concept of a consistently decorated structure, combined with repetition of pattern were, broadly speaking, Perpendicular ideas which point to influence from the "London School" of the 1330s in the West Country.[20] It should be noted, however, that Perpendicular tracery patterns were already used in the West Country and were part of the master masons' everyday working vocabulary by the mid-fourteenth century.[21]

It appears, finally, that all of the preconditions necessary for the debut of fan vaulting were either developed or present in the West Country by the mid-fourteenth century: (1) the tendency toward ribs of the same curvature, (2) the use of jointed masonry which made possible the flat central spandrel panel and simplified construction, (3) the use of a precise geometric form with attached ribs for a vault, and (4) Perpendicular tracery patterns.

The identification of the first example of the fan vault is not of real importance to the understanding of the origins of the form. What is important, however, is the realization that fan vaulting was an evolutionary rather than a revolutionary building innovation. The ingenuity of the designer in this development should not be forgotten, nor that of the mason who, by using the vocabulary and building methods of the past and improving upon them, created a new visual order. The development in the West Country of the new mode of building started a vogue which ultimately led to an important national architectural achievement.

18 Traditionally, the cloister at Gloucester has been considered the monument embodying the first structural fan vaults. From a study of the archaeological and documentary evidence, its vaulting probably should be dated to the period 1381-1412.[22] Recently, it was suggested that the Hereford Chapter House, which was built by 1371, was fan vaulted.[23] The evidence for this assertion rests on an interpretation of a drawing done in the eighteenth century by Stukeley. Only four walls of the structure were standing when Stukeley saw it.[24] The only parts of the vault that could have been in situ were the wall ribs and the tas-de-charge. It is certain that no part of the central pillar or any parts of the vaulting conoids above the tas-de-charge remained. Stukeley's drawing, by his own admission, is a proposed reconstruction of

19
20 how it might have looked.[25] The fragment, which now can be seen in the center of the chapter house, is not part of the central conoid, as has been

suggested, but it is a tas-de-charge from an angle. Clearly, it was designed to fit between two walls. This type of tas-de-charge does not necessarily suggest a fan vault, for it was also common to lierne vaults (cf. transept at Tewkesbury). Whether or not the Hereford Chapter House was fan vaulted remains problematic. Considering its early date, it seems more likely that a complex lierne vault was employed.

The answer to the question of whether the Gloucester cloister fan vault was the first to span a large space may never be known, especially considering that is impossible to determine the architectural contributions of the now destroyed West Country abbeys of Winchombe, Evesham,[26] and Cirencester,[27] which may have played an important role in the development of fan vaulting. However, a study of the several extant fan vaults from the end of the fourteenth century can contribute to our understanding of the early use of the form and help to define new questions.

4
21 The mid-fourteenth century monument to Hugh Lord Despencer in Tewkesbury Abbey has a proto-fan vault. The Trinity Chapel at Tewkesbury, built after 1375,[28] is perhaps the first structural fan vault to have been built. Since it is small and has only a span of 1.66 meters, it has often been referred to as a miniature, decorative, or toy fan vault.[29] Its vaulting, however, must be defined as structural in the same sense as the Gloucester cloister vaults are, because it is constructed of jointed masonry in which the extrados follows the intrados of the vault. The only difference is of scale
22 –the vaults at Gloucester have twice the span. The Founder's Chapel at Tewkesbury, built 1397,[30] has a similar fan vault to that of the Trinity Chapel. There was a strong and well-developed tradition for the building of fan vaults at Tewkesbury and Gloucester by the year 1400.

The influence of Gloucester was soon felt in the north porch of the west
23 façade of Exeter Cathedral. The fan vault there closely follows both the for-
24 mal and technical characteristics of the fan vaulting of the lavatorium located off the north walk of the Gloucester cloister. In addition, the Gloucester cloister vault most likely influenced the fan vault (now destroyed) begun
25 after 1393 in the entrance way of Old Wardour Castle, Wiltshire.[31] It should be noted that those two fan vaults were minor examples compared to those at Tewkesbury and Gloucester.

The first stone fan vaults probably influenced the wooden tester of the tomb of Edward III, which was built after 1378,[32] even though the ribs are not of equal curvature nor of equal length. Later, Hugh Herland, who may have been responsible for the tester of Edward III,[33] designed the wooden
26 fan vault for Winchester College Chapel (ca. 1390).[34] There, too, precise geometric forms for the vaulting conoids were not used. The master mason for Winchester College Chapel was undoubtedly William Wynford, who had earlier worked in the West Country,[35] and had to have known about West Country vaulting developments. It seems plausible that he may have given the idea of building a wooden fan vault to the master carpenter, Hugh Herland. If Harvey is right in his hypothesis that Wynford was the man responsible for Old Wardour Castle,[36] the almost immediate acceptance and spread of the fan vault during the last years of the fourteenth century could be accounted for by the mobility of masons, as much as it could be traced

to the men who commissioned them.

The idea that the West Country could influence architectural development in the East is not new: but can be seen, for example, in the vaulting of the Aerary Porch, Windsor, which was derived from the net vaults of the "Bristol School."[37] For another example, the mouldings, bases, and detail of Bishop Edyngton's work at Winchester Cathedral show extremely close imitation of Gloucester.[38] The complex lierne vaults of the west porches of Winchester Cathedral–which at first glance look as if they are a step in the development towards the fan vault–should be understood as merely reflecting the image of one. The mason who designed these Winchester vaults did not fully understand the concept of the fan vault; the vaulting conoids there are not regular geometric forms to which ribs are attached.

There is one aspect of the problem which has not been discussed–that of patronage. Unfortunately, we do not know where the first fan vault was built and in what context it was set. If the Gloucester cloister was first, fan vault patronage was monastic. If the small fan vaults of chantry chapel and tomb at Tewkesbury were first, patronage was secular–the Despencer family.[39] If this is the case, we have a great West Country family providing the funds and initiative for architectural innovation, which in part may explain why the form was to become common in the West Country itself during the fifteenth century. All of this is speculation, yet the associative value of architectural forms when seen in their social context should not be underestimated.

1. F. Bond, *Gothic Architecture in England* (London, 1905), 342. F. E. Howard, "Fan-Vaults," *AJ,* LXVIII (1911), 3. The exact date of construction is not known. Hugh Lord Despencer died on February 13, 1348/49, see J. Blunt, *Tewkesbury Abbey* (London, 1875), 68. The effigies have been dated to the 1350s, see L. Stone, *Sculpture in Britain: The Middle Ages* (Harmondsworth, 1955), 182.

2. The date is problematic; see R. D. Reid, *Wells Cathedral* (Leighton Buzzard, 1963), 83-84; L. S. Colchester in a letter of 26 February 1972 gives the date as 1319; the vaulting is still constructed of ribs and panels; the panels are tufa. However, the shape is geometric.

3. J. N. Dalton, *The Collegiate Church of Ottery St. Mary* (Cambridge, 1917), 12ff; "The ribs of the vaulting do not follow the construction but are mere ornament, . . . when the whitewash came to be picked away, the real arch, made of common masonry, was laid bare, crossing the church at proper intervals without any regard to the position of the ribs." J. D. Coleridge, "On the Restoration of the Church of St. Mary the Virgin, at Ottery St. Mary," *Transactions of the Exeter Diocesan Architectural Society,* IV (1853), 189-217.

4. J. Fitchen, *The Construction of Gothic Cathedrals* (Oxford, 1961), 79.

5. Letter of 26 February 1972 from L. S. Colchester.

6. G. Webb, *Architecture in Britain: The Middle Ages* (2nd ed., Harmondsworth, 1965), 41.

7. W. Hart, ed., *Historia et Cartularium Monasterii Sancti Petre Gloucesteriae* (London, 1863-67), I, 50.

8. See F. Bond, *An Introduction to English Church Architecture* (London, 1913), I, 322-27.

9. J. Harvey, "The Architects of St. George's Chapel, Part I, The Thirteenth and Fourteenth Centuries," *RSG,* IV, 2 (1961), 54. In England the idea that a vault should have articulated ridges goes back at least to the choir at Lincoln (after 1192). Transverse as well as longitudinal ridge ribs were employed at Westminster Abbey (1245) and Exeter (ca. 1300). There the transverse ridge ribs rise up to the longitudinal ridge rib because the bays were rectangular. It should also be remembered that in these examples the ribs have different curvatures. For dating, see N. Pevsner, *The Choir of Lincoln Cathedral* (London, 1963), 3, 11-12; H. M. Colvin, ed., *Building Accounts of King Henry III* (Oxford, 1971), 6; and H. E. Bishop and E. K. Prideaux, *The Building of the Cathedral Church of St. Peter in Exeter* (Exeter, 1922), 30ff.

0. J. Heyman, "Spires and Fan Vaults," *International Journal of Solids Structures,* III (1967), 252.

1. Reid, *Wells Cathedral,* 27.

2. Fitchen, *The Construction of Gothic Cathedrals,* 69, and Marcel Aubert, "Les plus anciennes

croisées d'ogives, leur rôle dans la construction" *Bulletin monumental,* XCIII (1934), 141ff.

13. R. Willis, "Architectural History of the Cathedral and Monastery at Worcester. Part I: The Cathedral," *AJ,* XX (1863), 113, n. 4.

14. For late Continental drawings of vaulting ribs, see Hans Koepf, *Die gotischen Planrisse der Wiener Sammlungen* (Graz, 1969), figs. 208, 326, 453, 454.

15. The planklike shape of the individual panels is probably a result of the influence of wooden vaults on stone ones. Wooden vaults were built in England from quite an early time. For example, Henry III ordered one for his chapel at Windsor in 1243, see P.R.O., *Calendar of the Close Rolls, Henry III, 1242-1247,* 39. The present 15th century south transept vault at York Cathedral replaced an earlier one of the first half of the 13th century, see J. Hughes, "The Timber Roofs of York Minster," *Yorkshire Archaeological Journal,* XXXVIII (1955), 474-95.

16. Large and well-worked stones were purchased, for example, for Westminster Abbey in the late 14th century, see G. G. Scott, *Gleanings from Westminster Abbey* (2nd ed., Oxford, 1863), 259.

17. First noted by R. Willis, "On the Construction of the Vaults of the Middle Ages," *Transactions of the Royal Institute of British Architects,* I (1842), 52.

18. For an outline of the concept of the "Bristol School," see N. Pevsner, "Bristol-Troyes-Gloucester," *Architectural Review,* CXIII, 674 (Feb. 1953), 89-98.

19. From 23 May 1337, see Oxford, Bodleian MS Ashmole 794, f. 57v, cited in *Engl. Med. Archit.,* 216.

20. J. Harvey, "The Origin of the Perpendicular Style," in E. M. Jope, ed., *Studies in Building History* (London, 1961), 134-216.

21. For example, Wells Presbytery, east window ca. 1335-38 and Gloucester choir, 1337, or soon after, see Harvey, *Studies in Building History,* 138-39.

22. See catalogue entry for complete discussion of the problem.

23. Norman Drinkwater, "Hereford Cathedral: Chapter House," *AJ,* CXII (1955), 61-75.

24. William Stukeley, *Itinerarium Curiosum* (2nd Ed.; London: Baker and Leigh, 1776), 71.

25. ". . . I endeavoured to restore the whole in drawing as well as I could . . ." *Ibid.,* 71.

26. The north cloister walk was rebuilt by Abbot Ombersby, 1367-1379, see BM Harl. MS 3763, f. 176.

27. Fragments of fan vaulting found during the recent excavation seem to date to the fifteenth century. However, the major fourteenth century extensions and transformed choir were not excavated, see P. D. C. Brown and Alan D. McWirr, "Cirencester, 1965," *The Antiquaries Journal,* XLVI (1966), 240-254.

28. BM Cotton MS Cleopatra C.III, f.220a. Printed in *Monasticon,* II, 62.

29. See, for example, John Harvey, *Gothic England* (London: B. T. Batsford, Ltd., 1947), 128.

30. BM Cotton MS Cleopatra C.III, f.220a, Printed in *Monasticon,* II, 60.

31. P.R.O., C.66/337, m.17. Cited in Laurence Keen, "Excavations at Old Wardour Castle, Wiltshire," *The Wiltshire Archaeological and Natural History Magazine,* LXII (1967), 67.

32. *Engl. Med. Archit.,* 131.

33. *Engl. Med. Archit.,* 131.

34. W. F. Oakeshott and John W. Harvey, "The King's Chief Carpenters," *British Archaeological Association Journal,* 3rd Series, XI (1948), 25.

35. *Engl. Med. Archit.,* 127-131.

36. Harvey, *Gothic England,* 56; *Engl. Med. Archit.,* 310.

37. Harvey, "The Architects of St. George's Chapel, Part I. The Thirteenth and Fourteenth Centuries," 55; The situation is more complex for London may first have influenced Bristol (crypt of St. Stephen's Chapel may date from 1292) see Pevsner, "Bristol-Troyes-Gloucester," 91. However, H. M. Colvin dates the vaulting of the crypt of St. Stephen's Chapel to the 1320's, see H. M. Colvin, ed., *The History of the King's Works* (London: HMSO, 1963), I, 517.

38. Harvey, "The Origin of the Perpendicular Style," 157n.83.

39. ". . . as far as the fabric of the Abbey goes, the Despencers may indeed be almost called its second founders," Blunt, *Tewkesbury Abbey,* 67.

3

The Diffusion of Fan Vaulting

Unless some fan vaults of considerable span have been lost, there is no link between the small fan vaults of Tewkesbury and Gloucester (before 1412) and the high chancel vault of Sherborne Abbey (after 1430).[1] In fact, no fan vaults seem to have been built at all in the period between 1412 and 1430, except perhaps the tower vault at Axbridge. Because fan vaults were more expensive to build than lierne vaults, the economic state of the country and building industry in the period 1400-30 may explain why. It has been postulated that there was no population growth in England during the period 1400-30,[2] and labor shortages raised the cost of building. In spite of an economic depression,[3] craftsmen in the period 1412 to 1430 commanded continually higher wages.[4] After 1430 the population and wealth started to increase again, and the 1426-40 generation seems to have lived longer than the preceding one.[5]

The fan vault reemerged as a fashionable mode of building in the late 1430s, a period of tax reductions.[6] Two distinct fan vault building schools can be isolated in this period.

The Sherborne chancel vault–perhaps designed around 1430 and completed by 1459–is different in both conception and execution from previously built fan vaults: (1) its vaulting conoids are polygonal in horizontal section, so the horizontal bounding ribs are composed of straight line segments rather than circular ones; (2) a longitudinal ridge rib is employed; (3) bosses are employed at the rib intersections; (4) the central spandrel panel is not flat; (5) the vaulting is constructed of a combination of ribs and panels and

11

jointed masonry, and a lighter material, tufa, was used for the infilling of the panels.[7] Therefore, the chancel vault at Sherborne is basically a lierne vault to which the fan vault look has been applied. Yet, because it spans 7.48 meters, it is the first apparent attempt to build a great fan vault.

The almshouse at Sherborne was begun in 1440 and was partly built of Ham Hill stone, as was the chancel of Sherborne Abbey. Both may have been designed or built by the same master mason, because of the similarity of architectural detail.[8] In the building accounts for the almshouse, Robert Hulle is named as master mason.[9] This Robert Hulle could be the same mason who worked on the nave of Winchester Cathedral after the death of William Wynford,[10] so it was not unreasonable for Fowler to suggest Hulle was the designer of the Sherborne chancel. Surely, Abbot Bradford would have looked for a man of some experience to built a long span vault. At any rate, if Hulle or another mason who had experience in building long span lierne vaults had been the designer of the Sherborne chancel, this could partially explain the amazing combination of fan and lierne type vaulting forms. The new solution was a different type of fan vault–one with polygonal conoids and a distinctly non-flat central spandrel panel. Whereas earlier fan vaults were constructed completely of jointed masonry, the Sherborne chancel brought together the use of rib and panels with jointed masonry. The combined technique was a result of scale: Sherborne is a long span vault, so the degree of surface articulation is not uniform across its surface. Where a high level of surface articulation was desired, jointed masonry was employed. This technique facilitated construction.

The influence of the Sherborne solution for a high vault, after the construction of the nave in the last quarter of the fifteenth century, can be seen in the neighboring Benedictine houses, such as at Milton Abbas and Muchelney. The idea that a fan vault have polygonal conoids was used in many less ambitious projects such as in the porches at Hilton, Crewkerne, and in the King's House at Salisbury, which at that time was the prebendal home in Salisbury for the abbots of Sherborne. More notable examples were Bishop Stillington's Chapel (1478-88) and the crossing at Wells, the Dorset Aisle at Ottery St. Mary (ca. 1520), and the Lane Aisle at Cullompton (ca. 1526).[11]

The Gloucester solution for the fan vault ultimately had the greatest impact, but the Sherborne chancel should be seen as a major work which formulated and redefined an alternative to the Gloucester solution. In doing so, it initiated a local building vogue which had some vitality. However, this local vogue did not commence until the closing decades of the fifteenth century.

At the same time of the rebuilding of the chancel at Sherborne, a series of fan vaults which follow in direct development from the Gloucester type were built: the chantry chapels located at Tewkesbury (1438), North Leigh (1438), Warwick (1441), Canterbury (1439), and the vestibule of the Chapel of All Souls College, Oxford (1438-42). None of these have long span vaults.

Isabel Despenser, who built the Beauchamp Chantry at Tewkesbury,[12] was married to Richard Beauchamp,[13] who before his death planned to build the Beauchamp Chapel at Warwick.[14] Archbishop Chichele, who was

12

responsible for the foundation of All Souls College, was Archbishop of Canterbury when the chantry chapel for Henry IV was under construction.[15] Stylistic features of the Wilcote Chapel at North Leigh bespeak the architecture of Richard Winchombe, a master mason working in Oxford.[16] While we only have documented the names of the masons employed at All Souls, a sculptor, John Massyngham, worked at Canterbury in the late 1430s,[17] at All Souls in the early 1440s[18] and was later employed on the Beauchamp Chapel at Warwick.[19] If the same sculptor was employed on these projects, perhaps the same mason was as well. The fan vault of the Wilcote Chapel, North Leigh, is related in style to that of All Souls College, Oxford; the slender octagonal bases and shafts of Henry IV's Chantry at Canterbury also suggest the influence of an Oxfordshire mason. The stones for the fan vault of All Souls were most likely carved at Burford,[20] and a fan vault with similar technical characteristics was built in the south porch there. The tower fan vault of the same period at Minster Lovell was probably built by an Oxford mason, Thomas Bedwell.[21] In conclusion, by the 1440s, a center for building fan vaults had established itself in Oxfordshire, which was to become very significant in the development of English architecture.

About one half of the fan vaults built before 1450 were located in chantry chapels, which is important in explaining why the fan vault gained acceptance. Besides being a beautiful solution to the problem of creating a visually unified and consistently decorated interior, it represents the transformation into architectural form of the tradition of epideictic rhetoric–the elaborate praising of personages of high degree.[22] The lierne vault exhibits a high degree of surface articulation, but the fan vault has one more important characteristic–clarity. It created an image easily remembered and thus capable of associative value. The employment of a fan vault in a chantry chapel context can in part be seen as a manifestation of the founder's love of ostentation and as an expression of his own individuality. Wycliffe (1320?-1384) condemned the founders of chantries for that very reason: Et raro vel numquam deficit eis luciferina superbia qua cupiunt nomen suum in terris perpetuari. (. . . seldom if ever free from the pride of Lucifer in wishing to perpetuate their name in the world.)[23]

The last and most important period for the construction of fan vaults was circa 1475-1540, when the mode of building had been accepted by the middle class and when three-quarters of the extant fan vaults were built. At least three regional nodes of fan vault building can be isolated for this period: Sherborne (already explained), London, and Somerset.

The first fan vaults to be used by royal masons during this period were located at St. George's Chapel, Windsor. The master mason was Henry Janyns,[24] probably the son of Robert Janyns, who was employed at All Souls College, Oxford, during the construction of the fan vaults there (1438-42).[25] Since the same masons' marks as at All Souls College appear on the fan vaulted south porch at Burford (ca. 1450),[26] Robert Janyns might have been involved in its construction. Perhaps the Janyns's made their permanent home in Burford.[27] If so, Henry Janyns came from an area and a family that was familiar with the fan vault, its design and construction. In this instance, the mason–more than the patron–should be seen as responsible

13

for transmitting the idea of building a fan vault, from Oxfordshire to Windsor. Once transmitted, the impetus for building fan vaults changed hands, and passed to the patron.

The influence of St. George's Chapel soon echoed in court circles.
41 Bishop John Alcock built a chapel at Ely in 1488.[28] Both the tracery pattern and the stone jointing pattern in the vaulting conoids were similar to the already existing pattern in the aisles of St. George's Chapel. As Comptroller of the Works under Henry VII, Alcock would have been familiar with the new works at Windsor.[29] Consequently, it is not surprising that he wanted to build in the latest court style. He had built a fan vault in his new palace
42 at Downham[30] but only fragments of it remain.

Bishop Edmund Audley of Hereford (1492-1502) was a canon of Windsor in 1474 and later Chancellor of the Garter in 1502.[31] Nowhere can the
43 influence of St. George's Chapel be better seen than in the chapel Audley
44 built for himself at Hereford. It duplicates the size and stone jointing pattern of the polygonal chantry chapels that were built at St. George's. Perhaps Audley employed the same master mason as well as a similar design. Audley was transferred to Salisbury in 1502.[32] Later, when Audley built a chapel
45 there (ca. 1516),[33] he built in the latest prevailing court style—that of Henry VII's Chapel, Westminster.

Bishop Nicholas West, who was involved with the completion of St.
46 George's Chapel in 1511,[34] built a chantry chapel at Putney soon after 1515.[35] The tracery pattern of the vaulting conoids is similar to the nave aisle vaults at St. George's. The employment of the fan vault at Windsor in the 1480s played a vital role in the reemergence and use of the form in court circles in the period 1475-1540.

Fan vaulting was confined for the most part to Southern England. When fan vaults were built in relative isolation, their presence usually can be traced to contacts with London and the court. For example, the Trinity Chapel in
47 St. David's Cathedral (Wales), which was under construction in 1522, was built by Edward Vaughan, who spent most of his life in the Home Counties before being appointed bishop of St. David's.[36] Another example is the Ver-
48 non Chapel at Tong (Shropshire). Anthony Fitzherbert, Henry Vernon's executor and a London man, was responsible for the construction of the chapel.[37] Sir Henry Vernon was a knight of Bath and Treasurer to Arthur, Prince of Wales.[38]

By the year 1500 the fan vault not only had become an accepted mode of building, but also had won high royal favor: it was employed in Henry
49 VII's Chapel, Westminster, which was conceived of as a vast chantry chapel and burial place for the Tudor dynasty. The influence of that chapel was soon felt in chantry chapels across the south of England: Lupton's chapel
50 at Eton, Audley's chapel at Salisbury, Ramryge's chapel at St. Albans, and
45
51 the Salisbury Chantry at Christchurch. In addition, there was a group of fan vaults—generally known as the Wastell type—principally built at Cam-
52 bridge, Peterborough, and Canterbury, which can be seen as reflecting royal patronage or taste, and Bishop Oliver King had court masons design the
53 vaulting for his new church at Bath (ca. 1502).[39] Without question, London and the court provided impetus for the spread and dissemination of the fan

vault during this last period.

While the construction of fan vaults in chantry chapels can be traced in the period 1475-1540 to London and the court, the construction of fan vaults in porches and towers can be ascribed in part to the rise of the new middle class who wanted to emulate the life style of the upper class.

Cloth-making was established in the fourteenth century at Castle Combe, but it was not until the first half of the fifteenth century that evidence of industrial growth stimulated by war orders for cloth became impressive.[40] About the rural character of the wool industry in England, a Frenchman in a Herald's Debate said, ". . . your clothiers dwel in great fermes abvode in the countrey havyning howses with commodities lyke unto gentylmen . . ."[41] For example, the typical fifteenth century entrepreneur began with a cottage, and gradually acquired mills, employed journeymen weavers and fullers, kept sheep, had wool dyed on their premises, and then sold it in London or Bristol.[42] This new class became interested in the arts and adorned their houses with goldsmith work.[43] It is not surprising then, that William Haynes, an owner of a mill, gave £20 in 1435 towards the building of a new tower at Castle Combe,[44] which eventually was to be fan vaulted.

The period of the 1470s and 1480s was an exceptional period of prosperity, when the population and rents began to rise.[45] Edward IV's reign was a period of financial stability for the crown, which coincided with an economic upsurge and a general redistribution of wealth.[46] Nowhere was the result of this expansion more apparent than in Somerset. In 1377 Somerset ranked twenty-third in lay wealth amongst the English counties; by 1515 it had moved to second place.[47] Notably, out of the total of over 120 fan vaults built in England, at least thirty-seven were built in Somerset during the period 1478-1540. Out of these thirty-seven, twenty-one appear in towers and nine in porches. Just as the new middle class had ". . . howses with commodities lyke unto gentylmen . . . ," the rebuilding of parish churches by this class has to be seen as a reflection of their new social status and civic pride, as well as of religious piety. However, it does not explain why fan vaults were chosen over any other type of vaulting.

54 The earliest fan vault in Somerset may be the tower vault at Axbridge. Even though the vaulting is square, the distortion of the tracery patterning and the irregularity of the stone jointing pattern suggest that this fan vault was an early experiment–perhaps as early as circa 1430. If so, since the majority of fan vaults erected in Somerset can be dated to the period 1478-1540, it was built in apparent isolation.

55 Bishop Stillington's Chapel at Wells Cathedral was fan vaulted before the form became common in Somerset. In 1476, Stillington, living for the most part in London,[48] made the only recorded visit to Wells during his episcopate; it was then that he decided to rebuild the cloister lady chapel to be his place of burial.[49] Construction began in 1478.[50] It is interesting to speculate that Stillington might have requested a fan vault: Not only because it was a form just becoming popular in court circles, but also because he must have been familiar with it from his student days at All Souls College, Oxford.[51] There the fan vault was employed in a commemorative context, since All Souls was founded as a chantry college. Although it is impossible

to determine the precise role he played in the design process, it can be assumed that he approved the design before it was built.

The fan vaulting of Stillington's Chapel (now destroyed), was characterized by polygonal fans, bosses at the rib intersections, and a branching type of tas-de-charge. Two types of material, Doulting stone and a lighter material, were used in its construction. The design points to the Sherborne solution for a fan vault as its source of inspiration. Thus while the building accounts for the chapel are not known to survive, it can be assumed that the master mason was a West Country man. John Harvey may well be right when he suggested that William Smyth, who was master mason of Wells Cathedral at that time, was designer of the chapel.[52]

56   The tower vault at Ditcheat is related in style to the vaulting of Stillington's Chapel. The visual similarity is especially evident in the subpanel layout, and, more subtly, in the way the vertical ribs rise up and beyond the horizontal bounding ribs and meet on the ridges. On the basis of style then, this fan vault should be dated to the 1480s. As the chancel at Ditcheat was rebuilt in the period 1473-91,[53] it seems likely that the crossing tower vault was added at the same time.

57   The west tower vault of St. John's, Glastonbury, was probably built in the last quarter of the fifteenth century. Although many of the stylistic details differ, the basic conception of the Ditcheat and Glastonbury fan vaults is similar. They both employ the same–but uncommon–stone jointing pattern.

58 The tower vault at Ilminster, it should be noted, has the same stone jointing pattern.

If the assumption is made that stone sizes available from the quarry were relatively consistent, individual workshops may be classified according to their stone jointing systems. Therefore, the hypothesis can be put forward that the Ditcheat, Glastonbury, and Ilminster fan vaults were built by the same workshop or by masons trained in a common workshop. The building of Stillington's Chapel at Wells, which was a major undertaking, meant that a major architectural workshop was located there. This workshop probably served as a training ground for masons who, after the completion of Stillington's Chapel in 1488, went on to do other work in the county. This could also account for the increasing popularity of fan vaults in Somerset in the period 1478-1540. Stillington's Chapel can be seen as giving impetus to fan vault building in Somerset.

Another major architectural workshop was located at Glastonbury. There, the Edgar Chapel was rebuilt toward the end of the fifteenth century.[54] Whether it was fan vaulted is conjectural, but fan vaults were built in the

59 abbey, as is evident from extant fragments. But these fragments are too few to assess the role that Glastonbury might have played in the introduction of fan vaulting to Somerset. Glastonbury had strong connections with London and the court,[55] so it is not far-fetched to hypothesize that since fan vaults were popular in court circles, the form would have been adapted at Glastonbury and thereafter in the surrounding area.

Abbot Selwood of Glastonbury, who was responsible for the building

60 of tenements at Mells,[56] may have given impetus to the rebuilding of Mells

61 Church, which contains two fan vaults. Near Mells, Doulting has an almost identical fan vault in its porch. Also, the fan vault at Buckland Dinham is similar to the Mells porch in rib profile and in articulation of the center ring in its central spandrel panel. The similarity of this group of fan vaults, when seen in respect to their close geographical proximity, might point to the emergence of a local workshop in the area, circa 1500.

For the most part, fan vaults erected in Somerset towers belong to the sixteenth century. Langport may have been built by John Heron, who was Surveyor to Henry VII.[57] Since the tower displays the Beaufort badge, and Lady Margaret Beaufort held Langport until her death in 1509, the tower was probably completed by that time. The tower is built of lias, with Doulting stone used for the west window trim and fan vault. The use of Doulting rather than Ham Hill stone suggests a connection with a north Somerset workshop rather than one from the south, where Ham Hill stone was more frequently used for carved dressings. The stone jointing pattern does not fall into any categorized group and is not consistent–perhaps irregular sizes of stones were only available from the quarry.

The tower fan vaults at Muchelney and Shepton Beauchamp, probably completed before 1507,[58] should be grouped together for reasons of style, workshop technique, patronage, and geographical proximity. The stone jointing patterns in both of them are the same, but their spans are different: 3.37 meters and 4.00 meters respectively. Wedmore, located in the north of Somerset, is the only other tower fan vault that has the same stone jointing pattern, though it is completely different in style. They could all have been built by the same mason; if so, the difference in style would be explained by the creativity of the mason in changing this imagery, while maintaining the same construction pattern.

The tower vaulting at St. Mary Magdelene, Taunton, was completed by 1514.[59] It most likely influenced the design of the neighboring tower fan vault at St. James, Taunton. While their spans are 5.20 meters and 4.34 meters respectively, their stone jointing patterns are the same, thus suggesting the same workshop. Taunton was a major center in Somerset in the early decades of the sixteenth century. It is estimated to have had a population of three to four thousand.[60]

The tower vaults at North Petherton and Weston Zoyland were most likely built by 1517.[61] They are almost identical in conception, size and stone jointing patterns. Since they are in close geographical proximity to each other and the stone jointing pattern is the same as that used in the Taunton churches, they were probably built by the same workshop. If they were built after the Taunton churches, a mason trained at Taunton may have been responsible for them. Perhaps one workshop was able to build in different styles, depending on what the patron wanted. The same stone jointing pattern also appears later on at Batcombe, circa 1540.[62]

The tower vaults at Shepton Mallet and Chewton Mendip were built circa 1540.[63] Their stone jointing patterns are identical. This stone jointing pattern was not common and apparently was employed only in one other fan vault, Curry Rivel. Stylistically, the Shepton Mallet and Chewton Mendip fan vaults are related to the Taunton ones, but because of the different stone jointing pattern, they were probably built by different masons.

The early sixteenth century fan vaults located in the porches of Ile Abbots, North Curry, and Kingston St. Mary follow the same basic model. Again, close geographical proximity and similarities in design and construction suggest that they were products of the same workshop. The evidence further suggests that the provincial mason, once getting the idea for a new form, was less creative with it and used it several times with little modification.

While the evidence is in no way conclusive, the theory can be put forward that there is a direct connection between local prosperity and the rebuilding of churches. The impetus for the inclusion of a fan vault in these structures probably came from the architectural workshops of Glastonbury and Wells; because not only were these well established workshops building fan vaults and might have served as training grounds for masons who later established local building practices, but also because Wells and Glastonbury were important centers of culture and taste. Surely, the new middle class wanted to build in the latest prevailing style.

Along with the dissolution of the monasteries in the 1530s-1540s the construction of fan vaults came to a virtual standstill. This is not surprising, because the overwhelming majority of fan vaults were employed in ecclesiastical structures. It was not until the early seventeenth century that the fan vault was to be revived and patronized by the heads of the Church of England in that stronghold of Anglicanism–the University of Oxford.[64]

1. First pointed out by Howard, "Fan Vaults," *AJ,* LXVIII (1911), 8.
2. Josiah Cox Russell, *British Medieval Population* (Albuquerque: University of New Mexico Press, 1948), 235, 269, 270.
3. John Saltmarsh, "Plague and Economic Decline in the Later Middle Ages," *The Cambridge Historical Review,* VII (1941), 381.
4. E. H. Phelps Brown and Sheila V. Hopkins, "Seven Centuries of Building Wages," in E. M. Carus-Wilson, edit., *Essays in Economic History* (London: Edward Arnold, Ltd., 1962), 11, 177; Materials do not go up appreciably in cost during the fifteenth century, see J. E. Thorold Rogers, *A History of Agriculture and Prices in England* (7 vols.; Oxford: At the Clarendon Press, 1866-1902), IV (1882), 433-525.
5. Russell, *British Medieval Population,* 272.
6. W. G. Hoskins, "The Wealth of Medieval Devon," in W. G. Hoskins and H. P. R. Finberg, *Devonshire Studies* (London: Jonathan Cape, 1952), 240.
7. The tufa was replaced in the nineteenth century, see R. H. Carpenter, "On the Benedictine Abbey of S. Mary, Sherborne with Notes on the Restoration of Its Church," *Royal Institute of British Architects Sessional Papers,* 1876-1877, 145.
8. P. N. Dawe for the late Joseph Fowler, "Sherborne Almshouse Building Accounts, 1440-1444," *Notes and Queries for Somerset and Dorset,* XXIX, pt. 290 (Sept., 1969), 74-75.
9. *Ibid.*
10. *Ibid.,* 77; *Engl. Med. Archit.,* 141.
11. See Catalogue Entries.
12. BM Cotton MS Cleopatra C.III, f.220a. Printed in Monasticon, II, 63.
13. On 23 November 1423, see J. Blunt, *Tewkesbury Abbey* (London, 1875), 76.
14. Licence granted on 11 May 1437, P.R.O., *Calendar of the Patent Rolls,* Henry VI, III (1436-1441), 429.
15. E. F. Jacob, "The Building of All Souls College, 1438-1443," in *Historical Essays in Honour of James Tait* (Manchester: Printed for the Subscribers, 1933), 121.
16. F. E. Howard, "Richard Winchcombe's Work at the Divinity School and Elsewhere," in T. F. Hobson, editor, *Adderbury "Rectoria,"* Oxfordshire Record Society, VIII (1926), 38.
17. He was paid 13s.4d. in August 1438 for "pro ymagine pre le syne et Sonne." Oxford, Bodleian MS Top. Kent c.3, f.149. Cited in *Engl. Med. Archit.,* 182.
18. Jacob, "The Building of All Souls College, 1438-1443," *op. cit.,* 130.
19. He was paid £66.0s.8d. by 1449. BM Add. MS 28564, f.257. This manuscript is a nineteenth century copy by Robert Bell Wheler. The original accounts are lost.

20. Jacob, "The Building of All Souls College, 1438-1443," 126.
21. E. A. Greening Lamborn, "The Lovell Tomb at Minster," *Oxfordshire Archaeological Society, Report* 83 (1937), 19.
22. Paul Frankl, *The Gothic: Literary Sources and Interpretations through Eight Centuries* (Princeton, N.J., 1960), 197.
23. Rudolf Ruddensieg, edit., *John Wycliffe's Polemical Works in Latin,* I, 272-273. Cited in K. L. Wood-Legh, *Perpetuul Chantries in Britain* (Cambridge: At the University Press, 1965), 305.
24. W. H. St. John Hope, *Windsor Castle* (2 vols.; London: Country Life, 1913), II, 378, 379. For Janyns' family connections between Windsor and Henry VII's Chapel, Westminster see W. Leedy, "The Design of the Vaulting of Henry VII's Chapel, Westminster; A Reappraisal," *Architectural History,* XVIII (1975), 9.
25. *Engl. Med. Archit.,* 146; Jacob, "The Building of All Souls College, 1438-1443," 128.
26. R. H. C. Davis, "Mason's Marks in Oxfordshire and the Cotswolds," *Oxfordshire Archaeological Society,* Report 84 (for 1938), 78.
27. The will of a Robert Janyns, who made his home in Burford in 1501, was proved 9 October 1506, P.C.C. 11 Adeane, printed in R. H. Gretton, *The Burford Records* (Oxford: At the Clarendon Press, 1920), 675-677. Could this be the son of Henry Janyns and the grandson of the Robert Janyns who worked at Oxford in the 1440s? Also, Burford was an important center for building. Henry Janyns rented a house there in 1481 for masons working on St. George's Chapel, Windsor, see Hope, *Windsor Castle,* II, 403.
28. The date on the foundation stone is 1488, see James Bentham, *The History and Antiquities of the Conventual and Cathedral Church of Ely* (Cambridge: Printed by the University Press, 1771), 183.
29. *Ibid.,* 183; *DNB,* I, 236.
30. VCH, *Cambridgeshire,* IV, 92.
31. Emden, *Oxford,* I, 75-76.
32. Emden, *Oxford,* I, 76.
33. Licence was granted in 1516, see *L & P Henry VIII,* pt. I, 832.
34. On 7 September 1511 a warrant was issued for the payment to him of £200 for the vaulting of the building, to be repaid by the Knights of the Garter to the Exchequer, see *L & P Henry VIII,* I, 1452.
35. See Catalogue Entry.
36. Emden, *Cambridge,* 607.
37. *L & P Henry VIII,* III, nr.102.(5).
38. George Griffiths, *A History of Tong, Shropshire* (2nd Edit.; London: Simpkin, Marshall, Hamilton, Kent & Co., Ltd., 1894), 46-49.
39. Robert and William Vertne, see catalogue entry for Bath.
40. E. M. Carus-Wilson, "Evidences of Industrial Growth on Some Fifteenth Century Manors," in E. M. Carus-Wilson, edit., *Essays in Economic History,* II, 160.
41. *Ibid.,* 151.
42. *Ibid.,* 164.
43. G. Poulett Scrope, *History of the Manor and Ancient Barony of Castle Combe...* (London: J. B. Nichols and Sons, for private circulation, 1852), 246.
44. *Ibid.,* 248.
45. F. R. H. DuBoulay, *An Age of Ambition* (London, 1970), 15.
46. *Ibid.,* 15.
47. R. S. Schofield, "The Geographical Distribution of Wealth in England, 1334-1649," *Economic History Review,* 2nd Series, XVIII, nr.3 (1965), 504.
48. H. C. Maxwell-Lyte, edit., *The Registers of Robert Stillington and Richard Fox,* SRS, LII (1937), xv
49. *Ibid.,* xv.
50. See Catalogue Entry.
51. T. W. Jex-Blake, "Historical Notices of Robert Stillington," *SANH Proc.,* XL, pt. II (1894), 3.
52. *Engl. Med. Archit.,* 246.
53. E. Buckle, "Ditcheat Church," *SANH Proc.,* XXXVI (1890), 27-28.
54. Leland, *Itin.,* I, 289.
55. See Ian Keil, "London and Glastonbury Abbey in the Later Middle Ages," *London and Middlesex Archaeological Society,* XXI, pt. II, 173-177.
56. F. Bligh Bond, "Mells Church," *SANH Proc.,* LVII, pt. I (for 1911), 54.
57. See Catalogue Entry.
58. On heraldic evidence, see E. Buckle, "Shepton Beauchamp Church," *SANH Proc.,* XXXVIII (1891), 42.

Diffusion
of
Fan Vaulting

59. (E. H. Bates) "St. Mary's Church, Taunton," *SANH Proc.,* LIV (for 1908), 30-31.
60. W. G. Hoskins, *Provincial England* (London: Macmillan & Co., Ltd., 1965), 72.
61. See Catalogue Entries.
62. See Catalogue Entry.
63. See Catalogue Entries.
64. See Alfred Clapham, "The Survival of Gothic in Seventeenth Century England," *AJ,* CVI, Supplement (for 1949, 1952), 4-9.

4

On the Theory, Design, and Construction of Fan Vaults

The traditional Gothic ribbed vault was conceived of as a series of supports, or ribs, between which were placed small vaults having warped surfaces, or webs. In this structural solution for a vault, the ribs perform three basic functions: (1) a load carrying function, (2) a permanent framework for erecting the webs, and (3) the aesthetic function of both masking the joints between intersecting groins of the vault and creating linearity, an important feature of early Gothic architecture.[1]

The erection of a traditional ribbed vault in theory is straightforward: the transverse arches and ribs were placed, then webs built up. In France and sometimes in England, after the vault was erected and the mortar cured, the ribs could be stripped away and the vault would still stand—as can be seen in some war-damaged buildings.[2] In these rare instances, the diagonal ribs were usually not rebated, and the webs formed a continuous structure over the top of the ribs.[3] The structural function of the ribs could be assumed by the webs, but only if the webs were of sufficient cross-sectional dimensions to carry the load,[4] and the web stones were laid like voussoirs in an arch.

Thus, in France and generally on the Continent, the ribs were structural, at least while the vault was being erected. In any case, their constructional function can not be denied. In England insofar as the ribs were rebated to receive the webs, they continued to be structural as well as aesthetic in function, even after the vaulting was erected. The stress levels in the webs of ribbed vaults were kept low and the diagonal ribs carried the load to the piers. This rib and panel system had the advantage of concentrating the vaulting thrusts as efficiently as possible on one point, permitting–when seen in conjunction with the high stilting of the wall ribs in French cathedrals–the opening and lightening of the structure until it became a skeletal stone framework.[5]

Whereas the vaulting conoid of a Gothic ribbed vault assumes an irregular shape, the vaulting conoid of a fan vault is a precise geometric form in the majority of cases. Compared to a ribbed Gothic vault in which the ribs comprise extremely rigid members which support the infilling or webs, no structural distinction is made in a fan vault between covering and supporting elements. In theory, a fan vaulting conoid functions as shell structure, which by definition is a three-dimensional structure with the thickness comparatively smaller than the other two dimensions, in which the major stresses act in directions parallel to the middle surface.[6] Shape and thickness are important as they can cause redistribution of load. The most important load is its own dead weight. Remember: if thickness is doubled, both the dead weight and the area upon which it acts are increased; but the stress remains unchanged.[7]

12 The most important characteristic of a fan vaulting conoid is that it is a doubly-curved structural form with anticlastic curvatures; that is, through any one point there are curvatures in opposite senses–concave one way, convex the other. Since it is extremely rigid (as is the shell of an egg), the assumed deflection is small.[8] Failure of a doubly-curved structure usually results from failure due to compressive or tensile stresses, rather than buckling. It can be assumed that, since stone has low tensile strength, and that slippage between stones cannot occur, a masonry structure will be stable (i.e., in equilibrium) as long as a line of thrust can be found which lies wholly within the masonry.[9] Heyman, in his structural analysis of a fan vault, has shown that a profile of any "reasonable" shape and quite small thickness can accommodate the curve of the equation needed to satisfy this requirement, and that stress levels were low even for long span fan vaults.[10] A fan vault is an essentially stable structure; however, it took a long time for the medieval mason to grasp the idea that stability was not prejudiced by size.

78 For equilibrium, a conoid in a fan vault must be continually supported along its edges and at its bottom. The walls support it vertically, the tas-de-charge supports its bottom, and the central spandrel panel provides the necessary compressive load along its upper edge. Since the central spandrel panel acts as a plate structure, structural and visual distinctions are made between the vaulting conoids and the central spandrel panel. The effective part of the fan vault which in theory works as a shell structure, is the part of the vaulting conoid that is above the tas-de-charge, or from above the rubble fill in the vaulting pockets (if they are not empty) to the central spandrel panel.[11]

The rubble fill present in the conoids of most fan vaults, enables the thrust surface to pass out of the fan vault shell into the solid interior; thus, the line of action of the horizontal thrust of the vault is dropped to a lower level. This, when seen in conjunction with the turning surface of the vault, allows a large margin of adjustment for the line of action of the total horizontal thrust,[12] so the thrust is more or less distributed across the surface of the wall. Also, the rubble fill contributes an inward movement about the springing, thereby counteracting some of the outward horizontal thrust of the vaulting. By contrast, the thrust in a Gothic ribbed vault is collected into the diagonal ribs, and little adjustment can be made to the line of action of the resultant total horizontal thrust; therefore, the flying buttresses must be placed at approximately their optimal position, or the ribbed vault will collapse.[13] The problem of buttressing is not as critical for a fan vault as it is for a ribbed vault. In this respect it should be noted that the nave of Sherborne Abbey does not have flying buttresses, but the chancel does. This is because the curvature of the nave vault is more steeply pitched than that of the chancel. Its total horizontal thrust is lower than that of the chancel, and it requires less buttressing than does the chancel vault.

In theory, fan vaults act as shell structures, but whether they were intended as such is a completely different matter. Though several of the more important fan vaults were completely constructed of jointed masonry, it is not possible to conclude that the medieval mason understood, even intuitively, that shell structures have both vertical and horizontal component forces acting over their entire vaulting surfaces.

The medieval mason was incapable of even the simplest structural calculation.[14] This lack of understanding was not important because stability, not strength, was the critical factor when designing a masonry structure, and stability was a function of geometry and proportion. The reasons for the employment of jointed masonry must have been practical rather than theoretical. It was easier to achieve the desired high level of visual articulation by carving the patterning out of large pieces of stone, so each stone is structural as well as decorative. Considering that the surface is doubly curved, as is the patterning on it, jointed masonry was the logical solution. The utilization of this technique in long span structures evolved out of its use in small tomb canopies. The techniques of the sculptor not only influenced but made possible a major development in monumental architecture.

In theory, once a fan vault has been erected and the centering struck, it should be impossible to remove any component part if the vault action is that of a shell structure, because both the vertical and horizontal component forces would be acting over the entire surface. During the restoration of Sherborne Abbey, the tufa panels of the chancel vault, which is constructed in part with ribs and panels, were lifted out and replaced with panels of Ham Hill stone. The fact that the lighter tufa was originally used suggests that the mason thought that only the rib in this location carried the load. And he was right. Consequently, a fan vault that is constructed in part of ribs and panels in theory should function as a shell structure but in reality can also function as a frame structure. The fact that it can function both ways makes it more viable; it can change its structural action in response to changes that might occur in the abutment system.

There is a direct relationship in stone fan vaults between the way they are constructed and the distances they span. All fan vaults under 2.00 meters are completely constructed of jointed masonry. Those which span between 2.00 and 2.50 meters for the most part are still constructed completely of jointed masonry. The notable exceptions, located at Corsham House (Wiltshire) and Hilton (Dorset), are constructed out of ribs and panels with jointed masonry used for their traceried parts. The total number of fan vaults that span between 2.50 and 3.00 meters is almost equally divided between those constructed completely out of jointed masonry and those constructed of jointed masonry in conjunction with ribs and panels. For spans over 3.00 meters, rib and panel construction with jointed masonry for the traceried parts predominates. Of the twenty-two fan vaults that span between 4.00 and 5.00 meters, only two are constructed completely out of jointed masonry. Of the eighteen fan vaults that span over 5.00 meters, only three are constructed completely of jointed masonry: the tower gallery at Mildenhall (5.25 meters), the tower vault at Fotheringhay (5.53 meters), and the main vault of Henry VII's Chapel, Westminster (10.58 meters). All of these fan vaults have more complex tracery patterns over their entire surfaces than the majority of fan vaults of greater span. The fan vault with the greatest span is the main vault of King's College Chapel, Cambridge. It spans 12.66 meters. Fan vaults constructed of ribs and panels with jointed masonry for the traceried parts outnumber those which are constructed completely of jointed masonry by three to two. The parts of fan vaults that are executed in ribs and panels have no traceried decoration. Jointed masonry was used because it facilitated construction, and not because it was considered conceptually or structurally better than rib and panel construction. The medieval mason followed the easiest method of construction that would satisfy his visual objectives.

Besides the self-supporting stone structural solutions noted above for fan vaults, the fan vault of the Ramyrge Chantry in St. Alban's Cathedral (built circa 1515) is a suspended stone structure, and the vaulting of Winchester College Chapel (built circa 1390) is constructed of wood.

Because of the geometric properties of a fan vault conoid in conjunction with a flat central spandrel panel, the fan vault is best suited to a square vaulting module. It is not surprising, then, that the overwhelming majority of fan vaults were built over square bays. All the early fan vaults had two-centered curves, but from the late 1430s onwards, fan vaults with four-centered curvatures were built. Notable examples of early four-centered fan vaults are located at North Leigh, Oxford, and Canterbury.

79 The first known rectangular bay to be fan vaulted was in the east walk of the Gloucester cloister. There, two-centered curves of the same radius were used in both directions. This solution resulted in intersecting conoids in the long direction that formed a ridge which distinctly rises up to the central spandrel panel. Early fan vaulting of rectangular bays appeared in the Trinity
22 Chapel at Tewkesbury (built after 1375). Although the bays of the chapel are rectangular, the vaulting module is square, and the vaulting conoids spring from side pendants. This design solution ultimately reached its apex in the
49 vaulting of Henry VII's Chapel, Westminster.

While the four-centered curves began to be used in fan vaults in the 1430s, it was not until quite late, circa 1500, that two- and four-centered curves were used together to fan vault a rectangular vaulting module. This solution allows the ridges formed by the intersecting vaulting conoids to remain relatively horizontal. The idea was executed at Maids Moreton, Saf-
80 fron Walden, and in the main vault of King's College Chapel, Cambridge. The solution which used four-centered curves, but of different curvatures

in both directions, came into general use about 1510 and was used in the side chapels of King's College Chapel, in Bishop West's Chapel, Putney, and in the Poyntz Chapel, Bristol. Because this solution for fan vaulting a rectangular module was not arrived at until quite late, it partly explains why fan vaults were not used to span large spaces, for large spaces usually had rectangular bays. The vaulting of the Sherborne chancel, completed by 1459, employs two-centered curves in both directions in similar fashion to the Gloucester cloister rectangular bay solution. But it does not have a flat central spandrel panel, and the vaulting conoids are polygonal in shape.

Although the main bays are rectangular in Henry VII's Chapel, the basic vaulting mode is square, that is, each bay is of such proportions (5:2) that it breaks down into ten squares from which the design is generated.

A unique solution for fan vaulting a rectangular bay can be seen in the porch vaults of Mells and Doulting. There, the design module is one-quarter of the east-west span, which is also the radius of each vaulting conoid and of the circular, central spandrel panel. This vaulting solution solves the problem of how to fan vault a rectangular plan without having intersecting vaulting conoids.

The fan vaults of the polygonal chantry chapels in St. George's Chapel, Windsor, and the Audley Chapel at Hereford, all built circa 1500, utilize fan vault conoids in their angles to support a flat saucer dome. The vaults of these chapels are constructed completely of jointed masonry. In addition, fragments found in the recent excavations of Cirencester Abbey suggest that the fifteenth century chapter house there (which was polygonal in shape) was fan vaulted. In conclusion, the majority of fan vaults were built over square bays, but other design solutions were possible, which shows the ingenuity of the master mason to adapt a basically square shape solution for use in non-square areas.

Based on archaeological evidence, it is possible to clarify the constructional process, which consisted of four basic steps for small fan vaults. First, a tas-de-charge was installed in each corner of the bay. Although they usually rested on shafts, they were deeply set into the walls and can be thought of as corbels upon which the vaulting sits. Tas-de-charge fragments can be seen at Muchelney Abbey and at Old Wardour Castle. Next, the wall ribs were installed with their keystones, as can be observed at Shelton and Littlebury. The wall ribs were usually inserted into indentations placed in the walls to create a condition of fixity as, for example, in the abbey tower at Evesham, and in the north porch at Cirencester. In these instances a crack or fissure was likely to develop between the first course of stones in the vaulting and the wall ribs, because no matter how carefully the individual stones were shaped and fitted to each other, their beds never precisely matched up. The stones then accommodate themselves to each other and to the abutments, in this case the wall ribs. The cracks would appear as the vaulting underwent deformation when compression was induced into it, that is, when the centering was struck or when there was settlement in the abutment system; afterwards, these fissures were usually filled in with mortar. This procedure was adopted in the main vault at King's College Chapel along the transverse arches. Joints in the transverse ridges close to the walls at

King's must have also formed hinges, because they opened up. In the nineteenth century iron clamps were put in between these stones. Similar cracks can be observed in the tower vault at Muchelney and in the porch vault at Saffron Walden amongst many others. The general principle is that masonry vaults naturally form hinges to accommodate themselves to the abutment system, and such cracks are usually harmless. Four hinges must be formed to turn the structure into a mechanism of collapse, and the geometry of a fan vault is such that four hinges most likely could never be formed. The fan vault is an essentially stable structure; the only real possibility for failure is if the abutment system gives way.

86
87 After the wall ribs were erected, the vaulting conoids were constructed starting from the bottom, working upwards in horizontal courses. As construction of the conoids progressed, the transverse ridge stones were placed. Finally, the central spandrel panel would be put in place. Most of this stonework had to be supported on a considerable amount of centering, the construction of which involved a whole series of problems: the amount of deformation the centering would undergo under partial and complete loading conditions, how it was struck, and how it was taken down.

The centering for a quadripartite ribbed vault would most likely be continuous under the ribs, because they were constructed first, then the webs, **88** or panels, were put in. Whereas, in a fan vault the keystone, that is, the central spandrel panel, was the last stone to be put up. This construction sequence must have had important consequences for the type of centering employed. In the vast majority of fan vaults, only the vaulting conoids had to be supported by the centering, because the central spandrel panel was one large stone spanning the distance between the vaulting conoids. Since it was the last stone to be placed, it was not necessary to support it from below. Furthermore, the weight of the central spandrel panel was of such magnitude that it created movement in the structure, thereby inducing compression and eliminating the problem of how the centering was to be struck. For example, the central spandrel panel in the north porch at Cirencester is almost 2.25 meters long and averages 18 centimeters in depth, and the central bosses in King's College Chapel weigh approximately one and one half tons each. When the Peterborough vault was rebuilt in the 1930s, no problems of decentering were encountered because the placement of the keystones in that situation induced compression into the vaulting.[15] This was probably not the case in the many jointed masonry vaults of short span. In these, wedges were used to induce compression as in the vaulting of **89** Prince Arthur's Chantry Chapel, Worcester. There, large pebblelike stones were pounded into the flat arch vault. In other instances, wooden wedges may have been used.

In large fan vaults where individual stones were purpose-cut, they were individually designated for a particular location and for their sequence in the constructional process. This procedure can clearly be seen in the main **90** vault in King's College Chapel. There, the vertical joints of most individual **91** stones were marked with a symbol to indicate its quadrant of the bay, and with Arabic or Roman numerals to indicate the horizontal level and precise location within the quadrant. The stone layers on the site had only to place each stone according to its markings; there was no question about the exact position. Because these position/assembly marks were used, the vault must have first been totally fabricated in the workshop. Prefabrication has a long history in masonry; it was also commonly employed in the making of roof trusses.

From a study of the markings, the typical bay in the main vault at King's College Chapel was constructed as follows. After the lateral walls were taken up to their full height and the roof was installed, as was the usual practice in the medieval period, the large transverse arches were erected first between bays. These arches established and helped to maintain vault curvature, augmented rigidity between adjacent bays, and helped to conceal visual discrepancies between bays. Second, the four conoids were built up from the long sides of the bays working inward, one horizontal level at a time. Third, the transverse ridge stones were placed as construction of the conoids progressed upwards; each transverse ridge stone functions as the keystone for its horizontal level. Fourth, the longitudinal ridge stones were placed, starting from both ends of the bay and working inward. Fifth, the stones which comprise the boss were dropped into place from above.

One of the last things to take place in the constructional process was the final carving of the ribs and other surface articulation. Because the sectional profiles of the surface articulation usually match up perfectly, the stones probably were partially carved in the workshop and finished after the vaulting was placed. If they had been completely finished in the workshop, deformation of the vaulting surface that would take place when compression was induced into the vaulting would have caused some shifting of individual stones. Also, there are no apparent marks on the vault surfaces which might have been made by the centering. After this was accomplished and the joints mortared in, the vaulting was sometimes painted, as was the Audley Chapel at Salisbury.

One important problem in the execution of fan vaults was that of stereotomy, the cutting of rough blocks of stone so they will form a predetermined whole when fitted together.[16] In 1842, Willis showed how the medieval mason could have determined the stone shapes by plane geometry projection methods.[17] Since no English medieval drawings for vaults are preserved,[18] Willis's theory cannot be substantiated, but from a large corpus of late Central European medieval drawings for vaults preserved in Vienna,[19] it can be seen that medieval designers did employ projection methods to determine vault heights and curvatures. Apparently, they did not do drawings for individual stones. Instead, the determination of individual stone shapes was left for the builder to resolve on the site after the basic design had been established.[20] It would seem that the problem of shaping individual component stones for a vault did not effect the overall design of the vault. Since some stones have a horizontal plane on them, Willis suggested that this plane might have been a "surface of operation"–a base from which the other surfaces of the stone were worked.[21] In the fan vaults that can be inspected from above, this feature appears consistently in Peterborough and King's College Chapel, and in some instances in the main vault of Henry VII's Chapel, Westminster. A fragment from a fan vault from Circencester Abbey also displays this "surface of operation." The technique seems to be the exception rather than the rule; it was by no means common to all fan vaults, nor to one workshop, nor does it appear in any conoidal stones in early fan vaults, where intrados generally follow extrados very closely. If Willis's theory is correct, this technique for shaping stones would seem to be a late development in workshop practice and may have been a result of scale, for it seems to have been used only in vaults of longer span. Since centering lines and arcs–which must have been made by beam compasses–are present on these horizontal surfaces and are continuous from stone to stone, these "surfaces of operation" must have been essential for determining and controlling the overall shape of the vault. Therefore, these "surfaces of operation" at least facilitated the construction of long span vaults. The lines that would have helped us understand the sequence of shaping the individual stones were probably cut away during carving.

96   Should a stone crack during carving, wooden bow-ties were inserted and cemented in with hot cement made in part of resin and wax, as can be seen at Cambridge and Peterborough. This economy measure posed no problem, because after placement these stones would be in compression; the crack would close up, and there would be no loss of structural strength.

Separate webs, when employed in fan vaults, were usually constructed of panels which spanned between the ribs. Exceptions to this rule can be
97 seen in Lady Chapel off the Martyrdom in Canterbury Cathedral, where small
98 blocks of stone were used, and at Cerne Abbas where the webs were con-
99 structed of small slats of stone. The webs in the main vault in King's College Chapel were often constructed of panels approximately five centimeters thick upon which a cemented rubble fill of another six centimeters or so is placed to bring the upper surface of the panel up to the level of the extrados of the rib stem. The shape of the panels for the most part are flat and rectangular. This results in straight beds, as can be seen in the crossing vault at Wells and in King's College Chapel. Some vaults have panels that are doubly-curved. In these cases, the resulting beds are concave, as in Peterborough. In fan vaults constructed completely of jointed masonry, the beds tend to be concave. A notable exception to the rule is the vault in the Jesus Chapel, Westminster.[22]

Some stones were chiseled down after erection. For example, stones
100 in the transverse ridges in King's College were cut away after they had been placed, and their dead load lightened almost by half. This was probably done for structural reasons; the vault was pulling away from the wall because too much weight was originally placed on the ridge, and it caused minor bending. This evidence reinforces the fact that it was impossible for the medieval mason to judge the cross-sectional dimensions required to provide adequate stiffness without first exploring the requirements in actual full scale construction.

As can be seen from a study of vaulting fragments at Cirencester, Wells, Downham, Muchelney, Littlebury, and other places, there is little archaeological evidence for the consistent use of dowels in small fan vaults. However, mutton bones were found to have been used as dowels in the long span fan vaulting at Peterborough.[23] These most likely were used for constructional rather than for structural reasons. In other words, they helped to align the stones while the vaulting was being erected. Oyster shell wedges were also used in the vault at Peterborough to help position individual stones. From this evidence, it seems likely that dowels may have been used in other long span fan vaults.

It is often suggested that one of the principal advantages of the fan vault lies in its cheapness which resulted from the use of standardized parts.[24] The fact it was not an economical way to build can be deduced from documentary evidence: Wastell was to be paid £20 to build a fan vault compared with £12 to build a vault of a ". . . more course worke . . ." of the same size in King's College Chapel.[25]

The use of standardized parts in some fan vaults was possible because of the repetitive pattern of the design, the use of jointed masonry, and the availability of standard stone sizes from the quarry. The fact that a pattern repeats itself does not necessarily mean it will be cheaper to execute. The important cost consideration here is the use of jointed masonry, and it takes more time and labor to carve a stone that is doubly-curved than one that is more simply shaped. Fan vaults have greater surface articulation than regular ribbed vaults, and consequently, the shaping of the stones for a fan vault required more skilled labor. Fan vaults were not, therefore, economical to build. Besides, it would hardly seem likely that Henry VII would have chosen fan vaulting for his chapel if it had involved any suggestion of economy to members of the court.

1. For a discussion of the role of the rib see John Fitchen, *The Construction of Gothic Cathedrals* (Oxford, 1961), 87 ff. Modern scholars are debating the load carrying function of the rib. For a discussion and analysis of the vaults of Cologne Cathedral which indicate that the ribs do not play a vital structural role see R. Mark, J. F. Abel and K. O'Neill, "Photo-elastic and Finite-element Analysis of a Quadripartite Vault," *Experimental Mechanics,* XIII, nr. 8 (1973), 322-329.
2. Fitchen, *The Construction of Gothic Cathedrals,* 68.
3. *Ibid.,* 69.
4. Jacques Heyman, "On the Rubber Vaults of the Middle Ages and Other Matters," *Gazette des Beaux-Arts, LXXI* (March, 1968), 183.
5. Fitchen, *The Construction of Gothic Cathedrals,* 80.
6. A. Paduart, translated by F. H. Turner, *Shell Roof Analysis* (London; C. R. Books, Ltd., 1966), 10ff.
7. *Ibid.,* 15.
8. *Ibid.,* 61, 91.
9. Jacques Heyman, "The Stone Skeleton," *International Journal of Solids Structures,* II (1966), 252-253.
10. Jacques Heyman, "Spires and Fan Vaults," *International Journal of Solids Structures,* III (1967), 256.
11. *Ibid.,* 254.
12. *Ibid.,* 256.
13. *Ibid.,* 256.
14. See H. Straub, *A History of Civil Engineering* (Leonard Hill, 1952); Ivor B. Hart, *The Mechanical Investigations of Leonardo da Vinci* (1925).
15. Information from the late Mr. G. G. Pace, who witnessed the reconstruction.
16. For modern solutions to the problem see Arthur W. French and Howard C. Ives, *Stereotomy* (2nd Edit., Revised; New York: John Wiley and Sons, Inc., 1920?).
17. Robert Willis, "On the Construction of the Vaults of the Middle Ages," *Transactions of the Royal Institute of British Architects,* I (1842), 47.
18. For a partial listing of extant English drawings see Martin Biddle, "A Thirteenth-Century Architectural Sketch from the Hospital of St. John the Evangelist, Cambridge," *Proceedings of the Cambridge Antiquarian Society,* LIV (1961), 106-108.

Theory,
Design,
and
Construction

19. For example, see Hans Koepf, *Die gotischen Planrisse der Wiener Sammlungen* (Graz, 1969), fig. 275. For description of other collections see F. Bucher, "Design in Gothic Architecture – A Preliminary Assessment," *Journal of the Society of Architectural Historians,* XXVII (1968), 49-71, and F. Bucher, "The Dresden Sketch-book of Vault Projection," *Acts of the XXII International Congress for the History of Art* (Budapest, 1972), 527-537.

20. See Lon R. Shelby, "Mediaeval Masons' Templates," *Journal of the Society of Architectural Historians,* XXX, nr. II (1971), 140-154.

21. Willis, "On the Construction of the Vaults of the Middle Ages," 46ff.

22. Willis, "On the Construction of the Vaults of the Middle Ages," 50.

23. Information from the late Mr. G. G. Pace.

24. John Harvey, *Gothic England* (London, 1947), 129.

25. Robert Willis and John Clark, *The Architectural History of the University of Cambridge* (Cambridge, 1886), I, 613-614.

5 Image and Meaning: An Illustration

From the earliest times, vaults carried symbolic overtones for some people. By the end of the Middle Ages, vaults – like window tracery – had developed into elaborate abstract patterns. On the Continent these had become virtuoso performances, which dazzled the eye and the mind with their almost incomprehensible patterns. By contrast, the stereometric simplicity and regularity of English fan vaults creates an unforgettable impression on the beholder. Spatial unity was achieved. The resulting image imparts the impression of circles or wheels revolving in space.

The largest number of fan vaults appear in chantry chapels, and, more importantly, the major fan vaulted buildings constructed during the period 1475-1540 were meant to function as chantries; this circumstance raises the question of the connection between the visual forms chosen and the context in which they were employed. Can we go beyond this to find a patron who might have been specifically attracted by an early remembered form of a fan vault and wanted to use the form to associate with a symbolic or allegorical concept? This occurrence would not be new. We only have to look at the way Durandus, Suger, or St. Hugh of Lincoln interpreted architectural forms.

Too little is known about the relationship between the designer and patron and the decision-making process for the determination of a building program in medieval England to adequately assess the role each played in the design process. It is generally agreed that patrons did take an active interest in the way their buildings were to look and what they were to communicate, which can be best illustrated by an examination of Henry VII's Chapel, Westminster.

In his will King Henry VII directed that the windows be glazed, etc., ". . . as is by us redily divised and in picture delivered to the Priour (Bolton) of Sainct Bartilmews besids Smythfeld, masitre of the works of our said Chapell . . ."[1] The role that Prior Bolton or some other[2] may have played in the design process should not be discounted. Although Bolton was an ecclesiastic, and most probably did not do actual design work, he or another person along with the master mason may have helped to determine the building program. It is recorded in connection with Lady Margaret's tomb for the Chapel that in 1513-14, Bolton was paid for ". . . his counsell in devisynge the seide tombe and for his labour and costis and expensis in surueyinge and controllynge the werkmen of the same tombe at diuerse and sondry tymes and for sendynge for diuerse werkmen from beyonde the sea for making of seide tombe."[3] From this account entry it is quite clear that Bolton played a role in the determination of the program for the tomb, as well as being involved in its actual construction. As it was contemporary practice to employ court poets to help with the symbolism of allegories for pageants and jousts,[4] it would seem likely that someone, whether Bolton or another, would have been employed to work out the complex iconographic program for the sculpture and glass of the chapel. Scholars, including Lawrence Stone, agree that the builders strove to influence public opinion through art by proclaiming the triumphant self-assertion of the new Tudor dynasty.[5] Consequently, the question can be asked whether the architecture, the dominant feature of which is the fan vaulted ceiling, was intended to work hand in hand with the sculpture and glass to achieve this same end.

More than most fan vaults, the vaulting of Henry VII's Chapel communicates the idea of the circle or wheel because of its pendants. It is necessary to investigate what symbolic connotations, if any, this visual image may have had at the time the chapel was designed, which was after 1498, when Henry VII decided to change his place of burial from Windsor to Westminster, and by October 1502, when construction was already underway. There is important evidence which relates Tudor political propaganda with sunwheel shapes. In connection with this, the following description of a London pageant held in 1501 may suggest relevant symbolism.

The fourth pageant, "The Sphere of the Sun," for the reception of Katherine of Aragon in 1501 was designed according to the court herald as a "celestiall place," and displayed an image of Prince Arthur, heir apparent to the throne of England and Katherine's spouse, seated upon a golden throne situated in the middle of a wheel admist a revolving cosmos: "Benethe his chare there was IIII great sterres, like IIII wheles, runnying very swyfte . . ." Above his wheel was a representation of the Father of Heaven. A host of angels ". . . havyng scriptours of *te Deum* and *tibi omnes etc.*," were grouped around the Father of Heaven. Much of the surrounding decoration was heraldic: the red dragon, the red lion, and the white greyhound. This elaborate mechanical cosmos was the most impressive visual feature of the entire pageant series.[6]

The sun at this time was considered according to the herald to be the "syngnfyour of kyngys." The herald concluded his description of this pageant by saying, "and this was named the sphere of the sunne, appropriat to the Prince of England, shewyng and declarying his fatall desposicaon and desteny." Sydney Anglo, in *Spectacle Pageantry, and Early Tudor Policy,* proves through an extensive iconographic study of the pageant that this pageant shamelessly identifies Prince Arthur both with Christ the Redeemer and with Christ the Sun of Justice.[7] While Prince Arthur in this fourth pageant is identified with God the Son, Henry VII in the fifth pageant is identified with God the Father: ". . . o wir Soverayn lord the kyng, May be Resemblid to the kyng Celestyall.[8] Anglo points out the relationship of this pageant with the cosmic vision of Boethius, who speaks of the Creator, His cosmic wheel, the revolution of the heavens upon the wheel, and finally the throne of the Creator to which the wheel is attached.[9]

Several interpretations for the circle are possible. For St. Augustine, the circle was the symbol of virtue.[10] For Boethius, the heavens revolved upon the wheel, and for Ezekiel the circle was the spirit of life.[11] There is no single iconographic interpretation for a circle; medieval images and symbols were often ambiguous and thereby gain richness through their associative power. For example, when Johannes Scotus Erigena spoke of the number eight, he thought of its relation to Sunday, Easter, Resurrection and regeneration, spring, and new life. All of these connotations he said are ever-present and vibrated in him whenever he thought of eight.[12] The circle, then, should be understood as a multivocal image.

The total context in which the vaulting is placed helps us to clarify its meaning, for underneath it are rows of statues of apostles, saints, and prophets, whose purpose Henry VII explained in his will: "I trust also to the singular mediacions and praiers of all the holie companie of heven . . ."[13] Clearly, Henry VII envisioned his chapel as a celestial place. Heraldic decoration, like that in the fourth pageant for the reception of Katherine of Aragon, abounds. The chapel was intended not only to be the burial place of Henry VII but also for Henry VI, whose mortal remains Henry VII had prepared for transfer to Westminster. It was through Henry VI that Henry VII, in part, laid claim to the throne. In this context the reasons for the construction of the chapel were both political and religious. The chapel was to be the visible evidence of the legitimacy and the practical power of the Tudor dynasty. In this regard, it is interesting to note that Henry VII had, until the day he died, a basic fear that his dynasty might be displaced.[14]

The architectural forms in the chapel, when seen in conjunction with the sculpture and glass, emphasize the chapel as a celestial realm and establish Henry VII's place there. Furthermore, his tomb was to be located in the center,[15] surrounded by a grille,[16] and was to be covered with a conical roof – the vaulting – just as Christ's tomb was supposed to have been.[17] That the roof of a church belongs to the heavens was not a new idea. Around 1225, St. Hugh of Lincoln described the various parts of a church: the foundation is the body, the wall the man, the roof the spirit; the body belongs to the earth, men to the clouds, the spirit to the stars.[18] Henry VII's Chapel is more than a concrete interpretation of that idea. When seen in the context of the symbolism employed in the fourth pageant for the reception of

Katherine of Aragon, "The Sphere of the Sun," it establishes a visual connection between the Tudor dynasty and Christ, thereby combining temporal and spiritual power. It can also be seen to symbolize eternal life by association with the Godhead.

This does not provide a complete symbolic explanation of the links between royal patronage and fan vaulting, but it illustrates the way in which the associative quality of the fan vault may have been exploited and endowed with symbolic meaning. If we accept the idea that the vaulting as well as the sculpture and glass of Henry VII's Chapel had symbolic connotations, we can only speculate to what degree such symbolism – which may have been a royal prerogative – was intended by those members of the court who had fan vaults built. If one fan vault was iconographically significant, perhaps the rest share some such meaning.

The design of temporary structures, such as for pageants, their symbolism, and their influence on the design of permanent structures in England for the period around 1500 has yet to be given due consideration. The relative roles the architect, the patron and the advisors played in the design process is the crucial issue here; it is at present unknown how much, and what kind of assistance the master mason received, which might have influenced the formal design.

1. Thomas Astle, *The Will of King Henry VII* (London, 1775), 6.
2. Bolton probably was not Master of the Works until after 1504. See Westminster Abbey Muniment 23582 where Sir William Tyler was entitled *magister operum domini regis.* Cited in H. M. Colvin, *History of the King's Works,* III, pt. 1 (London, 1975), 213.
3. Robert Forsyth Scott, "On the Contracts for the Tomb of the Lady Margaret Beaufort," *Archaeologia,* LXVI (1915), 370.
4. Joyselyne G. Russell, *The Field of the Cloth of Gold* (London: Routledge Kegan Paul, 1969), 34.
5. L. Stone, *Sculpture in Britain: The Middle Ages,* 229.
6. Francis Grose and Thomas Astle, *The Antiquarian Repertory* (4 vols.; London: Edward Jeffrey, 1807-1809), II, 273, and Sydney Anglo, *Spectacle Pageantry, And Early Tudor Policy* (Oxford: At the Clarendon Press, 1969), 77ff.
7. Anglo, *ibid.,* 82.
8. Anglo, *ibid.,* 88-89.
9. Anglo, *ibid.,* 76.
10. Augustine, *De quantitate anime,* cap. XVI, Migne, *Patrologique Cursus Completus, Series Latina,* XXXII, c. 1051f.
11. Ezekiel, I:10.
12. Cited in Richard Krautheimer, "Introduction to an 'Iconography of Medieval Architecture,'" *Journal of the Warburg and Courtauld Institutes,* V (1942), 9-10.
13. Astle, *The Will of King Henry VII,* 4.
14. *L & P Henry VIII,* I, 231-240 and S. B. Chrimes, *Henry VIII* (London, 1972), 308.
15. Astle, *The Will of King Henry VII,* 4.
16. To be made by Thomas Ducheman, P.R.O., E. 214/15, 52. Cited by Stone, *Sculpture in Britain,* 270n.79.
17. John Beckwith, *Early Christian and Byzantine Art* (Harmondsworth: Penguin Books, 1970), 25.
18. J. F. Dimock, edit., *Metrical Life of St. Hugh, Bishop of Lincoln* (Lincoln, 1860), 32ff.

6

Illustrations

*All photographs by author
unless otherwise noted.*

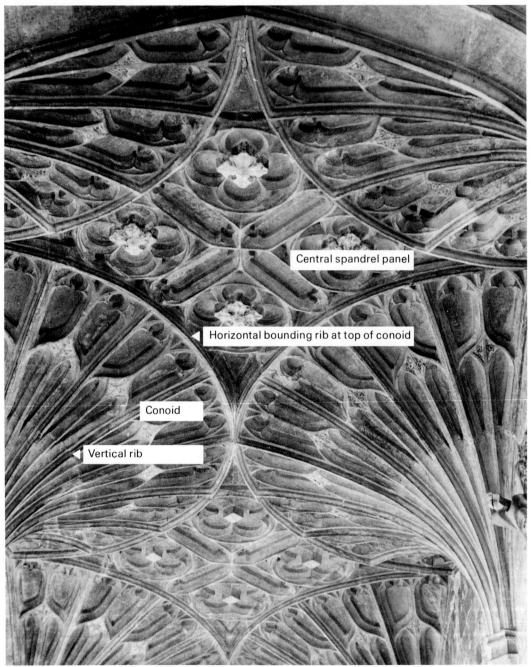

Central spandrel panel

Horizontal bounding rib at top of conoid

Conoid

Vertical rib

1 North Leigh, St. Marys; Wilcote Chapel, circa
1440.

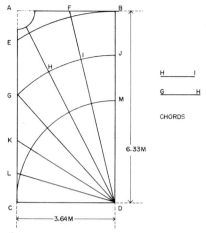

2 Cambridge, King's College Chapel, main vault, built 1512-15. Schematic plan of one quadrant of a bay showing rib positions.

3 Bosbury, Holy Trinity Church, Morton Chapel, built circa 1510, southeast corner.

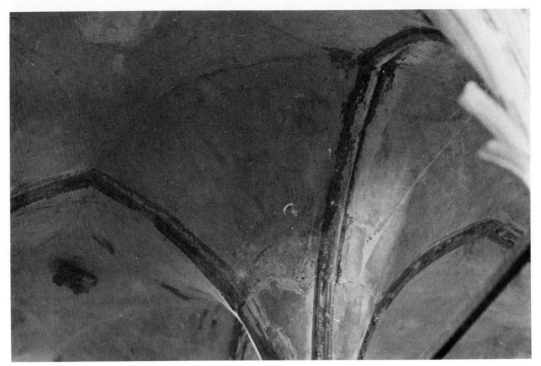

4 Tewkesbury Abbey, Despencer
Monument, canopy.

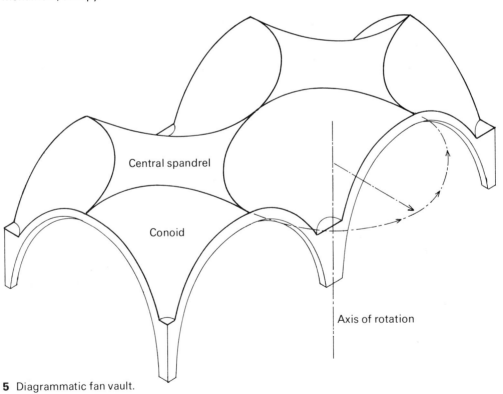

Central spandrel

Conoid

Axis of rotation

5 Diagrammatic fan vault.

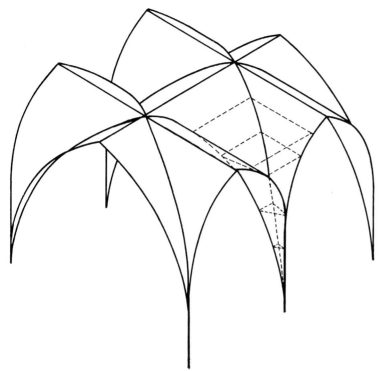

6 Diagrammatic French ribbed vault (after Fitchen).

7 Gloucester Cathedral, north transept.

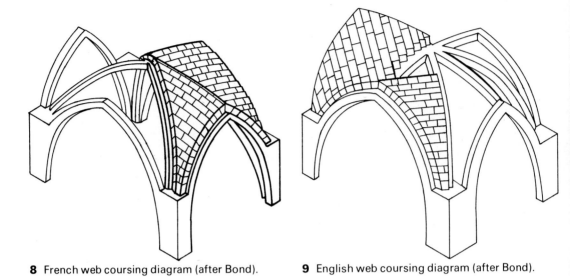

8 French web coursing diagram (after Bond).

9 English web coursing diagram (after Bond).

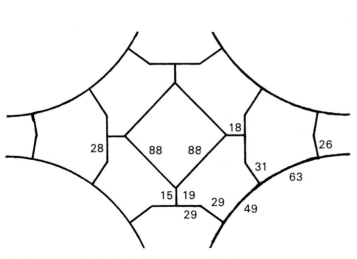

10 Gloucester Cathedral, cloister, stone jointing pattern.

11 Windsor, St. George's, Aerary Porch.

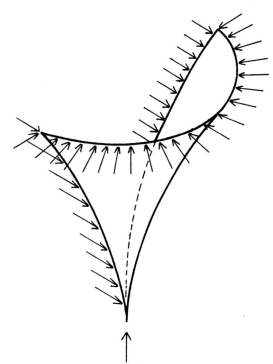

12 Fan vault, structural diagram.

13 Cirencester, St. John the Baptist, north porch. Originally ribs and panels were cut together; restoration work here on the ribs does not reflect medieval practice (photo: Wiltshire Newspapers, Swindon, England).

41

14 Wells Cathedral, tomb canopy of William
de Marchia.

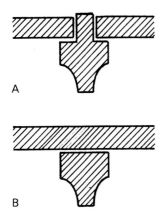

15 Rib to web relationship diagram, (A) rebated;
(B) not rebated.

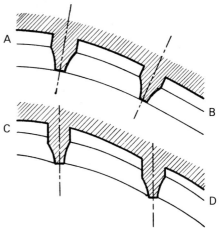

16 Rib to surface relationship diagram, (AB) ribs
perpendicular to the vaulting surface; (CD) ribs
perpendicular to the floor.

17 Wells Cathedral, chancel.

18 Gloucester Cathedral, cloister, late 14th century.

19 Hereford Cathedral, chapter house, vaulting fragment.

20 Side view of 19.

21 Tewkesbury Abbey, Trinity Chapel.

22 Tewkesbury Abbey, Founder's Chapel.

23 Exeter Cathedral, west façade, north porch.

24 Gloucester Cathedral, cloister, lavatorium.

25 Old Wardour Castle, entranceway.

26 Winchester College, chapel.

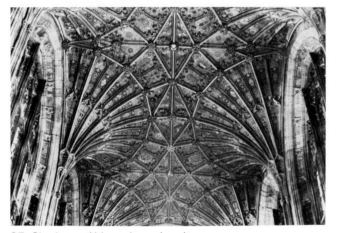

27 Sherborne Abbey, chancel vault.

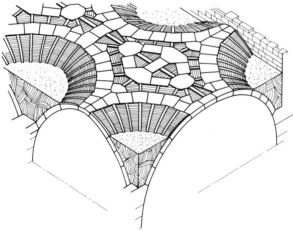

28 Sherborne Abbey, extrados of the chancel vault (after Carpenter).

29 Milton Abbas, crossing tower.

30 Crewkerne, south porch.

31 Wells Cathedral, crossing tower.

32 Ottery St. Mary, Dorset aisle.

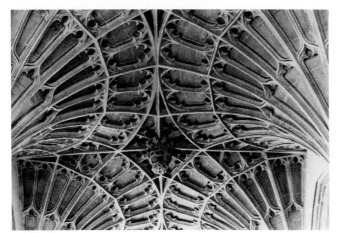

33 Cullompton, St. Andrews, Lane aisle.

34 Tewkesbury Abbey, Beauchamp Chapel.

35 Warwick, chantry chapel off Beauchamp Chapel (photo: Great Britain, National Monuments Record).

36 Canterbury Cathedral, Henry IV's Chapel (photo: Great Britain, National Monuments Record).

37 Oxford, All Souls College, chapel vestibule.

38 Burford, south porch.

39 Minster Lovell, crossing vault.

40 Windsor, St. George's Chapel, south chancel
aisle.

41 Ely Cathedral, Alcock Chapel (photo: Great
Britain, National Monuments Record).

42 Downham, Bishop's Palace.

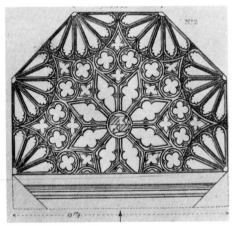

43 Windsor, St. George's Chapel,
Urswick, plan (Pugin).

44 Hereford Cathedral, Bishop Audley's Chapel,
plan (Howard).

45 Salisbury Cathedral, Audley Chapel.

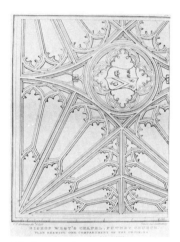

46 Putney, St. Mary the Virgin, Bishop West's Chapel, partial plan (Andrews).

47 St. David's Cathedral, Trinity Chapel.

53

48 Tong, St. Bartholomew, Vernon Chapel
(photo: Great Britain, National Monuments
Record).

49 Westminster Abbey, Henry VII's Chapel, main vault
from southeast apsidal chapel, before painting (photo:
Great Britain, National Monuments Record).

50 Eton College Chapel, Lupton's Chapel.

51 Christchurch Priory, Salisbury Chapel.

52 Cambridge, King's College Chapel.

53 Bath Abbey, east end of chancel.

54 Axbridge, St. John the Baptist, crossing tower.

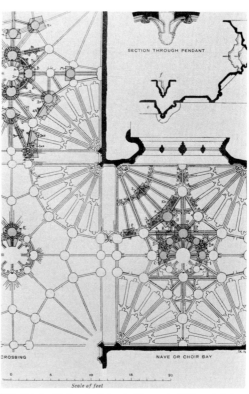

55 Wells Cathedral, Lady Chapel off the cloister, reconstructed plan (Buckle).

56 Ditcheat, St. Mary Magdalen, crossing tower.

57 Glastonbury, St. John's, west tower.

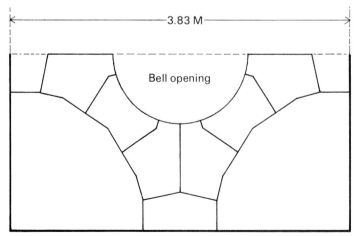

58 Ilminster, St. Mary, crossing tower, plan
showing stone jointing system.

58

59 Glastonbury Abbey, fan vault fragments.

60 Mells, St. Andrew's, south porch (photo:
Great Britain, National Monuments Record).

61 Doulting, St. Aldhelm, south porch.

62 Buckland Dinham, St. Michael's, south porch.

63 Langport, All Saints, west tower.

64 Muchelney, Sts. Peter and Paul, west tower.

60

65 Shepton Beauchamp, St. Michael, west tower.

66 Wedmore, St. Mary Magdalene, crossing tower.

67 Taunton, St. Mary Magdalene, west tower.

68 Taunton, St. James, west tower.

69 North Petherton, St. Mary, west tower.

70 Weston Zoyland, St. Mary's, west tower.

71 Batcombe, St. Mary, west tower.

72 Shepton Mallet, Sts. Peter and Paul, west tower.

73 Chewton Mendip, St. Mary Magdalen, west tower.

74 Ile Abbots, St. Mary, south porch.

75 North Curry, Sts. Peter and Paul, south porch.

76 Kingston St. Mary, St. Mary's, south porch.

77 Beaulieu Abbey, chapter house entrance recess.

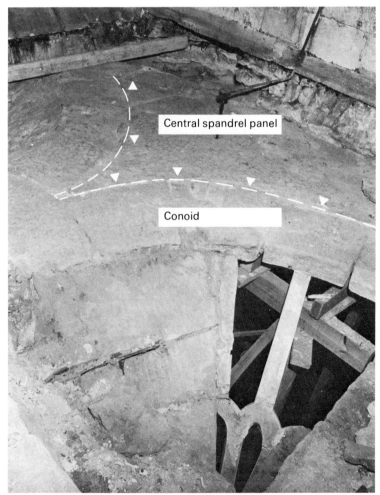

Central spandrel panel

Conoid

78 Cirencester, St. John the Baptist, north porch. Shows how the spandrel provides the necessary compressive load to keep the vaulting conoid in equilibrium. Originally ribs and panels were cut together; restoration work here does not reflect medieval practice. (photo: Wiltshire Newspapers, Swindon, England).

65

79 Gloucester Cathedral, cloister, east walk, rectangular bay.

80 Saffron Walden, St. Mary the Virgin, south porch.

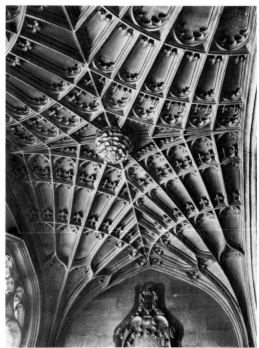

81 Cambridge, King's College Chapel, side chapel (photo: Great Britain, National Monuments Record).

82 Westminster Abbey, Henry VII's Chapel,
partial plan of nave vaulting bay (Cottingham).

Original wall line

83 Muchelney Abbey, cloister fragment, shows
how the tas-de-charge was set into the wall.

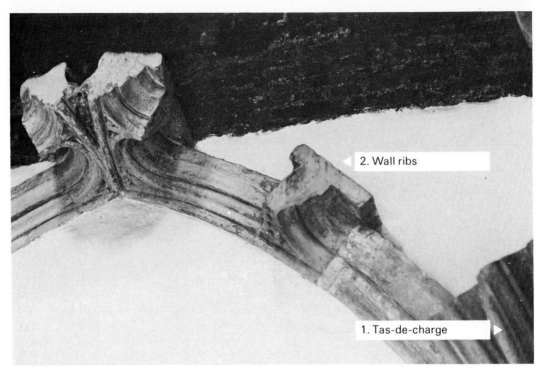

84 Shelton, St. Mary, south porch, showing the first two steps in the constructional process.

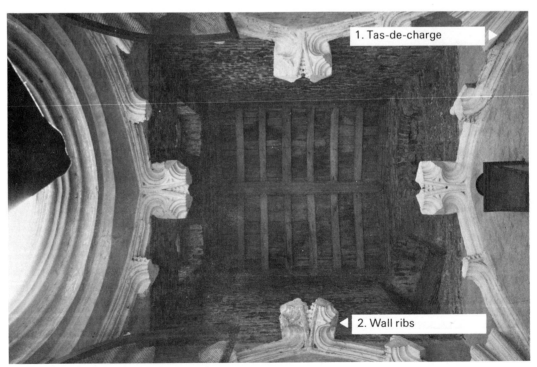

85 Shelton, St. Mary, south porch, showing the first two steps in the constructional process (photo: Great Britain, National Monuments Record).

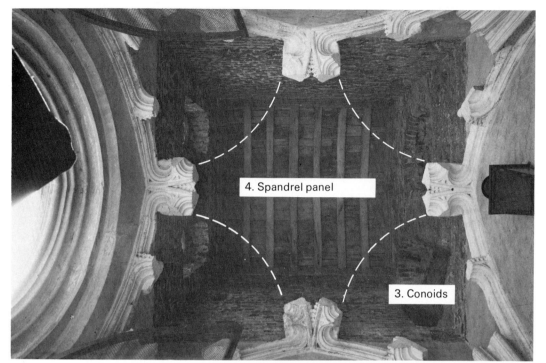

4. Spandrel panel

3. Conoids

86 Shelton St. Mary, south porch, showing the third and fourth steps in the constructional process.

4. Central spandrel panel

3. Conoids

87 Cirencester, St. John the Baptist, north porch, vault from above showing third and fourth steps in the constructional process (photo: Wiltshire Newspapers, Swindon, England).

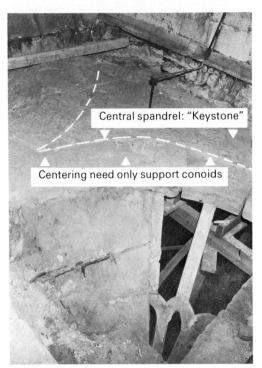

Central spandrel: "Keystone"

Centering need only support conoids

88 Cirencester, St. John the Baptist, north porch, showing necessary centering (photo: Wiltshire Newspapers, Swindon, England).

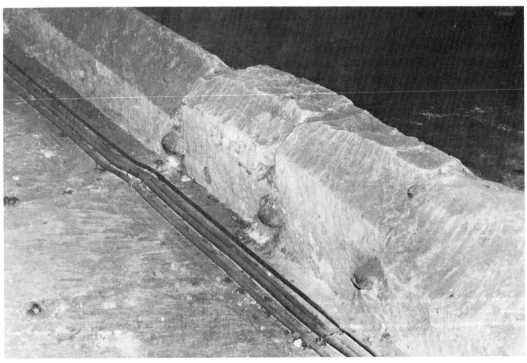

89 Worcester Cathedral, Prince Arthur's Chantry Chapel, extrados of vault.

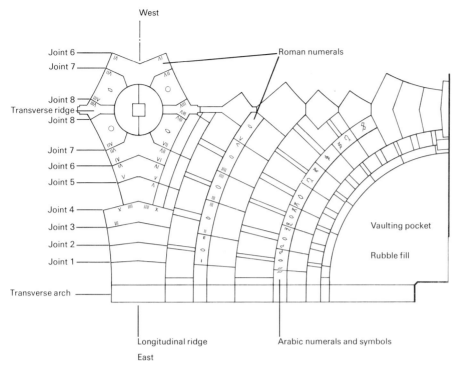

West

Joint 6 — Roman numerals

Joint 7

Joint 8

Transverse ridge

Joint 8

Joint 7

Joint 6

Joint 5

Joint 4

Joint 3

Joint 2

Joint 1

Transverse arch

Vaulting pocket

Rubble fill

Longitudinal ridge

East

Arabic numerals and symbols

90 Cambridge, King's College Chapel, main
vault, plan, typical quadrant of one bay showing
position/assembly marks.

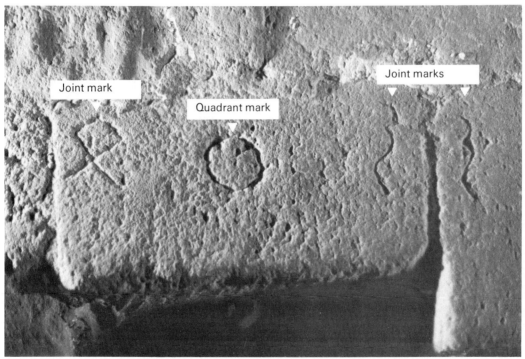

Joint mark

Joint marks

Quadrant mark

91 Cambridge, King's College Chapel, main vault,
extrados of typical stone showing joint and
quadrant marks.

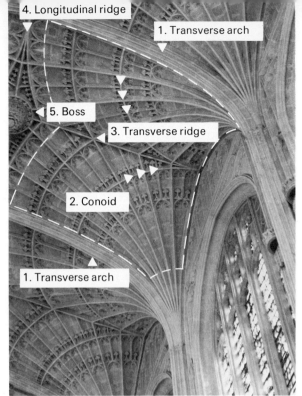

92 Cambridge, King's College Chapel, main vault, showing steps in the constructional process.

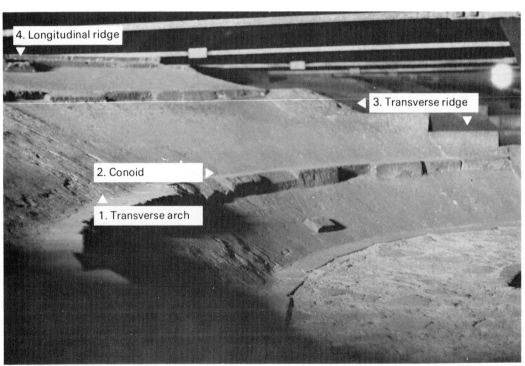

93 Cambridge, King's College Chapel, extrados of main vault, showing steps in the constructional process.

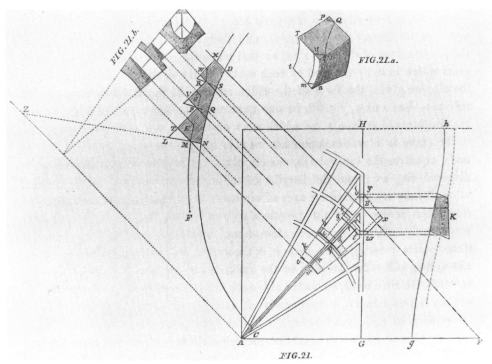

94 Plane geometry projection methodology, showing formulation of transverse ridge stones; see also, illustration 95 (Willis).

95 Peterborough Cathedral, new building, large fan, extrados, transverse ridge showing horizontal "surfaces of operation."

73

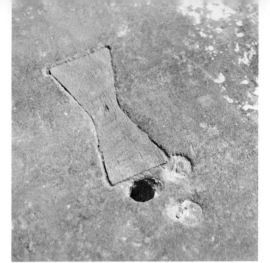

96 Cambridge, King's College Chapel, main vault, extrados, showing wooden "bow-tie" and lewis holes used for lifting stones.

97 Canterbury Cathedral, Lady Chapel off the Martyrdom.

98 Cerne Abbas, porch to the abbot's hall.

99 Cambridge, King's College Chapel, extrados of main vault, showing cemented rubble fill.

100 Cambridge, King's College Chapel, main vault, extrados, transverse ridge.

101 Bath Abbey, extrados of chancel vault.

102 Bath Abbey, north chancel aisle.

103 Bath Abbey, extrados of chancel vault, vaulting conoid.

104 Bath Abbey, extrados of chancel vault, first transverse ridge from west.

105 Bath Abbey, extrados of chancel vault, first
transverse ridge from the east.

106 Bath Abbey, extrados of north chancel aisle.

107 Bath Abbey, extrados of north chancel aisle, pendant from above.

108 Bath Abbey, Prior Bird's Chantry Chapel.

109 Beckington, St. George's west tower.

110 Bodmin, parish church, south porch.

111 Bosbury, Holy Trinity Church, Morton
Chapel, north side.

112 Bristol, St. Mark, Poyntz Chapel (photo: Great Britain, National Monuments Record).

113 Bristol, St. Stephen's, south porch (photo: Great Britain, National Monuments Record).

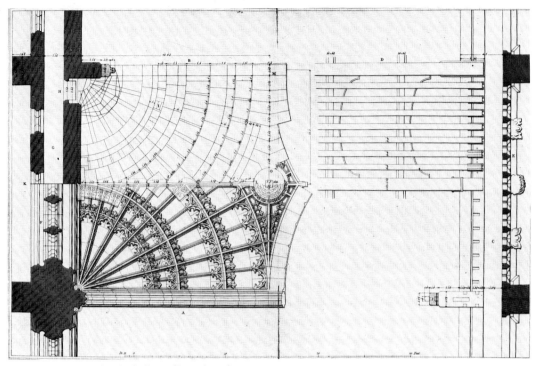

114 Cambridge, King's College Chapel, main
vault, plan (Mackenzie).

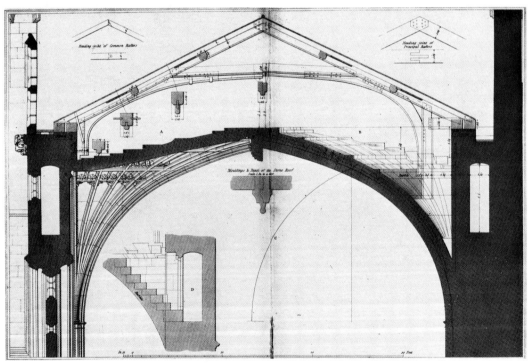

115 Cambridge, King's College Chapel, main
vault, transverse section (Mackenzie).

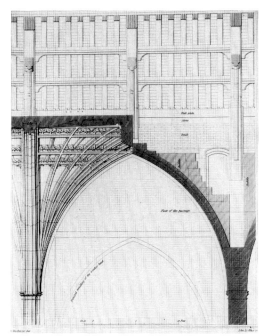

116 Cambridge, King's College Chapel, main
vault, longitudinal section (Mackenzie).

117 Cambridge, King's College Chapel, south
porch.

118 Cambridge, St. John's College, gateway.

119 Canterbury Cathedral, central tower.

120 Canterbury Cathedral, central tower,
extrados of vaulting ridge.

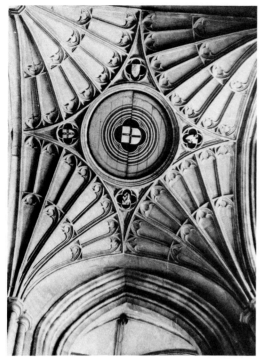

121 Canterbury Cathedral, southwest tower.

122 Castle Combe, St. Andrew's, west tower.

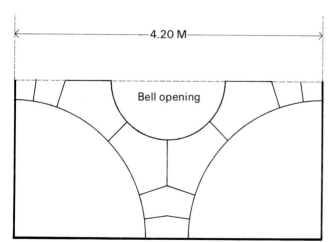

123 Chewton Mendip, St. Mary Magdalen, west tower, plan showing ridge stone layout.

124 Cirencester Abbey, vaulting fragment.

125 Cirencester, St. John the Baptist, north porch.

126 Cirencester, St. John the Baptist, St. Catherine's Chapel.

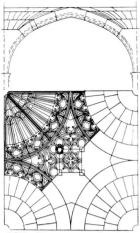

127 Cirencester, St. John the Baptist, south
porch, section and plan (Howard).

128 Cirencester, St. John the Baptist, south
porch.

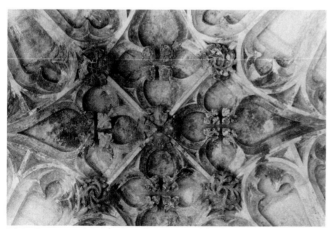

129 Corsham House, Bradford-on-Avon porch.

130 Cowdray House, hall porch (photo: J. A. Gotch, *Early Renaissance Architecture in Britain,* 1901, pl. IV).

131 Croscombe, St. Mary's west tower.

132 Crowcombe, Holy Ghost, south porch.

133 Cullompton, St. Andrews, Lane Aisle, extrados of vaulting conoid.

134 Cullompton, St. Andrews, Lane Aisle, extrados of boss.

135 Curry Rivel, St. Andrew's, south porch.

136 Curry Rivel, St. Andrew's, west tower.

137 Evesham, All Saints, Lichfield's Chapel.

138 Evesham, St. Lawrence, Chapel of St. Clement.

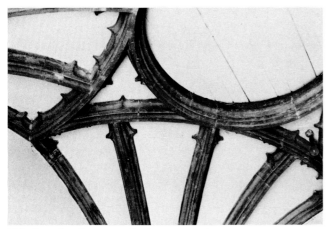

139 Eye, Sts. Peter and Paul, west porch.

140 Fotheringhay, St. Mary the Virgin and All Saints, west tower.

141 Glastonbury Abbey, vaulting fragments.

142 Glastonbury, St. John's, west tower.

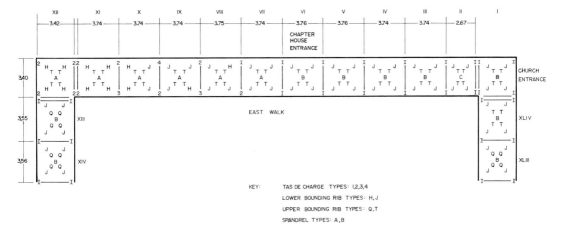

143 Gloucester Cathedral, cloister, plan.

144 Gloucester Cathedral, cloister, bay VI-VII, tas-de-charge, type I.

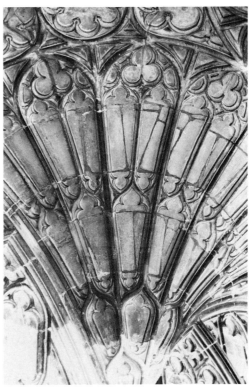

145 Gloucester Cathedral, cloister, bay XI, southeast, tas-de-charge, type II.

93

146 Gloucester Cathedral, cloister, bay IX, southwest, tas-de-charge, type III.

147 Gloucester Cathedral, cloister, bay IX, northeast, tas-de-charge, type IV.

148 Gloucester Cathedral, cloister, east walk.

149 Gloucester Cathedral, cloister, bay VIII, intrados.

150 Gloucester Cathedral, cloister, bay VIII, extrados.

151 Gloucester Cathedral, west entrance to the nave.

152 Gloucester Cathedral, east entrance into the cloister from the church.

153 Gloucester Cathedral, south chantry chapel off the Lady Chapel.

154 Great Malvern Priory, chantry chapel.

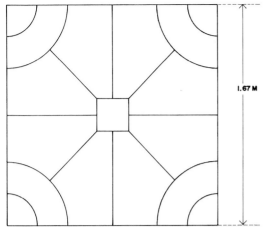

155 Great Malvern Priory, chantry chapel, plan, stone jointing layout.

156 Hereford Cathedral, Bishop Audley's Chapel, upper story.

157 Hereford Cathedral, Bishop Audley's Chapel, lower story.

158 Hereford Cathedral, Bishop Stanbury's
Chapel.

159 Hereford Cathedral, Vicars' Cloister porch.

160 Highworth, St. Michael's, west tower.

161 Hilton, All Saints, south porch.

162 Ilminster, St. Mary, crossing tower.

163 Iron Acton, St. James the Less, west tower.

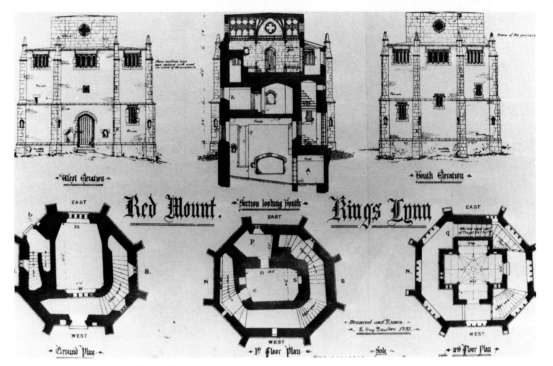

164 King's Lynn, Red Mount Chapel, plans and sections (Dawber).

165 King's Lynn, Red Mount Chapel, plan of fan vault (Howard).

166 King's Lynn, Red Mount Chapel, fan vault.

167 Lacock, St. Cyriac's, present Lady Chapel.

168 Littlebury, Holy Trinity, south porch.

169 Maids Moreton, St. Edmund's, vestry
(photo: Great Britain, National Monuments
Record).

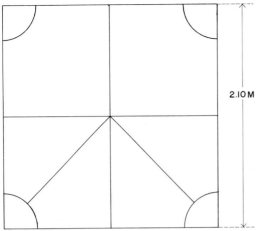

170 Maids Moreton, St. Edmund's, south porch, plan of stone jointing layout.

171 Maids Moreton, St. Edmund's, south porch, central spandrel panel.

172 Maids Moreton, St. Edmund's, north porch.

173 Maids Moreton, St. Edmund's, west tower.

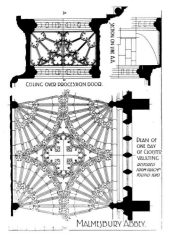

174 Malmesbury Abbey, cloister, plan
(Brakspear).

175 Mells, St. Andrew's, west tower.

176 Mildenhall, St. Mary's, west tower gallery.

177 Muchelney Abbey, cloister, vaulting fragment.

178 Norwich, St. Giles, south porch.

179 Ottery St. Mary, St. Mary, north porch.

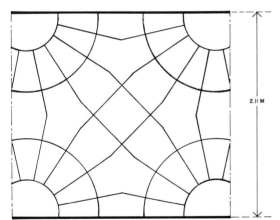

2.11 M

180 Oxford, All Souls College, chapel vestibule, plan of stone jointing layout.

181 Oxford, Christchurch, chantry chapel.

182 Oxford, Magdalen College Chapel,
Founder's Oratory, drawing of 1823/33 (photo:
Great Britain, National Monuments Record).

183 Oxford, Queens College, former gateway,
now destroyed (Skelton).

184 Peterborough Cathedral, new building, large
fan vault.

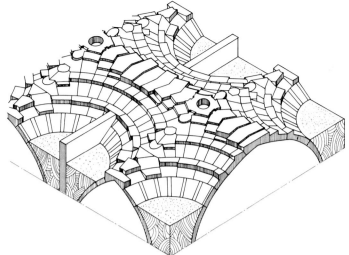

185 Peterborough Cathedral, new building, extrados of large fan vault (after Willis).

186 Peterborough Cathedral, new building, small fan vault.

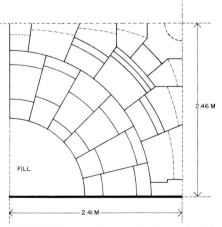

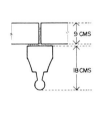

187 Peterborough Cathedral, new building, small fan vault plan of stone layout (after G. G. Pace).

188 Peterborough Cathedral, new building,
extrados of small fan vault.

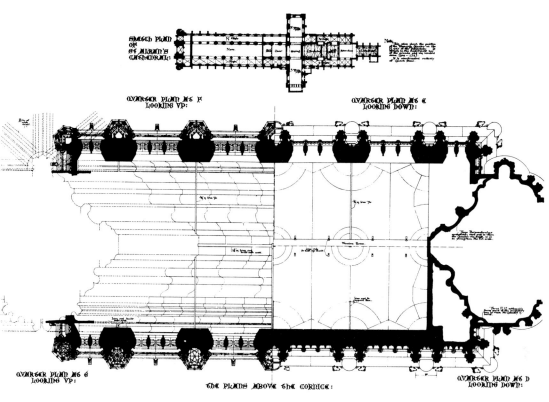

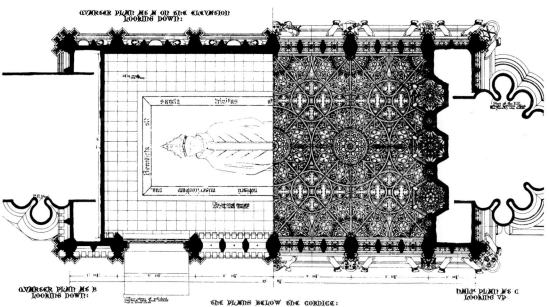

189 St. Albans Cathedral, Ramryge Chapel
The Builders Journal and Architectural Record,
3 Feb. 1897).

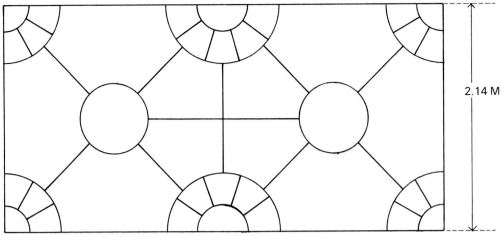

190 Salisbury Cathedral, Bishop Audley's
Chapel, plan of stone jointing layout.

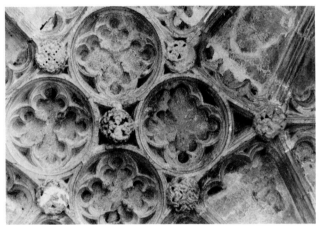

191 Salisbury, King's House, porch.

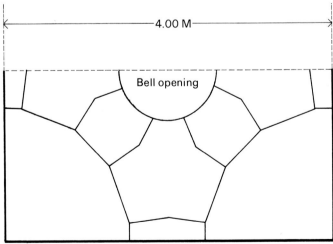

192 Shepton Beauchamp, St. Michael, west
tower, plan of stone jointing layout.

193 Sherborne Abbey, crossing.

194 Sherborne Abbey, nave.

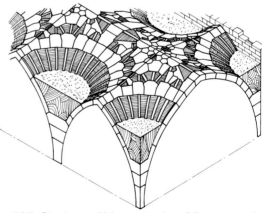

195 Sherborne Abbey, extrados of the nave vault (after Carpenter).

111

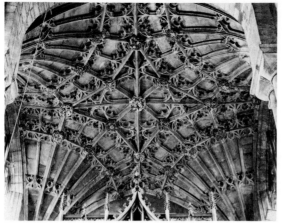

196 Sherborne Abbey, north transept (photo:
Fred H. Crossley and Maurice H. Ridgway,
Courtauld Institute).

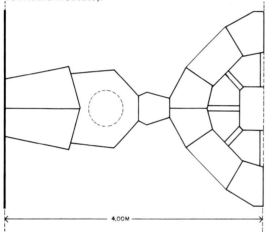

197 Sherborne Abbey, north transept, plan of
ridge layout.

198 Sherborne Abbey, St. Katherine's Chapel.

199 Sherborne Abbey, Wykeham Chapel.

200 Sherborne Abbey, extrados of chancel vault.

201 Sherborne Abbey, north transept, extrados, ridge.

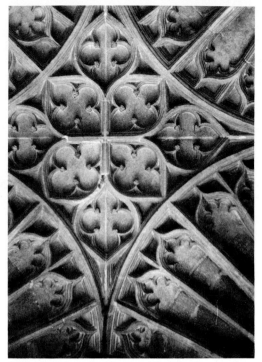

202 Spalding, St. Mary and St. Nicolas, north porch.

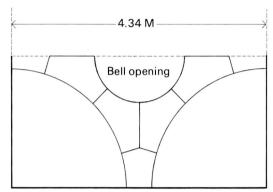

203 Taunton, St. James, west tower, plan of ridge stone layout.

4.34 M

Bell opening

204 Tewkesbury Abbey, cloister.

205 Tewkesbury Abbey, cloister.

206 Torbryan, Holy Trinity, south porch (Howard).

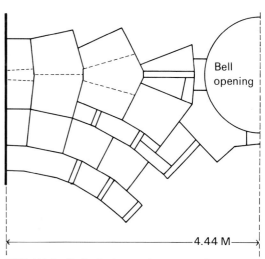

207 Wells Cathedral, crossing tower, plan of ridge layout.

115

208 Wells Cathedral, crossing tower vault,
extrados, ridge.

209 Wells Cathedral, crossing tower vault,
extrados, conoid.

210 Wells Cathedral, Lady Chapel off the cloister, vaulting fragments.

211 Wells Cathedral, Sugar's Chantry Chapel.

212 Westminster Abbey, Henry VII's Chapel,
nave vault (photo: Great Britain, National
Monuments Record).

213 Westminster Abbey, Henry VII's Chapel,
plan of east end of nave (Cottingham).

214 Westminster Abbey, Henry VII's Chapel,
partial plan of typical side aisle bay (Cottingha

118

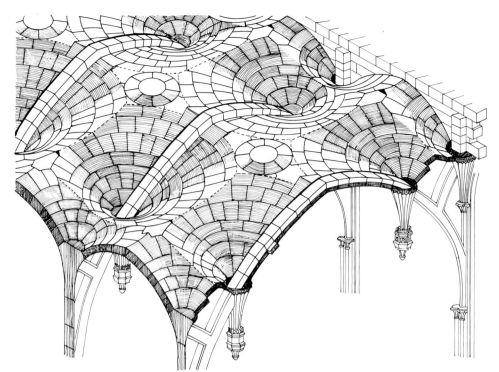

215 Westminster Abbey, Henry VII's Chapel, extrados of nave vault (after Willis).

216 Westminster Abbey, Henry VII's Chapel, extrados of nave vault, transverse arch.

217 Westminster Abbey, Henry VII's Chapel,
extrados of nave vault, side pendant.

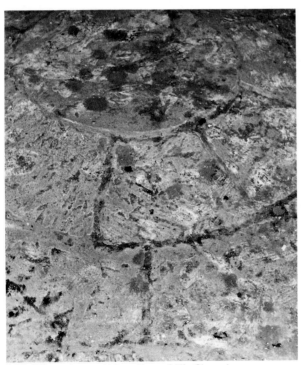

218 Westminster Abbey, Henry VII's Chapel,
extrados of nave vault, pendant in center of bay.

219 Westminster Abbey, Henry VII's Chapel, extrados of apse vault.

220 Westminster Abbey, Henry VII's Chapel, extrados of nave side aisle vault showing a diagonal arch.

121

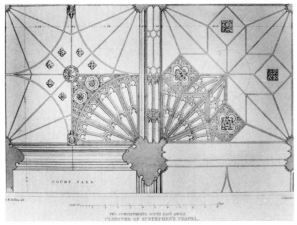

221 Westminster, St. Stephen's, cloister, plan, east walk (Britton).

222 Westminster, St. Stephen's, cloister, north walk (photo: Great Britain, National Monuments Record).

223 Westminster, St. Stephen's, cloister chapel (photo: Great Britain, National Monuments Record).

224 Westminster, St. Stephen's, cloister chapel, plan (Britton).

225 Winchester Cathedral, Cardinal Beaufort's Chapel (photo: Great Britain, National Monuments Record).

226 Winchester Cathedral, Bishop Waynflete's Chapel (photo: Great Britain, National Monuments Record).

227 Windsor, St. George's Chapel, Chantry of Edward IV.

228 Windsor, St. George's Chapel, nave aisle vault.

229 Windsor, St. George's Chapel, ambulatory, southeast bay.

230 Windsor, St. George's (Urswick) Chapel.

231 Windsor, St. George's Chapel, crossing (photo: Archives of St. George's Chapel, reproduced by kind permission of the Dean and Canons of Windsor).

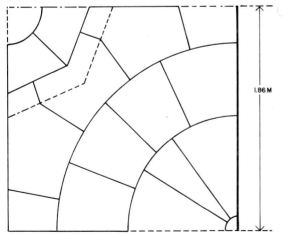

1.86 M

232 Windsor, St. George's Chapel, south choir aisle, plan of stone jointing layout.

125

233 Windsor, St. George's Chapel, south choir aisle, extrados of vault.

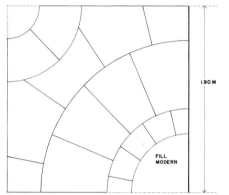

1.90 M

FILL
MODERN

234 Windsor, St. George's Chapel, nave aisle, plan of stone jointing layout.

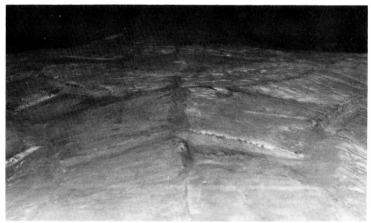

235 Windsor, St. George's Chapel, nave aisle, extrados of vault.

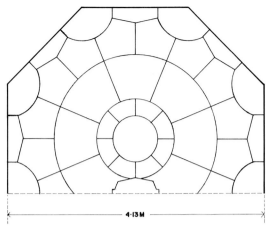

236 Windsor, St. George's Chapel, polygonal chantry chapels, plan of stone jointing layout.

237 Windsor, St. George's Chapel, Beaufort Chapel, extrados of vault.

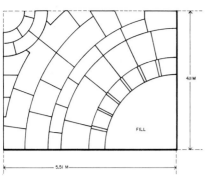

238 Windsor, St. George's Chapel, crossing, plan of stone jointing layout.

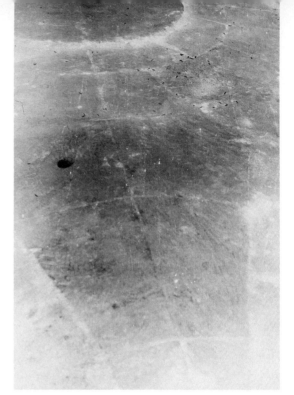

239 Windsor, St. George's Chapel, crossing, extrados of vault showing ridge.

240 Windsor, St. George's Chapel, crossing, extrados of vault showing conoid.

241 Wrington, All Saints, west tower.

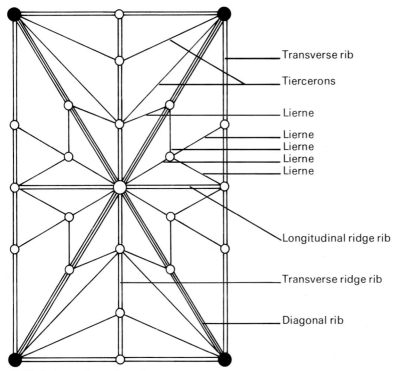

Transverse rib

Tiercerons

Lierne

Lierne
Lierne
Lierne
Lierne

Longitudinal ridge rib

Transverse ridge rib

Diagonal rib

242 Schematic vauling diagram.

7

Catalogue of the Major Fan Vaults Built to 1540

For the most part only structural fan vaults are included, thus fan vaulted oriel windows and the many niches and tomb canopies with decorative fan vaults are omitted. Furthermore, vaults which approach fan vaults, such as those at Rotterham (Yorkshire), Morton (Lincolnshire), Burwell (Cambridgeshire), and Holcumbe Rogus (Devonshire), are not included because their vaulting conoids are not bounded at the top by horizontal ribs.

The dimensions in meters were taken in the space above the vaulting whenever possible and only designate span. The east-west dimension is given first (east is defined as towards the main altar).

Fan vaults are an English phenomenon. Although there do not appear to be any medieval fan vaults built outside of England, the Lady Chapel at Caudebec-en-Caux (Seine-Maritime), France, has a pendant vault which is constructed in principle like the side aisle vaults in Henry VII's Chapel, Westminster, because the pendant is formed from a voussoir of an overflying arch.[1] The vaulting at Caudebec is constructed of ribs and panels, whereas the vaulting of Henry VII's Chapel is constructed of jointed masonry.

1. See Henri Jullien, "Clé de voûte de la chapelle de la vièrge à Caudebec-en-Caux," *Les monuments historiques de la France,* N.S., I (1955), 116-120.

54   Axbridge   St. John the Baptist: Crossing Tower
         Somerset   3.40m x 3.40m

Historical Analysis:

The capitals employed in the tower are similar to those in the south nave aisle and suggest one building campaign. The capitals of the north nave arcade differ. In the will of Thomas Lerbeck, dated 6 March 1429, preserved amongst the Axbridge archives, the testator expressed the desire to be buried in the porch (south?) which he himself lately built.[1] The exterior moulding of the south porch and the south nave aisle are identical and suggest one building campaign. Therefore, if Lerbeck had built the south porch, it seems likely that the interior tower remodelling with its fan vault could have been completed by 1429. Pevsner suggested a date of before 1420 for this fan vault, based on probable neighboring dates.[2]

General Description:

It is square in plan. The vaulting springs from shafts and foliated capitals. The top horizontal bounding rib is composed of circular segments. Trefoil cusping is employed in the subpanels. The areas between the conoids and central bell opening are articulated with sexfoils and trefoil cusped daggers.

Technical Description:

Two-centered curves are used. The tracery is executed jointed masonry. The other parts are rib and panel, in which case the panels are composed of irregularly shaped stones. In some instances rib and panel are joined (southeast conoid), but this may be due to later restoration.

1. *Royal Commission on Historical Manuscripts,* 3rd Report (London, 1872), 308.
2. Pevsner, *BE, North Somerset and Bristol* (1958), 80-81.

---

71   Batcombe   St. Mary: West Tower
         Somerset   4.04m x 4.04m

Historical Analysis:

The tower was under construction circa 1540 as documented by will bequests. In 1539, George George left 20s. for the construction of the tower and instructed that he be buried in the church,[1] and in 1540, Thomas Penny left stone for the building of the tower.[2] The fan vault was probably built at this time.

General Description:

It is square in plan with central bell opening. Each conoid is composed of four panels and springs from moulded capitals and shafts. Each panel is bounded at the top by a horizontal rib composed of circular segments. Trefoil cusping is employed in all panel divisions. The areas between the conoids and the bell opening are articulated with quatrefoils in circles and trefoil cusped daggers. A panelled arch leads on to the nave, on each side of which are escutcheons containing the Sanzaver arms.[3] Three pairs of angels on the exterior west front with various attributes allude to Christ's Passion.[4]

Technical Description:

The parts employed for tracery are jointed masonry. Above the tas-de-charge, the other parts are rib and panel. Four-centered curves are employed for the vaulting in contrast to the two-centered curves of the tower arch. The stone is from Doulting. The corner shafts look in some instances as if they were not planned from the start, for their courses do not match those of the wall in all cases–especially in the southeast corner near the top. A definite adjustment had to be made in the northwest corner to accommodate the vaulting. The wall ribs in each case are at varying dimensions from the wall, giving support to the theory that the vaulting was an afterthought. Another possibility is that the vaulting was designed and the stones cut at an off-site location, being erected later in the Batcombe tower; this would explain the problems of fitting.

1. F. W. Weaver, *Somerset Medieval Wills* (S.R.S. vol. XXI, 1905), 54.
2. F. W. Weaver, "Wells Wills," *SANH Proc.,* LXI (for 1915), 99.
3. F. J. Allen, "Batcombe Church," *SANH Proc.,* LIII (for 1907), 57.
4. *Ibid.,* 56.

Bath	Abbey: Chancel and Chancel Aisles
Somerset	*Chancel bay:* 6.13m x 9.14m
	Aisle bay: 6.13m x 5.10m

Historical Analysis:

Bishop Oliver King issued an injunction on 9 October 1500 in which he stated that he found the church in a ruinous condition, because the revenue of the priory had been spent on the monks instead of on the building under the rule of the former priors; he specified that in the future, allowances to the various offices were to be restricted to specified sums, and the balance to be spent on the fabric of the new church.[1] Letters apparently written in January 1503 between Bishop King and Sir Reginald Bray, indicate that Robert and William Vertue had been in Bath and devised the vaulting for the "chancelle" of the church.[2] King went on to state that he was confident that the roof would be completed before winter set in.[3] He died on 29 August 1503, and in his will specified that he be buried in the choir of the new church at Bath near the first arch on the north side towards the altar.[4] Since it was the usual practice to construct the roof first and then the vaulting, it seems likely that actual construction dates from 1504 or later. The coat of arms of Cardinal Adrian de Castello, who succeeded King and was deposed in 1518,[5] is found in various places on the vaulting of the chancel and its aisles, indicating that the vaulting was built between 1504 and 1518. The arms of James I appear in the easternmost bay of the chancel; they were probably added when the vaulting was repaired during his reign.[6]

The square east window of the abbey and the way in which the vaulting cuts across it, indicate that the present vaulting may differ from the Vertues' plan.[7] This reason is not substantial enough to propose that the vaulting as built was not designed by the Vertues, since the vaulting curve follows that of the tracery in the window and the idea of a curve cutting across a corner is not a foreign idea, but had been used by William Orchard in the Magdalen College (Oxford) Chapel doorway of circa 1480.[8] From King's correspondence with Bray, it is not clear whether the Vertues designed the whole building or just the vaulting. If a stone vault was originally intended, a rectangular window probably would not have been built. The west facade with its curved window was completed later, for Castello's arms were originally on the upper part of it.[9] Possibly the builders prior to January 1503 planned to have had another kind of roof articulation and only after the Vertues' visit decided to have a stone vault. The high quality of the internal stonework above the present vaulting and an indentation of uncertain function that runs around the wall at the height of the top of the vaulting lend credence to this theory. Therefore, it seems likely that the Vertues designed the vaulting for the abbey around 1503. However, they may have had little to do with the actual construction of the building, because Thomas Lynn, mason, was appointed by Robert Vertue to work at the abbey.[10]

53   The chancel is vaulted in three and one-third bays. The easternmost one-third is tunnel vaulted. Uniform bay size is employed both in the chancel and in the nave, suggesting that the whole church was laid out at the same time. The vaulting conoids intersect in the transverse direction forming ridges, and they just meet longitudinally. Each vaulting quadrant is composed of three tiers and four panels. The top bounding rib is articulated with a band of quatrefoils. Trefoil cusping is employed in all panel divisions. The spandrel panel in each of the three bays is composed primarily of quatrefoils radiating out from the center, which is articulated with a coat of arms.

102   The chancel aisles are four bays each in length. The vaulting conoids intersect to form ridges in the longitudinal direction and just meet in the transverse one. This solution is just opposite to what happens in the chancel vault. Each conoid is composed of two tiers and four panels. The top bounding rib is articulated with a band of quatrefoils. Trefoil cusping is employed throughout. The central spandrel panel in each bay has a pendant, except the easternmost bay in each aisle. Each pendant is divided into eight panels which are further subdivided. The central spandrel in the easternmost bay of each aisle is flat and articulated with sculptural decoration.

Technical Description:

103   The chancel vault is primarily rib and panel construction, with traceried parts and ridges executed in jointed masonry. Two-centered curves are employed throughout. The east-west ridge is horizontal, the north-south ridges rise up to the center. No one jointing pattern is employed; that is, for the same location in each bay a stone of the same size was not used. The thickness of panel is fairly constant, being about 9 cm. There is a major change in the constructive pattern from east to west, which **104** occurs in the way the stones are cut for the transverse ridges. The first two ridges from the west follow the same pattern; that is, a stone joint runs along its center **105** line. In the easternmost ridge, a joint runs along its center line in the first stones, but later shifts. In other words, the top of the ridge is composed of a series of single stones instead of a series of stones which abut each other along the center line of the ridge. Since the ridge, structurally speaking, is one of the weakest points in a fan vault, the single-stone solution is technically the more advanced design. This could mean that construction of the chancel vault started in the west and proceeded eastwards.

106
107   The chancel aisle vaults are composed of rib and panel with jointed masonry for the traceried parts. Four-centered curves are employed throughout. The east-west as well as the north-south ridges fall off in elevation from the central spandrel. The pendant is composed of two main parts. The upper part is a series of stones which forms a compression ring. The lower part of the pendant is then inserted into this ring, just as a boss could be, except that it is larger. This part of the pendant is hollowed out to lighten its weight.

---

1. Henry Maxwell-Lyte, ed., *The Registers of Oliver King and Hadrian de Castello* (SRS, LIV, 1939), 51. Printed in *Monasticon,* ii, 270; abstract in English in *VCH Somerset* II, 77.
2. ". . Robt. and William Vertu have been here with me. . . . And also of the vawte devised for the chancelle of the said church. . . ." Westminster Abbey Muniment 16,040, printed in J. Armitage Robinson, "Correspondence of Bishop Oliver King and Sir Reginald Bray," *SANH Proc.,* LX, pt. ii (for 1914), 4.
3. "This chirche as farre as I can see shalbe thoroughtely covered far beforne alhalowe tide . . . ," *ibid.,* 4.
4. ". . corpusque meum sub spe ut in die resurrectionis cum domino glorietur sepeliendum in choro novo ecclesie Balton inxta archam primam partis borealis proximam altari summo. . . ." printed in F. W. Weaver, edit., *Somerset Medieval Wills 1501-1530,* SRS, XIX (1903), 44.

5. *L & P Hen. VIII*, II, nos. 3781 and 4289.
6. R. Rawlinson, *The History and Antiquities of the Cathedral Church of Salisbury, and the Abbey Church of Bath* (London: W. Mears, 1723), 171.
7. Peter Kidson, et al., *A History of English Architecture* (Harmondsworth: Penguin Books, 1965), 139.
8. *Engl. Med. Archit.*, 198-201.
9. Edwin Morcombe Hick, *Bath Abbey* (The Homeland Handbook, no. 82; London: Frederick Ware and Co., 1913), 74.
10. "Thomas Lynn sone the most necessary mason for me that I can have and oone of theym that ys appointed by Robertu Vertue." Westminster Abbey Muniment 16,046, printed in Robinson, *op. cit.*, 4.

08	Bath	Abbey: Prior Bird's Chantry Chapel
	Somerset	Two bays, each 2.46m x 2.46m

Historical Analysis:

The intention to establish a chantry for Prior Bird goes back at least to circa 1503 when Bishop Oliver King mentioned it in a letter to Sir Reginald Bray.[1] Prior Bird died in 1525.[2] At the time of the Dissolution, the chapel was not yet finished and was only completed in the nineteenth century.[3] It has been suggested that construction of the chapel started circa 1515.[4]

General Description:

It is vaulted in two bays. Fan vaulting covers one and one-half bays. The remaining half bay, which is located over the altar, is covered with a panelled tunnel vault which displays the prior's arms.[5] The vaulting springs from moulded capitals. Complex panels and subpanels are developed. The basic tracery pattern of the subpanels is split by the vertical ribs. In the bay that is entirely fan vaulted, the areas left between the intersecting diagonal ribs in the central spandrel panel and the vaulting conoids are broken up into cusped subpanels. A foliate boss is located at the intersection of the diagonal ribs.

Technical Description:

Two-centered curves are employed. The construction is completely of jointed masonry.

1. Westminster Abbey Muniment, 16,040, printed in J. Armitage Robinson, "Correspondence of Bishop Oliver King and Sir Reginald Bray," *SANH Proc.*, LX, pt. II (for 1914), 4.
2. Richard Warner, *The History of Bath* (Bath, 1801), 250.
3. Edward Davis, *Gothic Ornaments Illustrative of Prior Birde's Oratory in the Abbey Church of Bath* (London: John Williams, 1834), n.p. The chapel was completed during the period 1859-74 by Rev. Charles Kemble, see *British Archaeological Association Journal*, N.S., XXVIII (1922), 14.
4. Davis, *ibid.; Engl. Med. Archit.*, 273.
5. Harold Brakspear, "Bath Abbey," *AJ*, LXXXVII (for 1930), 415.

09	Beckington	St. George: West Tower
	Somerset	3.21m x 3.29m

Historical Analysis:

No documentary evidence is known to exist. The tower itself is Norman; the fan vaulting and west window are late Perpendicular additions (sixteenth century?).[1] This general type of fan vault was employed in the north porch of St. John the Baptist, Cirencester, and possibly in the abbey there (chapter house?), both of which are fifteenth century.

General Description:

The vaulting springs from sculptured corbels which may be a later addition. Each vaulting quadrant is composed of four panels. No cusping is used. Panelled arches on both the window and nave sides were inserted to achieve a square plan for the vaulting.

Technical Description:

Two-centered curves are employed. The construction is of rib and panel, with jointed masonry for the traceried parts. The panel thickness is about 10 cm. The ribs are rebated to receive the panels.

1. F. C. Eeles, "Beckington Church," *SANH Proc.,* LXXVIII (for 1932), xliv.

---

110 Bodmin Parish Church: South Porch
Cornwall 2.98m x 2.98m

Historical Analysis:

There are several entries in the building accounts, dated 1469-72, for items relating to the porch.[1] Although none of the items directly refers to the vaulting, there is no reason to believe that the vaulting is not from this period.

General Description:

The vaulting is square in plan with a circular pendant in the middle. The vaulting has four conoids, each of which is composed of two panels and springs from a moulded capital and shaft. The horizontal rib of each panel is circular. Individual panels have cinquefoil cusping at the top, while the lower division is trefoil cusped. Between the conoids and pendant are trefoil cusped daggers. The pendant itself is composed of eight panels, each of which is trefoil cusped and decorated with an escutcheon. The exterior of the two-storied porch has niches for three statues, none of which survive.

Technical Description:

Tracery parts are all of jointed masonry. The other parts to the tas-de-charge are rib and panel construction. Four-centered curves are employed. The keystone of the wall rib is one piece of stone. From there a joint runs along the ridge of the vaulting until the lower part of the central pendant is reached. Between the ridges, all the tracery of the conoids are cut from one piece of stone, except that part which is included in the keystone of the wall rib, and part of the central pendant. The lower part of the pendant is carved from one block of stone, which was not structurally necessary as the four stones located around it form a compression ring, so it must have been included for ornamentation. The upper part of the vaulting is constructed of only five stones. The vaulting was most likely worked out in the workshop and erected later, as problems of matching occurred, for example, in the east end of the vaulting.

1. John James Wilkinson, "Receipts and Expenses in the Building of Bodmin Church, A.D., 1469-1472," *The Camden Miscellany,* vol. VII, N.S. vol. XIV (1875), 7, 20, 30, 38.

---

3 Bosbury Holy Trinity Church: Morton Chapel
Herefordshire 4.57m x 3.20m
Two bays, each 2.28m x 3.20m

Historical Analysis:

Thomas Morton was granted a license to found a chantry in the church of Bosbury with one chaplain and mortmain license to alienate lands of the annual value of £10 to the said chaplain on 12 December 1510 (2 Henry VIII).[1] The initials "T. M." are carved on the bottom of the boss of the pendant.[2] Therefore, the above license can be associated with the chapel, dating it circa 1510.

General Description:

A rectangular chapel located on the south side of the church. A panelled arch opens on to the nave; a moulded arch opens on to the south aisle. Each is four-centered. It is vaulted in two compartments; the vaulting springs from corbels and from a pendant suspended from the arched opening of the north side. Individual panels of the vault are not cusped. The spandrel panel in the middle of each bay is flat and is decorated with a quatrefoil enclosing a boss, carved with a tun and the capital letter "M."

Technical Description:

The wall ribs around the north and south walls are two-centered, while those on the east and west walls are four-centered. The vaulting module is rectangular. The east-west ridge is horizontal, while the north-south ridges rise only slightly toward the center. The ribs change curvature as each conoid is developed; that is, each individual conoid has a two-centered section along the north-south walls, and a four-centered section along the east and west walls. The ribs in between are graduated from a two-centered curve to a four-centered one. By changing the rib curvature the designer was able to achieve relatively horizontal ridges in both directions, thus eliminating the domelike effect which would have emphasized the individual compartments instead of placing emphasis on the space as a whole.

The construction is rib and panel above the tas-de-charge until the horizontal ribs are reached. These are of jointed masonry, as part of the adjoining panel is carved from the same stone as the rib itself at this upper level. Also, the central spandrel panels are of jointed masonry.

The wall ribs are not integrated into the structure of the wall itself. This is unusual and suggests that the vaulting may not have been planned from the start, but was an afterthought. Further evidence to support this theory is the poor integration of the west arch opening and the way in which the wall rib cuts across it, the detailing of the northwest corner, and the fact that the proportions are such that the chapel cannot be divided into square vaulting compartments.

---

1. *L & P Henry VIII,* I, pt. i, 364.
2. RCHM, *Herefordshire,* II (1932), 18.

---

2 Bristol   St. Mark's: Poyntz Chapel
          Two bays, each 1.83m x 2.74m

Historical Analysis:

Built by Robert Poyntz as shown by his will, dated 19 October 1520: "To be buried in the Church of the Gaunts besides Bristol in the Chapel of Jesus which latelie I have caused to be new edified and made of my costs and charges . . . the said new chapel which I lately edified is not in all things perfect and finished, yet according to mine intent, that is to wit, the glazing of the windows thereof and making of two pews with in the said chapel . . ."[1] The vaulting may have been complete by 1520. The glass in the east window bears the date 1527, which may be when the chapel was dedicated.[2]

General Description:

The vaulting springs from corbels. Since it does not spring from shafts and the vaulting curvature does not follow that of the windows, the decision to vault the chapel may have been made after construction began. Cinquefoil cusping is employed throughout, except in the upper articulation of the lower horizontal band, which is trefoil cusped. The boss in the east bay displays the arms of Henry VIII and Katherine of Aragon, and that in the west, the arms of Sir Robert Poyntz and his wife, Margaret Woodville.[3]

Technical Description:

Four-centered curves are employed throughout. The longitudinal ridge is horizontal, the transverse ridges rise up slightly to the center. It is constructed completely of jointed masonry.

1. John Maclean, *Historical and Genealogical Memoir of the Family of Poyntz* (Exeter, 1886), 98.
2. G. Rushforth, "The Painted Glass in the Lord Mayor's Chapel, Bristol," *BGAS,* XLIX (for 1927), 314.
3. W. R. Barker, *St. Mark's, or The Mayor's Chapel, Bristol* (Bristol, 1892), 191-192.

---

113   Bristol   St. Stephen's: South Porch
                                   Decorative Details

Historical Analysis:

William Worcestre noted in 1480 that the (south) porch was the work of Benedict (Crosse) the freemason.[1] It seems likely that it was constructed circa 1480. The vaulting was probably built at that time, because there is no indication that it was added at a later date.

General Description:

Rectangular in plan, the vault is a combination of a pointed tunnel vault with "fan vault conoids" at the corners. The designer seems to have been after an overall surface effect, as can be seen by the complex surface patterning.

Technical Description:

Two-centered curves are used throughout. It is constructed completely of jointed masonry.

1. John H. Harvey, edit., *William Worcestre Itineraries* (Oxford Medieval Texts; Oxford: At the Clarendon Press, 1969), 314, 315.

          Bruton   St. Mary's: West Tower
          Somerset

Analysis:

The present fan vault is modern. However, in 1878 it was noted that the springers and shafts of an original fan vault (?) remained, and the rest of the vaulting was plaster. It was hoped then (1878) that before long the whole would be rebuilt in stone.[1] There is no known record of what the original vault might have looked like.

1. Carpenter, "Parish Church of Bruton," *SANH Proc.,* XXIV (1878), 33.

---

62   Buckland Dinham   St. Michael's: South Porch
          Somerset   3.03m x 3.00m

Historical Analysis:

No documentary evidence is known to exist. The fan vaulting is a later addition to an already existing porch.[1] It most likely dates from the last decades of the fifteenth or early years of the sixteenth century, as fan vaults with "traceried wheels" were common to this period (cf. porches at Kingston St. Mary, Mells, etc.).

General Description:

The vaulting conoids spring from moulded capitals and shafts. Each vaulting conoid is composed of four panels, each of which is trefoil cusped. The top horizontal bounding rib is composed of circular segments. The central spandrel is articulated with eight radiating panels, each of which is trefoil cusped. The central boss is missing. Foliate bosses (one is a Tudor rose) are employed at four main rib intersections in the central spandrel panel, as well as at the apex of the wall ribs. The panelled arch which leads to the outside was most likely added when the vaulting was inserted.

Technical Description:

Two-centered curves are employed throughout. The construction is rib and panel, with jointed masonry used for the traceried parts. The central spandrel panel is constructed of wedge-shaped pieces of stone which form a compression ring.

1. Pevsner, *BE, North Somerset and Bristol* (1958), 147.

38	Burford	St. John the Baptist: South Porch
	Oxfordshire	Two bays, each 2.44m square

Historical Analysis:

No documentary evidence can be associated with this porch. However, Symond's notes of 1644 record the coats of arms of seven of the eight shields located on the exterior of it.[1] One of these shields is that of the Nevilles: the bear and the ragged staff.[2] The town passed in 1449 to the Nevilles, by the marriage of Lady Anne Beauchamp to Richard Neville.[3] The Beauchamp coat of arms does not appear on the porch. The chapel just to the east of the south porch was most likely remodelled between the years 1439 and 1449, when the manor was held by the Beauchamp family, for their arms are included in it.[4] Apparently, the chapel remodelling and the building of the south porch were carried out within a short time as the integration of the staircase of the porch with the chapel and its adjoining stonework appear to be of the same building operation. Therefore, it is possible that construction started between 1439 and 1449 and finished after 1449, when the upper shields of the porch were carved. At any rate, it certainly was finished by 1471, when the manor passed from the Nevilles to the crown.[5]

General Description:

It is a two-storied porch, fan vaulted in two square bays. Each vaulting conoid is composed of four panels and springs from moulded capitals and shafts. Each panel is bounded at the top by a circular segment. Panel divisions are trefoil cusped. The central spandrel is composed of four quatrefoils in circles. The tracery patterns are subordinate to the overall panel layout.

Technical Description:

Four-centered curves are employed. It is completely constructed of jointed masonry. The central stone in each bay is square and is placed diagonally to the sides of the bay. The corners of this stone coincide with the centers of the quatrefoils located in the central spandrel panel. From this point, joints run off to the corners of the bay, running part way down the axes of subordinate tracery ribs. After this, two stones are used: one for the tas-de-charge and another for the course directly above it. All of it shows great skill in both design and execution; no adjustments had to be made for fit.

1. Mary Sturge Gretton, *Burford Past and Present* (new edit.; London: Faber and Faber, 1945), 46-47.
2. *Ibid.*

139

3. William C. Emeris, "The Church of St. John the Baptist, Burford," in R. H. Gretton, *The Burford Records* (Oxford: At the Clarendon Press, 1920), 120.
4. *Ibid.*, 119.
5. *Ibid.*, 91.

Cambridge	King's College Chapel
Cambridgeshire	*Main Vault:* Twelve bays, each 7.37m x 12.66m
	Side Chapels: 6.25m x 3.62m
	North and South Porches: 4.24m x 3.50m

Historical Analysis:[1]

There were three major periods in the construction of King's College Chapel, Cambridge. The first two were 1446 to 1461 and 1483 to 1485. In 1499 the scholars of King's reminded King Henry VII of his uncle, Henry VI's, abandoned work, a splendid beginning left standing as an unsightly fragment.[2] Their plea for assistance went unheard until 1506, when after spending St. George's Day at King's,[3] Henry VII contributed £100 toward the fabric. It was not until 1508 that Henry VII started to give serious support to the project: £1,400 donated in 1508 was followed by £5,000 in 1509.[4] Another £5,000 was later given in 1511 by Henry VII's executors to complete the work.[5] Seemingly, Henry VII contributed only when he became conscious of his approaching death, and he was still unsuccessful in having his uncle, Henry VI, canonized, and transferring his uncle's body from Windsor to the new chapel at Westminster, which was then near completion. Political policy and piety–Henry VI was deemed a Saint by the populace–demanded that Henry VII not forget his links with the House of Lancaster. What better way could both objectives be immediately realized than by the completion of this chapel begun by his ". . . uncle of blessed memory." Thus began the third period of construction, 1508-1515.

Henry VII specifically directed that the chapel was to be completed exactly as it had been devised by his said uncle.[6] Actually, alterations were made in the design which reflect change in both taste and conceptual purpose. In the original plan of 1446, Henry VI specifically forbade curious works of "entaille and besy moldyng,"[7] but these wishes were not respected by Henry VII. Instead, the parts of the chapel to be completed were highly decorated with arms and badges to proclaim the triumphant self-assertion of the new Tudor dynasty. The elaborate fan vaulting that makes King's a notable building was constructed during this last period, 1508-1515.

On 7 June 1512 John Wastell and Henry Semark, one of the wardens of the masons, entered into an agreement by which Wastell would have the sole profit, and bear the whole charge of building the great vault of the church.[8] The contract for the great vault specifies that it was to be built ". . . accordyny to a platt thereof made and signed with the handes of the lordes executours unto the kyng of most famous memorye Henry vij[th] . . ."[9] Wastell was to be paid £100 per bay ". . . in fourme folowyny from tyme to tyme asmoche money as shall suffise to pay the Masons and other rately after the numbre of workmen."[10] Wastell and Semark were to provide the materials and pay the masons' wages and the vaulting was to be finished in 1515.[11] Clearly, Wastell was at this time seen by the college to be a master contractor. In this respect he was paid for items under purveyors' costs in the accounts, 1509-1515.[12] From the accounts it can be seen that the college paid for materials and wages; the £100 per bay, that was to be paid to Wastell, does not seem to have entered into the accounts. This fact is indeed puzzling. Wastell entered into another contract (this time by himself), on 4 August 1513 for the vaulting of the two porches, the seven chapels in the body of the church, the nine chapels behind the choir, and the construction of all the battlements of the porches and chapels.[13] All the vaults were to be built according to designs made for them. The nine chapels behind the choir were to be of ". . . a more course work . . ." and were contracted for £12 each, while the chapels of the antechapel, which were to be fan vaulted, cost £20 each. Since all the chapels have the same dimensions, it is clear that the fan vault was not the most economical way to build. The vaulting of each of the porches was £25; the stone specified for the porch vaults was Yorkshire, the stone for the chapels was Weldon. This difference of material may reflect the difference in cost–£25 versus £20–between the western chapels and porches, all of which have similar fan vaults. John Wastell was a master contractor at this time, but was he also the designer of the vault?

G. G. Scott, and more recently Arthur Oswald, have proposed that the intention to construct a fan vault goes back to the second major period of construction,[14] when Simon Clerk was master mason, circa 1480.[15] Their argument is based on two facts: (1) Wastell and Clerk were known to have worked together at Saffron Walden in 1485, thus Wastell must have been familiar with Clerk's ideas and intentions; and (2) the western piers of the chapel have seven shafts, while the eastern piers are composed of only five, which correspond to the vaulting above.[16] Since the eastern piers rise from the corbel level, Scott conjectured that they were built later (ca. 1480) than those in the west which he correctly dated as between 1448 and 1461. However, Scott failed to notice that the easternmost corbels were constructed of Huddleston stone, a material employed only in the first period of construction of the chapel, 1448-61. Willis and Clark not only pointed this out, but added that the corbelled piers also originally had seven shafts that were later altered.[17] Therefore, on the basis of the number and placement of shafts, it cannot be established that a fan vault was decided upon in circa 1480. Furthermore, the fan vault built at Saffron Walden shortly after 1485 is an early experiment in fan vault design which eventually leads to the design for King's rather than a design that leads away from it. For example, the solution for intersecting conoids had not yet been resolved–the cross section of the transverse ridge ribs is not the same as for the vertical ribs.

By 1483 the five easternmost bays of the chapel were roofed in.[18] When it became evident that funds were no longer available to carry on construction, the brick walls above the vaulting level in these bays were most likely plastered over,[19] for they would have been visible from the floor of the chapel. Also–as pointed out by the Royal Commission on Historical Monuments–the relieving arch in the fifth bay is of makeshift construction, and the through stones for the intended vaulting were omitted.[20]

One of the weakest design aspects of the chapel is the way in which the wall area is treated between the top of the windows and the vaulting. Although the design is consistent in all the bays, it was executed differently in the westernmost six bays, which is especially evident in the wall rib. In the easternmost six bays, the wall rib looks as if it had been remodelled. The upper parts of the walls at this end were built by Simon Clerk. It seems plausible that the wall facing already started by Clerk, was later altered during the period 1508-15 to conform to a new vaulting plan. Therefore, the decision to build a fan vault was most likely made during the final period of construction of the chapel.

The decision to build a fan vault, rather than a more simple vault as originally proposed by Henry VI in 1446, might have been made because of the iconographical connotations the fan vault may have carried. Henry VII's Chapel, Westminster, which was nearing completion in 1508, also has the fan vault as its main architectural feature. When seen in this perspective, the vaulting at King's reinforces an association between Henry VI and Henry VII; if so, the vaulting and the sculpture should be understood as a political document attesting the legitimacy of the Tudor dynasty.

If the theory is acceptable that the vaulting was designed shortly before 1512, the designer of it remains open to question. John a Lee is named chief mason in a small payment to him by the college on 8 July 1507, just after the last payment to the previous mason, Henry Smith.[21] John Wastell was master mason 1508-09 and was paid £13.6s.8d. per annum, and he and John a Lee, joint master masons, were paid at the rate of £26.13s.4d. between them during the years 1510-15. For the year 1509 the accounts do not show the master masons' salaries separately but simply add them to the total masons' wages for the fortnights in which their quarterly payments fell.[22] The generally accepted argument is that since Lee was frequently paid for the purveyor's costs, he had no part in the design; but it is not convincing, because Wastell was also frequently paid for purveyor's costs.[23] Lee was a royal mason, Wastell was not, and beginning in the late 1490s Lee received payment for works directly from the crown.[24] Before work on the chapel began in earnest on 1 May 1507, Lee, Henry Smith, and William Vertue, all royal masons, were entertained at the college.[25] Lee was the master mason of record; Wastell was yet to be appointed as joint master mason. Vertue visited again in 1509, this time in the company of another royal mason, Henry Redman. At this time they were paid a reward of 37s.4d.[26] On 30 July 1512, Vertue dined in Hall, having Wastell as a companion.[27] While these are the only recorded visits of Vertue, et al. to the college, there may have been more. It seems likely Vertue and Redman came to advise or check up on the building operations for the executors of Henry VII. What role they may have played in the design of the chapel and its vaulting is unanswerable. Perhaps they suggested that a fan vault be built, and let the detailing of it to Wastell and John a Lee. It is known that Wastell did design work in the 1490s at Canterbury,[28] and there is great similarity between the design and especially the execution of the vaulting of the Bell Harry Tower to the vaulting at King's. This combined with the fact that the parapet designs at King's and the Canterbury tower are identical, is strong evidence that Wastell was responsible for the design of the vaulting of King's College Chapel. But it cannot be confirmed.

General Description:

52   The Main Vault: The chapel is vaulted in twelve rectangular bays which are separated from each other by bold transverse arches. The vaulting springs from

114
115 moulded capitals and shafts. As the radius of the vaulting conoids is one-half the
116 north-south span, the vaulting conoids intersect in the middle of each bay forming a transverse ridge and just meet on a longitudinal ridge rib. In the central spandrel panel in each bay the ridge ribs and vertical ribs of the conoids are turned into a circle which frames a large sculptured boss. These bosses in alternate bays are carved with Tudor roses or portcullises which are framed by cresting that resembles crowns. Each vaulting quadrant is composed of six main panels which are further subdivided in the upper regions of the vaulting. Each subpanel is cinquefoil cusped under a two-centered head. Bratticing is placed along the horizontal bands. The horizontal bounding ribs are composed of circular segments. The vertical ribs are not equally spaced. An estimate was made for the painting and gilding of the vault.

81   The Side Chapels of the Antechapel: They are rectangular in plan. The vaulting is much like that of the main vault. However, there are several major stylistic differences: (1) the vaulting springs directly from moulded shafts; (2) the ridge and vertical ribs are not turned into a circle which frames the boss, but they directly intersect it; (3) the type of bratticing used is different at each level. In the lowest level fleur-de-lys are employed; in the level directly above, there are cross paty. The uppermost row of bratticing seems to be only decorative, and the boss employed in each case is a Tudor rose. The lowest horizontal band is composed of ogee curves.

117   The North and South Porches: They are rectangular in plan. The vaulting springs directly from moulded shafts. The radius of the vaulting conoids is one-half the north-south span, which is shorter than the east-west span. Therefore, the conoids do not intersect in the porch vaults as they do in the others. The east-west ridge ribs rise up to the center, while the north-south ridges are parallel to the floor. Each vaulting quadrant is composed of four main panels which are further subdivided. The subpanels are cinquefoil cusped under two-centered heads. Bratticing is placed along the horizontal bounding ribs, the upper row are cross paty, the lower fleur-de-lys. The central spandrel is articulated with a large Tudor rose surrounded by eight smaller ones.

Technical Description:

The Main Vault: Two and four-centered curves are employed. The construction is of ribs and panels with jointed masonry used for the traceried parts. The ribs are rebated to receive the panels. The panels vary in thickness from 5 to 15 cm. In some cases the panels are only about 5 cm thick with a cemented rubble fill placed on top to bring them up to the surface of the vault. The beds of the panels are straight. Rib and panel taken together reach a depth of about 32 cm. Mortar joints are usually .5 to 1 cm wide. Large crevices (now filled with mortar) are present between the vaulting conoids and the transverse arches. The apexes of the transverse arches and the apexes of the vaulting conoids are out of alignment. These discrepancies could have resulted when compression, and therefore movement, was induced into the vaulting. A thin layer of cement originally covered the extrados of the vault, sections of which can still be seen.

While the large transverse arches that separate one bay from another did not play a structural role, they aided in the constructional process, for the vaulting stones were laid from these arches toward the center of each bay. The extrados of the transverse arch follows the upper surface of the vaulting.

The overall stone jointing pattern is fairly consistent throughout the bays. The transverse ridges are composed of stones which abut each other and are shaped like irregular hexagons or Vs. The longitudinal ridge, which is at all places parallel to the floor, is composed of all V-shaped stones until the center of each bay is reached. There, stones around the central boss form a compression ring into which the boss stones were set. Most stones have centerlines traced upon them and have lewis holes for lifting. Placement/assembly marks also appear, which mark the joints and the quadrant of the bay into which each specific stone was to go. This vault probably was prefabricated in the workshop. When stones developed tensile cracks during carving, bow-tie shaped pieces of wood were inserted to "tie" the stone together; when the stone was put in place and compression induced, the tensile cracks disappeared. These "bow-ties" were cemented in with a hot cement made in part of wax and resin, as evidenced by the building accounts for the period 1508-1515. The irregularly shaped holes in the vaulting over the windows were apparently chopped through after the vaulting was erected and have been explained by Roger North as ". . . holes thro' which cords pass for carrying chaires when the inside of the roof is cleaned . . ."[29]

The material of construction is Weldon stone, known for its durability and frost resistance. It is composed of oolite spherules and shell fragments bound together by micro-crystalline calcite. It was quarried eight miles north of Kettering on the road to Stamford, and a large portion of it, at least in 1508, came to the college by road.[30] Weldon is buff to light brown in color with light brown markings and weighs approximately 2400 kg/cm.[31]

The Side Chapels of the Antechapel: Four-centered curves are employed. The construction is of ribs and panels with jointed masonry used for the traceried parts. Since the same basic stone jointing pattern was used for the ridges as in the main vault of the chapel, span did not determine the jointing pattern. The material of construction is Weldon stone.

The North and South Porches: Two-centered curves are employed. The construction is of ribs and panels with jointed masonry used for the traceried parts. The same basic stone jointing pattern was used for the ridges and in the main vault of the chapel. The material is magnesian limestone from Hampole (Yorkshire).[32]

1. The major works on the chapel are, Robert Willis and John Clark, *The Architectural History of the University of Cambridge* (4 vols.; Cambridge: At the University Press, 1886); John Saltmarsh, "King's College," in VCH, *Cambridgeshire*, III (1959), 376-407; RCHM, *An Inventory of the Historical Monuments in the City of Cambridge*, pt. 1 (1959); For architectural drawings of the vaulting see F(redrick) Mackenzie, *Observations on the Construction of the Roof of King's College Chapel, Cambridge* (London: John Weale, 1840).
2. King's College Muniments, Ledger Bk, I, 168b. Printed in *Calendar of the Close Rolls,* Henry VII, II, 71-73; noted by Saltmarsh, *ibid.,* 389.
3. Elias Ashmole, *Order of the Garter* (1672), 558.
4. P.R.O. E. 36/214, ff. 57, 72, 157, 179, 274, and King's College Muniments, Ledger Bk, I, 218a, Printed by Willis and Clark, *op. cit.,* I, 476.
5. King's College Muniments, Bk, I, 229a, b. Printed by Willis and Clark, *op. cit.,* I, 478, 479.
6. King's College Muniments, Ledger Book, i, ff. 217b-219a, and Willis and Clark, *op. cit.,* I, 476-8.
7. J. W. Clark and M. R. James, *The Will of King Henry the Sixth* (Cambridge, 1896), 7.
8. Willis and Clark, *op. cit.,* I, 608-609.
9. Willis and Clark, *op. cit.,* I, 608.
10. Willis and Clark, *op. cit.,* I, 608.
11. Willis and Clark, *op. cit.,* I, 494.
12. *Engl. Med. Archit.,* 284.
13. Willis and Clark, *op. cit.,* 613.
14. *Engl. Med. Archit.,* 63 and George Gilbert Scott, *An Essay on the History of English Church Architecture* (London: Simpkin, Marshall and Co., 1881), 183.
15. *Engl. Med. Archit.,* 60.
16. Scott, *op. cit.,* 183.
17. Willis and Clark, *op. cit.,* I, 495.
18. Willis and Clark, *op. cit.,* I, 472-475, 489-491; Henry Malden, *An Account of King's College Chapel in Cambridge* (1769), 17. This part of Malden was contributed by Edward Betham, see Saltmarsh, *op. cit.,* 389n.69.
19. RCHM, *An Inventory of the Historical Monuments in the City of Cambridge,* I, 102.
20. *Ibid.*
21. *Engl. Med. Archit.,* 245.
22. King's College Muniments, Chapel Buildings Accounts.
23. *Engl. Med. Archit.,* 159, 284.
24. BM Add. MS 7099, ff. 42, 44, 46.
25. *Engl. Med. Archit.,* 159.
26. King's College Chapel, Building Accounts, 1509-15. Cited in *Engl. Med. Archit.,* 284.
27. *Engl. Med. Archit.,* 284.
28. *Engl. Med. Archit.,* 279, 281.
29. John Wilson, edit., *Roger North on Music* (London: Novello and Co., Ltd., 1959), 268. Roger North died in 1734.
30. Donovan Purcell, *Cambridge Stone* (London: Faber and Faber, Ltd., 1967), 37, and King's College Muniments, Chapel Building Accounts, 1508-09. Transport by road was more expensive than by waterway. The building campaign was just getting started; it must have been important to stockpile stone before winter set in.
31. Arthur Warnes, *Building Stones* (London: Ernest Benn, Ltd., 1926), 107.
32. Purcell, *op. cit.,* 40.

118   Cambridge   St. John's College: Gateway
          Cambridgeshire   4.87m x 5.94m
                                  Two bays, each 4.87m x 2.97m

Historical Analysis:

Between 1511 and 1516, £4772 was spent on the fabric of the college,[1] but construction of the college was not completed until 1520.[2] Oliver Scales was clerk of the works;[3] the builder of the first court was William Swayn of Chesterton.[4] The designer of the vaulting is not named, but John Wastell has been suggested because of the stylistic similarities between this vault and that of King's College Chapel.[5] It is known that Wastell and Swayn worked together on the Great Gate of Trinity.[6] Because the overall effect of this fan vault is far richer than any other Wastell-type fan vault, it may not be from his hand.

General Description:

It is vaulted in two rectangular bays. Each vaulting conoid springs from foliated corbels, no two of which are alike. Each conoid is composed of six panels and two tiers. The lower tier is cinquefoil cusped with carved cusp points; the upper tier has trefoil cusping with subcusps and carved cusp points. Spaces formed by the cusping of the upper tier are filled with leaf ornament, daisies, and other flowers; one has a Prince of Wales's feather, another has an eagle of St. John.[7] Bratticing is carved along the top of the horizontal circular ribs, and in the middle of each bay is a carved boss; one has a rose, the other a portcullis and daisies. The vaulting has modern painting and gilding.[8]

Technical Description:

Four-centered curves are employed throughout. It is of rib and panel construction, except for tracery parts and ridges which are of jointed masonry. The longitudinal ridge is horizontal; transverse ridges rise up toward the center.

1. Edward Miller, *Portrait of a College; A History of the College of St. John the Evangelist Cambridge* (Cambridge: At the University Press, 1961), 6.
2. *Ibid.,* 8.
3. *Ibid.,* 6.
4. John Saltmarsh, "John Wastell at St. John's," *The Eagle,* LXIV (Jan. 1970), 14.
5. *Ibid.,* 16.
6. *Ibid.,* 14.
7. *Ibid.,* 15.
8. RCHM, *City of Cambridge,* pt. II (1959), 189.

9	Canterbury	Cathedral: Bell Harry Tower
	Kent	7.62m square

Historical Analysis:

The only documentary evidence that can be associated with the vaulting is in the obituary notice of Prior Goldstone II, prior from 1495 to 1517, which states that he finished the tower with its most beautiful vaulting.[1] The stone part of the vaulting has four carved bosses with coats of arms. The northeast boss is for Archbishop Morton (1486-1500), the southeast boss for King Henry VII, the northwest boss for Prior Goldstone II, and the southwest boss for Archbishop Warham (1503-32).[2] As Warham did not ascend until 1503,[3] the vaulting must have at least been completed after that date and before 1517 when Prior Goldstone died. Therefore, the vaulting dates from the early years of the sixteenth century.

The design of the vaulting has been attributed to John Wastell, not only because of its visual similarity to the vaulting of King's College Chapel, but because of his mention in an undated letter from Prior Sellinge to Archbishop Morton: ". . . John Wastell your mason, berer hereof to perceyve of hym what forme and shappe he will in resying of the pynacles of your new towre here: He drew unto us ij patrons of hem."[4] The letter goes on to say that ". . . these pynalces may be finished and accomplyshed this next somer following, the whiche if it mytt be so then your toure outwarde shuld appere a werke perfite."[5] The latest possible date for the letter is 29 December 1494, when the prior died.[6] That would put the expected completion date for the tower in the summer of 1495. However, extant fabric rolls of 1494-97 indicate that extensive work was done on the tower throughout that period, and that it was complete or nearly so by 1498 when the bells were hung by Ambrose the Smith.[7] Therefore, the decision to build a fan vault may have been made after the tower was completed. On 7 April 1496 Wastell was received into fraternity by the prior and chapter as master mason *(magister latomorum).*[8] While it is not known how long Wastell was master mason at Canterbury, he probably provided the design for the fan vault of the tower.

General Description:

It is square in plan. The vaulting springs from moulded capitals and shafts in the corners and from corbels located in the middle of each wall. The vaulting is planned in two tiers separated and bounded at the top by horizontal ribs which are composed of circular segments. Bratticing is placed along the top of the lower horizontal bounding rib and is visually emphasized by the triangular indentations placed behind it. The vertical ribs in each case are spaced equidistantly. The central spandrel consists of the bell opening around which are bratticing and sculptured decoration. Between the bell opening and the vaulting conoids are the initial of and three gold stones standing for Prior Thomas Goldstone.

Technical Description:

Two-centered curves are employed. The design module is based on one-quarter of the span. The ridges between the vaulting conoids rise slightly upwards until the bosses are reached. The central spandrel is horizontal. The vaulting is constructed of ribs and panels with jointed masonry for the traceried parts. The beds are straight. From what can be seen from above, the bosses are not hollowed out to lighten their weight as they are at Peterborough. The ridges are composed of stones which abut each other, being irregular hexagons in shape until the bosses are reached. Bricks, which add dead weight, were used–perhaps to stablize the vaulting and prevent buckling. These bricks were most likely added after compression was induced into the structure and the centering was removed, for the boss stones show signs of failure.

120

---

1. H. Wharton, *Anglia Sacra,* I, 145.
2. W. B. Messenger and Philip Blake, "The Heraldry of Canterbury Cathedral. Volume II; The Christchurch Gate and the Main Building," (1951), 54. Typescript in the Society of Antiquaries, London.
3. John LeNeve, *Fasti Ecclesiae Anglicanae IV Monastic Cathedrals (Southern Province),* compiled by B. Jones (London: The Athens Press, 1963), 5.
4. *Engl. Med. Archit.,* 280-281. Letter in Canterbury Cathedral Chapter Archives, Christ Church Letters, vol. I, f. 147. Printed in *Camden Society,* N.S. XIX (1877), no. LVIII and in William Danks and C. Eveleigh Woodruff, *Memorials of the Cathedral and Priory of Christ in Canterbury* (London: Chapman & Hall, Ltd., 1912), 208. Both printed versions are inaccurate, and ignore the numerous crossings out and interlineations. See William Urry, "Cardinal Morton and the Angel Steeple," *Friends of Canterbury Cathedral, 38th Annual Report* (1965), 20. Urry also mentions the fact that the drawing of pinnacles which has been attributed to Wastell (most recently in *Engl. Med. Archit.,* 280) was found amongst the uncatalogued Archives by J. B. Sheppard and was inserted into the volume of letters by him. Therefore, there is little evidence indeed to connect the letter and the drawing.
5. *Ibid.*
6. LeNeve, *op. cit.,* 5.
7. Urry, *op. cit.,* 22-23, and Cecil Hewett and Tim Tatton-Brown, "New Structural Evidence Regarding Bell Harry and the South-East Spire at Canterbury," *Archaeologia Cantiana,* XCII (1976), 129-136.
8. BM MS Arundel 68, f. 8; cited in *Engl. Med. Archit.,* 281.

Canterbury	Cathedral: Chantry Chapel of Henry IV
Kent	Two bays, each 2.08m x 2.69m

Historical Analysis:

Henry IV gave instructions in his will that his ". . . body for to be beryed in the chirch at Caunterbury . . . also y devys and ordeyn that ther be a chauntre perpetuall of twey preestis, for to sing and prey for my soul in the aforeseyd chirch of Caunterbury, in soch a place and aftyr soch ordinaunce as it seemeth best to my aforseyd cousin of Caunterbury."[1] The will was dated 21 January 1409, and was superseded by a later one, though the text of the subsequent one has not been preserved.[2] Henry IV died on 20 March 1413.[3] Neither the tomb of Henry IV nor the chapel were erected until after the death of the Queen Consort (1437); meanwhile the coffin rested upon a wooden hearse which was sold after the death of the Queen Consort by the prior and convent.[4] The chapel was dedicated in 1439.[5]

General Description:

The plan is composed of two rectangular bays. There is no longitudinal ridge rib, but a transverse rib visually divides the space into two bays, each a reflection of the other. The vaulting springs from moulded capitals and shafts. Each vaulting quadrant is divided into four main panels that are cusped. The spandrel panel in each bay is composed of circles within circles, some of which are cusped and subcusped. In the center of each bay and in the spaces formed by the intersection of the central spandrel and vaulting conoids along the longitudinal axis are placed shields for coats of arms.

Technical Description:

Four-centered curves are employed throughout. This enabled the designer to achieve ridges that are almost parallel to the floor. The central spandrel panel is flat. The vaulting is completely constructed of jointed masonry.

---

1. J. Nichols, *A Collection of All the Wills Now Known to Be Extant of the Kings and Queens of England, etc.* . . . (London: Printed by J. Nichols, 1780), 203.
2. James Hamilton Wylie, *History of England under Henry the Fourth* (4 vols.; London: Longmans, Green and Co., 1884-1898), III, 235.
3. *DNB*, XXVI, 41.
4. William Danks and C. Eveleigh Woodruff, *Memorials of the Cathedral and Priory of Christ in Canterbury* (London: Chapman & Hall, Ltd., 1912), 191.
5. "Item hoc anno primo die mensis Marcii (1439/40) dominus episcopus Rossensis dedicauit altare in honore sancti Edwardi regis et confessoris in capella que est exparte boriali ad feretrum sancti Thome." In William Gearle, edit., *The Chronicle of John Stone,* Cambridge Antiquarian Society Publication, XXXIV (1902), 26.

Canterbury	Cathedral: Lady Chapel off the Martyrdom
Kent	11.87m x 6.40m

Historical Analysis:

Obituary records of Prior Thomas Goldstone I indicate that he constructed this chapel and was buried in it.[1] The foundation stone for the chapel was laid on 9 September 1448,[2] and by 1449-50 enough of the chapel was completed to permit a burial there.[3] The chapel was first used on the fourth Sunday of Advent, 1455.[4] Prior Goldstone died in 1468 and was buried in this chapel,[5] at which time the vaulting was complete, for there is direct reference to it in his obituary notice.[6]

General Description:

The chapel is not rectangular in plan but is composed of two rectangular bays plus a small triangular area at the west end. When seen from above, the fan vaulting appears to have been intended from the start. The vaulting is well integrated into the chapel; it springs from moulded capitals and shafts, and follows the curve of the windows and wall panelling. There is a constancy of quality.

The vaulting conoids only intersect in the transverse direction. The transverse rib between the bays, the "diagonal" ribs formed by dividing each vaulting quadrant into two, and the top horizontal bounding ribs are all of the same section. The central spandrel of each bay is articulated with a circular pattern composed of eight radiating panels. While these panels are aligned with the ridges of the intersecting conoids, they are not aligned with the "diagonal" ribs of each vaulting quadrant. The arrangement imparts a feeling of movement and vitality to the vaulting.

Each vaulting quadrant is divided into two major panels, each of which is further subdivided. There are two horizontal bounding ribs, a major one at the top and a minor one below it. In the triangular area at the west end, a continuation of the same vaulting pattern is employed which ends abruptly along the west wall.

Technical Description:

Jointed masonry is employed for the central spandrel and horizontal bounding ribs; the remainder is constructed of ribs and panels. The panels are composed of small stones which were plastered over. The pockets above the vaulting are filled to the top. Two-centered curves are employed throughout. The vaulting ridges are horizontal.

---

1. "Aedificavit in Boreali parte hujus Ecclesiae Capellam in honorem B. V. Mariae, in qua et sepultus est." In H. Wharton, *Anglia Sacra,* I, 144-145. And ". . . in nova capella beate Marie quam erexit juxta martirium sancti Thome martiris prope hostium quod ducit ad claustrum in monumento suo novo quod exciderat de petra ubi nondum quisquam positus fuerat." In William Gearle, edit., *The Chronicle of John Stone,* Cambridge Antiquarian Society Publication, XXXIV (1902), 104-5.
2. Lambeth MS 20 f.208, cited in J. Wickham Legg and W. H. St. John Hope, editors, *Inventories of Christchurch Canterbury* (Westminster: Archibald Constable & Co., Ltd., 1902), 163. Also, *The Chronicle of John Stone op. cit.,* 44.
3. *The Chronicle of John Stone, op. cit.,* 48.
4. *The Chronicle of John Stone, op. cit.,* 65.
5. *The Chronicle of John Stone, op. cit.,* 104-5.
6. "Quam videlicit Capellem cum testudine lapidea valde artificiosa coopertura de plumbo . . . ," Wharton, *op. cit.,* I, 145.

---

121   Canterbury   Cathedral: Southwest Tower
             Kent   4.57m (approximately)

Historical Analysis:

Construction of the tower went on from 1423-34, when work was halted.[1] In 1459 the Bishop of Ross blessed a great bell named Dunstan *in navi ecclesie.*[2] This may mark the completion of the tower, and took place during the priorate of Thomas Goldstone I (1449-1468) who, according to his obituary notice, added certain ornamentation to the tower: "Turrem quoque sive campanile in australi parte navis Ecclesie ab altitudine porticus Ecclesie supra pulchro artificio consummari fecit."[3] While this probably refers to the exterior, it could well be that Goldstone completed the interior with the addition of a fan vault. The decision to insert a fan vault was taken after construction of the tower was well underway, for there is no correspondence of parts between the shafts and the vault itself.

This fan vault belongs to the same visual group as the vaulting of the Lady Chapel off the Martyrdom, which Goldstone built; yet it is different in certain aspects of construction, detailing, and geometry. If Goldstone was responsible for its construction–and this seems likely–it probably was added between the time he became prior (1449) and when the bell was blessed (1459).

General Description:

Each vaulting conoid is composed of four main panels with subpanels which are trefoil-cusped. The horizontal bounding ribs are circular segments. At the corners of the central spandrel panel between the conoids and bell opening are quatrefoils containing coats of arms.

Technical Description:

Four-centered curves are employed. A complex constructional pattern may have been used, but it is impossible to be certain, because the jointing system has been covered over. There are a few cracks visible, which run vertically on the centerlines between the ribs in the panels immediately along the walls. The construction pattern suggests a vault made completely of jointed masonry. Sections further in, however, seem to be composed of ribs and panels. All tracery parts are definitely of jointed masonry. It is impossible to determine what is original and what came from later restoration. No parts of this vaulting are visible from above.

1. For the building operations see C. Eveleigh Woodruff, "The Rebuilding of the South-West Tower of Canterbury Cathedral in the Fifteenth Century," *Archaeologia Cantiana,* XLV (1933), 37-47.
2. William Gearle, edit., *The Chronicle of John Stone,* Cambridge Antiquarian Society Publications, XXXIV (1902).
3. H. Wharton, *Anglia Sacra,* I, 145. Wharton printed *ad altitudimem* instead of *ab altitudine* see BM MS Arundel 68, Plut. clxiii, F. For Goldstone's dates see John LeNeve, *Fasti Ecclesiae Anglicanae IV Monastic Cathedrals (Southern Province),* compiled by B. Jones (London: The Athlone Press, 1963).

22	Castle Combe	St. Andrew's: West Tower
	Wiltshire	4.21m x 4.28m

Historical Analysis:

Construction on the tower began in 1434-35.[1] It has been suggested that the estate of Sir John Fastolf may have contributed to the erection of the tower after 1459.[2] There is no documentary reference to the construction of the vaulting, which appears to be a later addition, probably built in the last half of the fifteenth century.

General Description:

The vaulting springs from moulded corbels. Each vaulting conoid is composed of four panels. Cinquefoil cusping is employed on both horizontal bands. Four quatrefoils with daggers articulate the spandrel panel around the bell opening.

Technical Description:

Four-centered curves are employed throughout. The vaulting may have been built elsewhere and installed later in the tower, as the walls have been partly cut away and altered to receive it. Furthermore, the wall rib above the tas-de-charge is just laid up against the wall and is not placed in an indentation to receive it, which lends credence to the idea that the vaulting is a later addition. The construction is mostly of jointed masonry; however, parts appear to be rib and panel.

1. G. Poulett Scrope, *History of the Manor and Ancient Barony of Castle Combe . . .* (London: J. B. Nichols and Sons, for private circulation, 1852), 248. Date based on a memorandum written by William of Worcester.
2. *Ibid.,* 188-189, 318.

Cerne Abbas   Abbey: Porch to Abbot's Hall
        Dorset   3.97m x 3.36m

Historical Analysis:

The entrance porch to the Abbot's Hall was built from 1497 to 1509 by Abbot Thomas Sam.[1] It may have been erected after 1504, because a shield on the exterior of the porch (O with an owl above) may be that of Hugh Oldham, who was made bishop of Exeter in that year.[2] The rebus of Abbot Sam appears both in the center of the vaulting and on the exterior of the porch.

General Description:

The vaulting springs from moulded and foliate corbels; the panels of each vaulting conoid are trefoil-cusped. The horizontal bounding rib is composed of circular segments. The central spandrel is articulated with four quatrefoil panels grouped around a central quatrefoil, which contains the rebus of Abbot Sam. There are foliate bosses located at most rib intersections.

Technical Description:

Four-centered curves are employed. It is of rib and panel construction with jointed masonry employed for the traceried parts. The panel infilling is composed of small pieces of stones of about 8 cm thick, and the adjoining ribs are rebated to receive them. The ridges are executed in a combination of rib and panels and jointed masonry. The part of the ridge that is composed of rib and panels is not the same size in each case but varies to accommodate and fit the vaulting into the space provided. The jointing system employed is irregular.

1. RCHM, *Dorset West,* I (1952), 77.
2. *Ibid.,* and *DNB,* XLII, 105.

Chewton Mendip   St. Mary Magdalen: West Tower
        Somerset   4.43m x 4.20m

Historical Analysis:

This tower was under construction in 1541 as evidenced by the will of Thomas Halston de Chewton, in which he bequeathed xvi d. to the ". . . bylding of the tower of Chewton. . . ."[1] Leland wrote, "There is goodly new high tourrid steple at Chuton."[2] Iconographic similarities of the exterior west facade connect this tower with that of Batcombe, which was under construction at the same time. Differences in their fan vaults might indicate a common source for the iconographic program (Bath Abbey?) and a different workshop for their construction. The vaulting is almost identical to that of Shepton Mallet, which is 4.38m x 4.34m.

General Description:

The vaulting conoids spring from moulded capitals and shafts. Each capital is slightly different, and in the southwest corner, for example, the center line of the tas-de-charge and capital with its shaft is not in alignment. Each vaulting conoid is divided into four main panels and further subdivisions occur in the second tier. Trefoil cusping is employed throughout. Located around the central bell opening are quatrefoils, each of which contains a foliate boss.

Technical Description:

Two-centered curves are employed throughout. The construction is of rib and panel with jointed masonry for the traceried parts. In some cases rib and panel were cut together. The wall rib is laid up against the wall and not placed in an indentation, which suggests that the tower may have been vaulted after construction began. On the other hand it seems probable that the vaulting was prefabricated on the ground and then installed, as there are many problems of fit which were solved by twisting the vaulting out of shape. Most likely, this distortion would not have happened if each stone had been cut as the vault was going up.

1. P. H. Ditchfield, "Chewton Mendip," *British Archaeological Association. Journal,* N.S., XXVIII (1922), 27.
2. Leland, *Itin.,* I, 144.

| 51 | Christchurch | Priory: Salisbury Chantry Chapel |
| | Hampshire | 4.14m x 2.49m |

Historical Analysis:

The chapel was founded by Margaret, Countess of Salisbury, and was to be her burial place. She was executed in 1541.[1] The commissioners appointed by Thomas Cromwell to visit the priory wrote: "In thys churche we found a chaple and a monument curiously made of cane stone pr'pared by the late mother of Raynolde Pole for herr buriall, which we have causyd to be defacyd and all the armys and badgis clerely to be delete. . . ."[2] John Harvey has suggested that the designer was Thomas Bertie, because of the introduction of Italian details; he dates the monument as circa 1529.[3] This suggestion would place it contemporary with the chantry of Prior John Draper which is inscribed 1529 and which displays Renaissance detail of a similar nature. The Salisbury chantry is a much more elaborate and finely detailed work, and may have been built after Draper's chantry screen, or it could just have been more costly. The chapel was surely finished by 1538 when the countess was arrested.[4]

General Description:

The plan of the chapel consists of two rectangular bays of fan vaulting separated by a tunnel vault. In the middle of each of the three sections are large sculptured bosses. On the east boss were the armorial bearings of the Countess of Salisbury, on the middle boss a representation of the Trinity, and on the west boss the arms of Sir Richard Pole within a garter.[5] The fan vaulting springs from sculptured corbels. Each vaulting conoid is composed of four panels. Trefoil and cinquefoil cusping are employed. The main distinguishing feature is the emphasis placed on the horizontal bounding rib with its bratticing.

Technical Description:

Four-centered curves are employed throughout. The construction is completely of jointed masonry. The material is Caen stone.

---

1. *DNB,* XLVI, 29.
2. BM Cotton Cleopatra. E. IV., f. 267b. printed in Benjamin Ferry, *The Antiquities of the Priory of Christchurch, Hampshire* (Second edit., revised by John Britton; London: Henry F. Bohn, 1841), 11.
3. John Harvey, *Introduction to Tudor Architecture* (London: 1949), 92.
4. *DNB,* XLVI, 29.
5. Ferry, *op. cit.,* 40.

| 24 | Cirencester | Abbey: Fragments[1] |
| | Gloucestershire | |

During the recent excavations of the abbey, fragments were found to indicate that the Chapter House was fan vaulted. It was most likely rebuilt in the fifteenth century and was an extended octagon in plan. Since a grave was found in the center, there may not have been a central support, which would make the span about 7.50 m.[2] Not enough fragments were found to reconstruct the vaulting plan.

Fragments from the western closets of the chapter house indicate that they also were fan vaulted. They had plain pointed panels; the ribs were painted white, the background pink. The vault was constructed of jointed masonry. This type of fan vault can also be found in the north porch of the parish church at Cirencester, and probably dates from the second half of the fifteenth century.

A third fan vault was in the south transept or adjacent chapel of the abbey.[3] Its span was about 3 m, and it was built completely of jointed masonry. This example is quite late, and on stylistic grounds dates to the early decades of the sixteenth century (cf. porches at Ile Abbots, Kingston St. Mary, etc.).

A few fragments indicate that iron dowels were used.

1. Acknowledgement and regards to P. D. C. Brown, who told me in a letter of 14 Sept. 1971 of the fan vaulting fragments found during the recent excavations. I visited the Corinium Museum where I examined the fragments.
2. For plan of Chapter House as recovered by the recent excavations see John S. Wacher, "Cirencester, 1964," *The Antiquaries Journal,* XLV, pt. 1 (1965), pl. XLII.
3. I have seen a reconstruction drawing of the fragments by P. D. C. Brown.

| **125** | Cirencester | St. John the Baptist: North Porch |
| | Gloucestershire | 3.04m x 3.08m |

Historical Analysis:

There is no known documentary evidence that can be definitely associated with the porch. Clearly it was added after the Trinity Chapel was built, 1430-38,[1] for its walls just abut on the chapel's and the east wall of the porch is the same as the chapel's. The design and constructive details differ from those of the south porch vaulting, built circa 1492-1501,[2] and other later work in the church. Perhaps when John Gerveys wished in 1453 to be buried in the porch and left £10 toward it, it was the north porch he was referring to.[3] Certainly, the north porch dates from sometime between 1440 and 1490.

General Description:

The vaulting springs from moulded capitals and shafts. Each vaulting conoid is divided into two horizontal bands; each band has four panels, though they are not placed directly above each other. None of the panels are cusped. The central spandrel contains four quatrefoils in a circle.

Technical Description:

13   Two-centered curves are used throughout. The vaulting was originally all jointed masonry. The joints ran right along the ribs. In other words, each rib was part of the panel but placed at its edge. Each panel was rebated to receive the next. The central spandrel panel reaches a depth of about 18 cm and is cut from one large piece of stone. The beds are concave. During the recent restoration (1971) ribs and panels were substituted for jointed masonry, especially in the northwest corner.

1. E. A. Fuller, *The Parish Church of St. John the Baptist, Cirencester* (Cirencester: Baily & Son, 1882), 61.
2. *Ibid.,* 8 n. 4.
3. *Ibid.,* 9 n.1.

Cirencester   St. John the Baptist: St. Catherine's Chapel
Gloucestershire   3.87m x 16.46m

Historical Analysis:

The date 1508 appears on a boss in the easternmost bay. Tradition says that the vaulting was erected at the expense of Bishop Thomas Ruthall and his family.[1] The fact that one boss bears the initials "T. R." supports the traditional view. However, E. A. Fuller, writing in 1882, suggested that the vaulting was moved from the Cirencester Abbey cloister or some other chapel in the abbey church in 1539.[2] He cited as evidence the fact that workmen doing alterations in the abbey house in the nineteenth century found large portions of the same kind of roof.[3] Since these fragments have long disappeared, it is difficult to know exactly how similar they actually were. Little evidence was found in the recent excavations of the abbey to suggest that the cloisters were rebuilt in the sixteenth century,[4] and the proportions of the vaulting for a chapel within the abbey church would indeed be strange. Furthermore, if the vaulting was moved from the abbey, who paid for its re-erection, and why were the old bosses reused? The iconography of the bosses was valid for 1508 (the royal arms of Henry VII and the badges of the Prince of Wales and Katherine of Aragon);[5] it was not so for 1539. It seems plausible that a greater rebuilding program may have been envisioned in 1508 for the entire eastern end of the church. Leland stated with reference to the new work that Ruthall ". . . promisid much, but preventid with deth gave nothing."[6] Perhaps the vaulting was already prefabricated in the workshop when a change of plan on the extent of the rebuilding to be done took place, thus explaining the peculiarities of the vaulting as it is seen today.

General Description:

It is vaulted in four and two-thirds bays. The vaulting springs from moulded capitals and shaft remains. Each vaulting quadrant is composed of two major panels, each of which is further divided into subpanels. Cinquefoil cusping is employed throughout. The central spandrel panel consists of four quatrefoils in circles which are separated by four irregular lozenges. Trefoil cusped daggers are located in the "corners" of the central spandrel panels.

Technical Description:

Four-centered curves are used throughout. The vaulting is constructed of jointed masonry. The longitudinal ridge is horizontal, the transverse ridges rise slightly to the center. The vertical joints run in the middle between the ribs and not along the sides of them. Irregularities in the cusping pattern along the top horizontal bounding rib indicate that adjustments were necessary to make the vaulting fit, thus suggesting that the vaulting was prefabricated in the workshop. Apparently the vaulting was cemented over in the nineteenth century, when it was rebuilt by G. G. Scott,[7] so the stone joints are not visible from above. The vaulting pockets are two-thirds filled with rubble in some cases and completely filled in others.

1. Samuel Lyons, *A Collection of Gloucestershire Antiquities* (London: Cadell and Davies, 1804), 20.
2. E. A. Fuller, *The Parish Church of St. John the Baptist, Cirencester* (Cirencester: Bailey and Son, 1882), 8.
3. *Ibid.,* 8n. 3.
4. John S. Wacher, "Cirencester, 1964," *The Antiquaries Journal,* XLV, pt. 1 (1965), 109.
5. Fuller, *op. cit.,* 52.
6. Leland, *Itin.,* I, 129.
7. Fuller, *op. cit.,* 26.

| 127 | Cirencester | St. John the Baptist: South Porch |
| 128 | Gloucestershire | Each bay, 2.97m x 3.10m |

Historical Analysis:

There are bequests in wills from 1492 to 1501 toward the construction of this porch.[1] Robert Stone in 1492 left forty sheep *"ad reparationem novi porticus."*[2] John Avening, who died in 1501, made a bequest toward the "worke of the newe porch."[3] Leland states that "One Alice Aveling, aunt to Bishop Ruthall by the mother side, gave an hundreth markes to the building of the right good porche . . . And Ruthalles mother contributid, and other, to the performent of it."[4] It has been suggested that the porch was built by the abbots of Cirencester Abbey on land belonging to them for secular business with the royal commissioners on financial matters.[5] The vaulting was taken down and rebuilt in 1865 by G. G. Scott,[6] at which time parts of it were suspended from the timbers above. The "new" stones display a different jointing pattern.

General Description:

Vaulted in three and one-half bays, the vaulting is abruptly cut off at the southern end. The vaulting springs from moulded capitals and shafts. Each vaulting conoid is articulated with two major panels, each being further subdivided. Trefoil cusping is employed throughout. The top horizontal circular bouding rib is composed of circular segments. The central spandrel of each bay is circular with four quatrefoils inside. In the middle of each quatrefoil is a foliate boss, except in the middle bay, where each quatrefoil contains an angel with a shield on which are initials.

Technical Description:

Four-centered curves are employed throughout. The vault is constructed entirely of jointed masonry. The joints run in the middle between the ribs, and not along the side of them.

---

1. E. A. Fuller, *The Parish Church of St. John the Baptist, Cirencester* (Cirencester: Baily and Son, 1882), 8.
2. *Ibid.,* 9.
3. *Ibid.,* 8.
4. Leland, *Itin.,* I, 129.
5. Welbore St. Clair Baddeley, *A History of Cirencester* (Cirencester: Cirencester Newspaper Company, Ltd., 1924), 290.
6. Fuller, *op. cit.,* 26.

| 129 | Corsham House | Bradford-on-Avon Porch |
| | Wiltshire | 2.44m square |

Historical Analysis:

This fan vault was reconstructed at Corsham House in 1967 and presumably came from a house in Bradford-on-Avon which was owned by Thomas Connington in 1478.[1] The house was destroyed in 1938.[2] The vaulting most likely dates from the last quarter of the fifteenth century.

General Description:

The vaulting springs from sculptured corbels. Each vaulting conoid is divided into four main panels which are trefoil cusped. The central spandrel panel is articulated by intersecting diagonal ribs which form four cinquefoil cusped panels. Foliate bosses are placed at the intersections of the diagonal ribs and the horizontal bounding ribs of the vaulting conoids. Therefore, the distinction between central spandrel panel and vaulting conoids was retained. The horizontal bounding ribs are composed of circular segments.

Technical Description:

Four-centered curves are employed. The construction is of ribs and panels with jointed masonry for the traceried parts.

---

1. The information on the porch and house is written on a plaque erected in the porch in 1967. The architect responsible for the reconstruction of the fan vault was Mr. Ernest Tew of Bath.
2. *Ibid.*

30	Cowdray House	Hall Porch
	Sussex	3.66m x 3.96m

Historical Analysis:

The arms of Henry VIII are located above the doorway to the porch in a Renaissance niche.[1] In between the ribs of the vaulting are badges referring to the appointment of the Earl of Southampton, William Fitzwilliam, as Lord High Admiral in August, 1536.[2] Since he held this position until 1540, the porch was most likely vaulted between 1536 and 1540.[3] The center boss was carved with three ostrich feathers encircled by a crown, and probably was made after 1537 when Edward VI was born.

General Description:

Each vaulting conoid is composed of four panels which are cinquefoil cusped with subcusping. Bratticing is placed along the horizontal bounding ribs. The central spandrel is articulated with a traceried wheel which is surrounded by subcusped quatrefoils enclosing bosses and cinquefoil cusped daggers. There are ridge ribs in both directions. The main lines of the vaulting are Gothic, the detailing is Renaissance in character.

Technical Description:

Four-centered curves are employed. The vaulting is constructed entirely of jointed masonry.

---

1. W. H. St. John Hope, *Cowdray and Eastbourne Priory in the County of Sussex* (London: Country Life, 1919), 21.
2. Mrs. Charles Roundell, *Cowdray: The History of a Great English House* (London: Bickers & Son, 1884), 9; J. D. Mackie, *The Earlier Tudors,* 1485-1558 (Oxford, 1966), 650.
3. Mackie, *op. cit.,* 650.

30	Crewkerne	Church of St. Bartholomew: South Porch
	Somerset	3.24m x 3.31m

Historical Analysis:

No known documentary evidence can be associated with it. F. C. Eeles and C. E. W. Slade date the rebuilding of Crewkerne to the last half of the fifteenth century;[1] John Harvey dates the nave and west end to circa 1475-90 and says that it is in the style of William Smyth.[2] The tower may have had a stone fan vault, as there are stone tas-de-charges in place; the present wooden one is modern and has the date 1904 on it.

General Description:

Each vaulting conoid has four trefoil-cusped panels and springs from moulded capitals and shafts. The central spandrel panel is articulated with four quatrefoils in circles; they are separated from each other by ribs which intersect in the middle. The spandrel panel is domical in shape. There are foliate bosses at all the rib intersections. The horizontal bounding rib is composed of straight rib segments.

Technical Description:

The lower parts are of rib and panel construction; the upper parts are jointed masonry. The beds are straight. The vaulting is constructed of Ham Hill stone.

1. F. C. Eeles and C. E. W. Slade, "Church of St. Bartholomew, Crewkerne," *SANH Proc.,* LXXXV (1939), 9.
2. *Engl. Med. Archit.,* 246.

---

131   Croscombe   St. Mary's: West Tower
          Somerset   3.22m x 3.02m

Historical Analysis:

This fan vault is an addition to an earlier tower,[1] and may have been completed by 1476, since the churchwardens' accounts 1475-1548 do not mention it.[2] The Patton family were the chief land owners to 1449. The last Patton made an addition to the endowments and the fabric of the church circa 1449.[3] Perhaps the vaulting was inserted at this time.

General Description:

The vaulting springs from moulded corbels. Each vaulting conoid is composed of three tiers which are divided by circular horizontal bounding ribs, and each is divided vertically into two main panels. Quarter foliate bosses decorate the rib intersections between panels. Trefoil cusping is used throughout. The four daggers that surround the central bell opening are also trefoil-cusped.

Technical Description:

Two-centered curves are employed. The construction is of jointed masonry, at least for the traceried parts. Although it is impossible to determine, it is likely that the lower part is composed of ribs and panels.

1. Pevsner, *BE, North Somerset and Bristol* (1958), 178.
2. Bishop Hobhouse, edit., *Church-Wardens' Accounts of Croscombe, etc.,* SRS, IV (1890), 2.
3. *Ibid.,* 3.

---

132   Crowcombe   Holy Ghost: South Porch
          Somerset   2.70m x 2.72m

Historical Analysis:

No known documentary evidence is available. On the basis of the pattern of construction, the vaulting can be compared with the porches of North Curry, Kingston St. Mary, and Ile Abbots. This would date the vaulting as circa 1500. However, the unusual way in which the tracery is handled suggests a later date, possibly in the 1520s. The vaulting of the Vaughan Chapel in St. David's Cathedral, under construction in 1522, has a tracery pattern which is similar in concept. Pevsner suggested a date of just before 1534 for the completion of the south aisle,[1] the construction of which may have coincided with the vaulting of the porch.

General Description:

The vaulting springs from moulded capitals. Each vaulting conoid is divided into two main panels, each of which is subdivided. The tracery is handled in an individual manner, for the "lancets" along the top banding rib are divided in half by the vertical ribs of the vaulting. The same method of dividing the applied tracery into halves also occurs in the central spandrel panel. The lower banding is trefoil cusped; the upper employs cinquefoil cusping. The spandrel is articulated with a small pendant. There are transverse and longitudinal ridge ribs which are horizontal until they drop down to form the pendant.

Technical Description:

Four-centered curves are employed. It is of rib and panel construction with jointed masonry for the traceried parts. The central stone of the spandrel panel, from which the pendant is formed, acts as the keystone for the vaulting and is circular in plan.

1. Pevsner, *BE, South and West Somerset* (1958), 141.

---

3 Cullompton   St. Andrews: Lane Aisle
Devonshire   4.57m (span)

Historical Analysis:

The chapel was built by John Lane, a clothier or clothman,[1] who died on 15 February 1529,[2] and was buried near the altar as he had instructed in his will.[3] The inscription on his brass notes that Lane was founder of this chapel.[4] His initials and the emblems of his trade appear as part of the sculptural program of the chapel.[5] Construction most likely began before his death, for an inscription on the exterior (located below the window level) bears the date 1526.[6] Because of the location of the inscription, construction probably began about that time but may have continued after Lane's death, perhaps until 1552.[7] It has been suggested that the vault was an afterthought and that originally only a wooden roof had been planned,[8] for the piers and arches are not square with the windows and the springing of the vaulting is not always in alignment with the buttresses. This may well have been the case, but the decision to vault the chapel was surely made at an early stage in construction, since the internal stonework of the walls above the vaulting is very rough in comparison to the stonework below.

General Description:

While the chapel is vaulted in five bays of equal width, there is an additional space at the east and west ends between the end of the fan vaulting and the walls. At the east end this space is filled in by a transverse stone band, which in conception is a narrow tunnel vault. At the west end this space is treated as a recessed panel. Since the buttresses of the exterior wall are not spaced equidistantly, they do not line up with the vaulting module. This lends credence to the theory that the vaulting may not have been originally intended, but was decided upon after construction had begun.

The vaulting module is rectangular. There are transverse and longitudinal ridge ribs. The vaulting springs from sculptured corbels and shafts. Each vaulting quadrant is composed of four main panels, which are further subdivided. Trefoil and cinquefoil cusping was employed. A major difference occurs in the way in which the upper and lower horizontal bounding ribs are handled: the upper is composed of circular segments, the lower is of straight segments. The vertical ribs are spaced equidistantly.

157

Technical Description:

133
134
Two-centered curves are employed. Rib and panel construction with jointed masonry for the traceried parts is employed. The beds are straight. The transverse ridges are composed of single stones until the second stone from the boss (keystone for the vaulting) is reached. From there the ridge is composed of two stones, the joint between them running along the center line. The longitudinal ridge has no joints along its center line. No uniform jointing pattern is employed; that is, for the corresponding location in different bays, the shape and size of corresponding stones vary. This is particularly true for the area just below the ridge stones. In some cases rib and panel are cut together, in other cases they are separate. From above, the easternmost boss is hollowed out, while those to the west are solid. The mortar joints are various widths from about 1 to 2 cm.

1. E. Carus-Wilson, "The Significance of the Secular Sculpture in the Lane Chapel, Cullompton," *Medieval Archaeology,* I (1957), 113.
2. *Ibid.,* 114; will dated 3 February 1529, Somerset House, P.C.C. 4 Jankyn, printed by W. H. H. Rogers, "Two Tudor Merchants of the Staple of Tiverton and Cullompton, Devon," *Devon Notes and Queries,* II, pt. ii (April, 1902), 55.
3. "I desire to be buried in the New Chapel of Our Lady in Cullompton . . . ," Rogers, *op. cit.,* 55; and George Oliver, *Ecclesiastical Antiquities in Devon* (Exeter: W. C. Featherstone, 1840), I, 111.
4. ". . . Johs Lane . . . Q^e Capelle Fudator . . . ," Oliver, *ibid.,* I, 111.
5. For description of the sculptural program see Edwin S. Chalk, "The Church of St. Andrew, Cullompton," *Devonshire Association,* XLII (1810), 197-203.
6. For different readings and interpretations of this inscription see Oliver, *op. cit.,* I, 111, and Edward Smirke, "Notice on Some Obscure Words in the Inscription on the Lane Chantry at Cullompton," *Exeter Diocesan Architectural Society Trans.,* III (185?), 62-5. They both agree on the date, however.
7. Mary D. Cox, "Cullompton Church," *AJ,* CXIV (1959), 142.
8. Philip Chilwell Delagarde, "An Account of the Church of S. Andrew, Cullompton," *Exeter Diocesan Architectural Society Trans.,* III (185?), 60.

---

135   Curry Rivel   St. Andrew's: South Porch
             Somerset   3.10m x 3.11m

Historical Analysis:

No known documentary evidence is available. The Beaufort portcullis and the feathers of the Prince of Wales (Arthur?)[1] are displayed on a band of quatrefoils on the outside of the porch. This would suggest a date in the late fifteenth century or early years of the sixteenth century for the porch. The similarity of the fan vaulting to that of the porches of North Curry, Kingston St. Mary, and Ile Abbots supports this date. The rib profile is similar to the chancel vault of Bath Abbey, built 1504-18.

General Description:

The vaulting springs from moulded corbels. Each vaulting conoid is divided into four panels. Trefoil cusping is employed throughout. The central spandrel is a square which is composed of four framed quatrefoils which is surrounded by four more quatrefoils and daggers. In each quatrefoil is a foliate boss.

Technical Description:

The curvature of the vaulting is imprecise. The spandrel is horizontal. Rib and panel construction with jointed masonry for the traceried parts is employed. The ribs seem to be rebated to receive the panels. The central stone in the spandrel panel (keystone of the vaulting) is square. The vaulting is constructed of Ham Hill stone.

1. Pevsner, *BE, South and West Somerset* (1958), 147; A. K. Wickham, *Churches of Somerset* (New edit., London: MacDonald, 1965), 37; G. W. Saunders, "Church of St. Andrew, Curry Rivel," *SANH Proc.,* LXXI (1926), lvii.

6	Curry Rivel	St. Andrew's: West Tower
	Somerset	3.96m square

Historical Analysis:

No documentary evidence can be associated with the vaulting of the tower. The tas-de-charge type is similar to the type employed in the last quarter of the fifteenth century at Sherborne, and the ridge stone jointing pattern is similar to the tower vaults at Shepton Mallet and Chewton Mendip, which were built circa 1540. Therefore, the vaulting was probably built in the sixteenth century.

General Description:

The vaulting springs from moulded corbels. Each vaulting conoid is composed of four trefoil cusped panels. The horizontal bounding ribs are composed of circular segments. Between the vaulting conoids and the central bell opening are placed trefoil cusped daggers. There are foliate bosses at the apexes of the wall ribs.

Technical Description:

Two-centered curves are employed. The construction is of ribs and panels with jointed masonry for the traceried parts.

6	Ditcheat	St. Mary Magdalen: Crossing Tower
	Somerset	4.14m x 4.19m

Historical Analysis:

No known documentary evidence is available. The lower part of the tower dates from circa 1300;[1] the fan vault is a later insertion. At the end of the fifteenth century the chancel was rebuilt.[2] Heraldry on its parapet include the arms of Bishop Robert Stillington (1466-91), Dean John Gunthorpe (1473-98), and Abbot John Selwood (1457-93).[3] The fan vault of the tower may have been included in the building program of the later years of the fifteenth century, and may date from 1473-91. This dating seems plausible when the vault is compared to that of St. John's, Glastonbury which was built circa 1485. The treatment of their central spandrels is almost identical, but the Ditcheat fan vault is far more developed and richer in the tracery forms. Although unlikely, it is possible that it was added as late as the 1540s, when there were will bequests designated for ". . . the reparations of the tower."[4]

General Description:

The vaulting springs from sculptured corbels. There are two main panels which are subdivided. The lower horizontal banding is trefoil cusped top and bottom. The top horizontal bounding rib is composed of circular segments. There are bosses at all rib intersections.

Technical Description:

Two-centered curves are employed. The construction is of ribs and panels with jointed masonry for the traceried parts.

1. Pevsner, *BE, South and West Somerset* (1958), 149.
2. E. Buckle, "Ditcheat Church," *SANH Proc.,* XXXVI (1890), 27-8.
3. *Ibid.*
4. D. O. Shilton, R. Holworthy, edits., *Medieval Wills from Wells,* SRS, XL (1925), 206, 214.

61   Doutling   St. Aldhelm: South Porch
             Somerset   3.02m x 3.66m

Historical Analysis:

No known documentary evidence is available. The fan vaulting is almost identical to the vaulting of the porch at Mells. The ogee gable of the porch and the way in which the angle buttresses are handled directly compare to the porches of Yatton and North Cadbury, and the towers of Batcombe, Chewton Mendip, and Ile Abbots. These comparisons suggest a date in the last decades of the fifteenth or early decades of the sixteenth century. Pevsner was correct in dating the porch circa 1500.[1] The porch was entirely rebuilt ". . . along old lines . . ." in the nineteenth century.[2]

General Description:

The porch is rectangular in plan; the vaulting springs from sculptured capitals and shafts on the east and west walls and from sculptured corbels in the middle of the north and south walls. The design module for the vaulting is 75 cm, one-quarter of the east-west span. This dimension is the radius of each vaulting conoid and of the circular central spandrel. Between this spandrel (with a pendant in the center) and the vaulting conoids, are four smaller circles, each of which enclose quatrefoils with large foliate cusp ends. The southwest quatrefoil has three cusp ends which are foliate and one that is articulated with a ram. This particular vaulting is the solution to the problem of how to fan vault a rectangular plan without having intersectioning conoids and shows the ingenuity of the designer.

Technical Description:

Two-centered curves are employed throughout. The construction is completely of jointed masonry. The vaulting apparently was completely renewed in the nineteenth century, but seems to follow the old plan.

1. Pevsner, *BE, North Somerset and Bristol* (1958), 181.
2. "Doutling Church," *SANH Proc.*, XXX (1884), 32: "The south porch had been entirely rebuilt along old lines (says Mr. Ferry) and was very like that at Mells Church."

---

42   Downham   Bishop's Palace: Entrance Way
             Cambridgeshire   1.52m x 3.30m

Historical Analysis:

The palace was rebuilt by Bishop John Alcock of Ely, 1486-1500.[1] The exterior doorway is four-centered with continuous mouldings and has an ogee gable flanked by shields. One shield is charged with the arms of Ely and the other is blank.[2] The rebus of Bishop Alcock, a cock standing on a globe, is below the shields.[3] The rib profile and cusping pattern–but not the stone jointing pattern–connects this fan vault with those that have been attributed to John Wastell.

General Description:

The use of the entrance way is uncertain. It seems likely that this fan vaulted chamber was a vestibule because of its size and proportions, and because there once was a door at its opposite end. The side walls of this chamber are no longer standing. Only fragments of the fan vault remain in situ. It was vaulted in two almost square bays. Each vaulting conoid was composed of four panels, which were cinquefoil cusped.

Technical Description:

Four-centered curves are employed. The construction is completely of jointed masonry. The vertical joints above the tas-de-charge run on the centerlines between the vertical ribs, and not along side of them. The beds appear to have been straight. No dowel holes are present in the fragments. The panel thickness is about 9 cm; rib and panel together reach a depth of about 18 cm.

1. VCH, *Cambridgeshire,* IV, 92.
2. *Ibid.*
3. *Ibid.*

Ely   Cathedral: Alcock Chapel
       Cambridgeshire   4.67m square

Historical Analysis:

Bishop John Alcock is buried in the middle of the chapel.[1] A stone with the following inscription was found while opening a grave near the chapel: "Iohanne Alkcoc epus Eliensis hauc fabricam fieri fecit MCCCCiiij[xx]viij."[2] This most likely marks the foundation of the chapel, since Alcock was not Bishop of Ely until 1486.[3] The chapel was probably finished by 1500, when Alcock died.[4] Harvey attributes the design of Alcock's Chapel to Adam Lord, who was a mason of Ely in 1490, and suggests that Lord may have been identical with Adam Vertue.[5] The source of inspiration for the fan vault must have come from St. George's Chapel, Windsor, for the chancel aisle fan vaults have similar tracery and jointing patterns. Alcock was Comptroller of the Royal Works and Buildings under Henry VII,[6] so he would have been familiar with the building program at Windsor and the work of Henry Janyns.

General Description:

The chapel is formed from the north chancel aisle by enclosing the west and south sides with screen walls. Since the chapel is square in plan, the vaulting conoids only touch each other. In the middle of the chapel is an openwork pendant which terminates in a foliate boss. The central spandrel panel has as its "corners" cinquefoil daggers. The wall ribs on three sides of the chapel are cusped. Each vaulting conoid is composed of four panels. The subpanels have cinquefoil cusping under two-centered heads.

Technical Description:

Four-centered curves are employed. The vault is constructed of ribs and panels, with jointed masonry for the traceried parts. A regular stone jointing pattern is employed for the most part. A variance in the jointing pattern occurs in the lower part of the southwest conoid. The first course of stonework above the tas-de-charge runs vertically on the center lines located between the vertical ribs, thus the rib is in the center of each piece of stonework. The next stone course is rib and panel, followed by a course of jointed masonry. The ridges have joints along their center lines, starting from the second stone in, until the central pendant is reached. The back panel of the central pendant is composed of thirty-two wedge-shaped pieces of stone work located around its outer edge. The next stage is composed of eight pieces. The top of the vaulting is covered over.

1. William Stevenson, *A Supplement to the First Edition of Mr. Bentham's History and Antiquities of the Cathedral and Conventual Church of Ely* (Norwich: Stevenson, Matchett, and Stevenson, 1817), 68-69.
2. James Bentham, *The History and Antiquities of the Conventual and Cathedral Church of Ely* (Cambridge: Printed at the University Press, 1771), 183. The foundation stone is now located in the northwest corner of the Chapel.
3. *DNB,* I, 236.
4. *Ibid.*

5. Cambridge University Library, Add. Ms. 6392, f. 417. Cited in *Engl. Med. Archit.*, 171.
6. Bentham, *op. cit.*, 183; *DNB*, I, 236.

---

50   Eton   Eton College Chapel: Lupton's Chapel
           Buckinghamshire   4.27m x 3.52m

Historical Analysis:

Built as a chantry chapel by Roger Lupton (d. 1540), who was provost of Eton from 1505 to 1535,[1] the exact date of the chapel is unknown. But an entry for a spout on the new chapel appears in the Audit Book for 1514-15: "Et Hugoni lyne . . . remouendo vnum le spowte super nouam capellam,"[2] so the chapel was complete or nearing completion at that time. John Harvey has attributed the design to William Vertue,[3] based partly on the fact that Vertue and Redman were working on Lupton's Tower at Eton in 1516.[4] Perhaps they designed the chapel together.

General Description:

The vaulting springs from moulded capitals and shafts. The vaulting conoids intersect in the east-west direction and just meet in the north-south direction. Each vaulting conoid is composed of four panels, with subpanels that are cusped and characterized by straight-line tracery. The major subpanels are quatrefoils in lozenges with carved devices at their centers. The central spandrel panel is articulated with a pendant, at the bottom of which is a shield that displays Lupton's arms.[5]

Technical Description:

Four-centered curves are employed. The construction is completely of jointed masonry. Since the roof is leaded in, it is presently impossible to inspect the vaulting from above.

1. H. C. Maxwell Lyte, *A History of Eton College* (4th Edit.; London: Macmillian and Co., Ltd., 1911), 93, 108, 135.
2. Robert Willis and John Clark, *The Architectural History of the University of Cambridge* (4 vols.; Cambridge: At the University Press, 1886), I, 417.
3. *Engl. Med. Archit.*, 272.
4. Willis and Clark, *op. cit.*, I, 418n.2.
5. Lyte, *op. cit.*, 98-9.

---

137   Evesham   All Saints: Lichfield's Chapel
           Worcestershire   5.20m x 2.60m

Historical Analysis:

Abbot Clement Lichfield was buried at the entrance to this chapel in 1546.[1] On the central pendant boss is the monogram "C. L. P."[2] The chapel was most likely built by Prior Lichfield before 1514, the year he became Abbot of Evesham.[3] In 1928, the vaulting was repaired and rejointed, and a concrete support was built inside the walls above it.[4]

General Description:

Fan vaulted in two square bays. The vaulting springs from moulded corbels, except in the middle of the north side, where it springs from a pendant. Each vaulting conoid is composed of two panels, each of which contains elaborate subpaneling with trefoil and cinquefoil cusping. The central spandrel is circular and contains four quatrefoils which are sub-cusped. The "corners" of the central spandrel have cinquefoil-cusped daggers.

Technical Description:

Four-centered curves are employed. The vaulting is constructed completely of jointed masonry. The tas-de-charge of the middle north side, which is pendant, is also the keystone for the entrance archway. A regular stone jointing pattern is employed. After the first stone, joints run along the ridges of the vaulting. A joint does not occur along the center line of the transverse arch between the bays.

1. William Trindal, *History and Antiquities of Evesham* (1794), 41.
2. "The Bosses in the Sixteenth Century Chapels in All Saints and St. Lawrence Churches, Evesham," *Worcestershire Archaeological Society,* XVIII (1942), 47.
3. E. A. B. Barnard, "Clement Lichfield, Last Abbot of Evesham," *Worcestershire Archaeological Society,* V (1929), 40.
4. *Ibid.,* 50.

---

88 | Evesham | St. Lawrence: Chapel of St. Clement
| Worcestershire | 5.48m x 4.88m (approximately)

Historical Analysis:

The chapel may have been built as a chantry chapel for Abbot Clement Lichfield.[1] Although there is no inscription on it, it is known as a chantry: Edward VI in his endowment of the free grammar school at Stourbridge gave the land, etc., belonging to the chantry of St. Clement to the School.[2] Construction must have been well under way in 1528 when William Carpynter of Evesham bequeathed 40d. to the chantry and 20d. ". . . to the guilding of St. Jerome and his tabernacle."[3] Later, in August 1530, John Holewey, gentleman of Evesham, bequeathed 12d. toward the building of the Chapel of St. Clement in St. Lawrence Church.[4] Therefore, the chapel was under construction in 1530.

General Description:

The vaulting springs from moulded capitals and shafts. Each vaulting conoid is composed of four panels. Elaborate subpanels are developed. The center is articulated by a pendant with a foliated boss. Between the pendant and vaulting conoids are cinquefoil and cusped daggers.

Technical Description:

Four-centered curves are employed. The construction is completely of jointed masonry.

1. William Tindal, *The History and Antiquities of the Abbey and Borough of Evesham* (London, 1794), 40.
2. E. J. Rudge, *A Short Account of the History and Antiquities of Evesham* (Evesham: J. Agg, 1820), 88.
3. Worcestershire Prerogative Register, III, f.3. Cited in E. A. B. Barnard, "Clement Lichfield, Last Abbot of Evesham," *Worcestershire Archaeological Society Trans.,* V (1929), 42.
4. Worcestershire Prerogative Register, III, f.18. Cited in Barnard, *ibid.,* 42.

---

23 | Exeter | Cathedral: North Porch of the West Front
| Devonshire | 1.60m x 1.61m

Historical Analysis:

No known Exeter building account cites this vault, which closely parallels that of the lavatorium of the cloister at Gloucester, completed by 1412. However, there are differences between them: (1) the springers and capitals are articulated differently; (2) the diagonal rib at Exeter intersects the center quatrefoils, which does not happen at Gloucester; (3) although the top stones are cut in the same way, the series of stones directly beneath are cut differently; (4) at Exeter the vertical joints run along the centerlines between ribs, whereas at Gloucester they run along the rib edges. Therefore, the fan vault at Exeter may have been built in imitation of Gloucester but by a different master mason and workshop.

General Description:

The vaulting springs from moulded capitals and shafts. The horizontal bounding rib is composed of circular segments. The top panels of the vaulting conoids are cinquefoil cusped. The central spandrel is composed of four quatrefoils in circles.

Technical Description:

Two-centered curves are employed. The construction is completely of jointed masonry. The beds are straight.

---

139 Eye Sts. Peter and Paul: West Porch
Suffolk 4.37m x 4.25m

Historical Analysis:

John Pope of Eye bequeathed 6s.8d. in 1462 "to the reparacion of the steeple;" in 1469 John Darwent of Eye gave "ad reparacionem nove campanile eccl'ie de Eye Xs.," and Robert Turner of Eye bequeathed "ad fabricacionem nove campanile xlvis.viiid."[1] Material was borrowed for the construction of the tower in 1470.[2] Because the tower is not square, the fan vault may have been added at a later date, when the west porch was formed out of the ground story of the tower. The coat of arms of John de la Pole (d. 1493) appears on the tower; his wife was Elizabeth Plantagenet, sister of Edward IV and Richard III.[3]

General Description:

The vaulting springs from moulded capitals and shafts. Each vaulting conoid is composed of four panels, which are "flat" cusped. In the space left between the vaulting conoids and the bell opening at the east end is a sculptured rose.

Technical Description:

Two-centered curves are employed. It is constructed of ribs and panels with jointed masonry employed for the traceried parts.

1. Henry Creed, "The Church of Sts. Peter and Paul, Eye," *Suffolk Institute of Archaeology, Statistics, and Natural History,* II (1859), 125-148.
2. *Great Britain, Royal Commission on Historical Manuscripts,* Report X (4), 531.
3. Raymond B. Jones, *A Short History of SS. Peter and Paul, Eye* (Ramsgate: The Church Publishers, n.d.), 5.

Fairford St. Mary the Virgin: South Porch
Gloucestershire

Historical Analysis:

The vaulting is modern. Henry Taunt, in his guide to Fairford, wrote that "Inside the porch may be seen the stoup . . . and the remains of panelling upon the walls."[1] Surely he would have mentioned if the porch were vaulted, since he mentioned the panelling. Therefore, it cannot be assumed that the present fan vault is a replica of a former vault.

1. Henry W. Taunt, *Fairford Church* (3rd Edit.; Fairford: Thomas Powell, n.d.), 5.

| Fotheringhay | St. Mary the Virgin and All Saints: West Tower |
| Northamptonshire | 5.53m square (vaulting only) |

Historical Analysis:

The date 1529 appears on the northwest springer of the fan vault.[1] The vault was inserted into an already extant tower, the construction of which goes back to 1434.[2] It may have replaced an older vault, for the contract of 1434 specifies that the tower as to be ". . . vawthid with stone."[3] The design for this vault shows the influence of King's College Chapel, Cambridge.

General Description:

The vaulting springs from sculptured corbels, which depict angels holding shields. Each vaulting conoid is composed of six main panels. The subpanels are cinquefoil cusped. Bratticing is employed on the lower horizontal bounding rib and around the central bell opening. There are transverse and longitudinal ridge ribs.

Technical Description:

Two-centered curves are employed. It is constructed completely of jointed masonry.

1. This date has sometimes been interpreted as 1457, see H. R. Bonney, *Historic Notices in Reference to Fotheringhay* (Orundele: Printed by and for T. Bell, 1821), 49. The VCH, *Northampton,* II, 575, confirms, however, the 1529 reading.
2. *Monasticon,* VI, 1414.
3. *Ibid.*

| Glastonbury | Abbey: Fragments |
| Somerset | |

Analysis:

Based on the evidence of one boss which was found during the excavation of the chapel by F. Bligh Bond, it has been hypothesized that the Edgar Chapel, built by Abbot Beere (1493-1524) and finished by Abbot Whiting,[1] was fan vaulted.[2] According to Bond's interpretation, the setting-out lines found on the back of the boss for twelve radiating ribs implied a wheel of tracery between fans.[3] In another article he describes this boss in greater detail, indicating that the upper side was flat, had a lewis hole, and had four main ribs with eight lighter ribs between them.[4] This could mean that the vaulting had transverse and longitudinal ridges, and might have had a complex lierne form. On the other hand, the four main ribs could have been oriented toward the corners of the vaulting bay, as they are in the porch of Kingston St. Mary (Somerset), a fan vault of the early sixteenth century. This interpretation would support Bond's hypothesis. Although the evidence is not substantial enough to ascertain whether or not the Edgar Chapel was fan vaulted, vaulting fragments now preserved in the abbey's kitchen do indicate that there were fan vaults in the abbey. These fragments are from short span fan vaults that were completely constructed of jointed masonry. On the basis of style, they may be dated to the late fifteenth century. The idea of a fan vault was not foreign to the abbey. Since Glastonbury was one of the wealthiest of English monasteries,[5] it would seem likely that Beere decided upon a fan vault for the Edgar Chapel. After all, it was the most fashionable way of building at that time, and Abbot Beere had strong connections in London (he was part of the English Embassy to Rome in 1503 to congratulate the Pope on his election),[6] and was a man of learning (he corresponded with Erasmus).[7]

1. "Abbate Beere buildid Edgares chapel at the est end of the chirch: But Abbate Whiting performid sum part of it." Leland, *Itin.,* I, 289.
2. Frederick Bligh Bond, *The Gate of Remembrance* (2nd Edit.; Oxford: B. H. Blackwell, 1918), 72. Not a scholarly work, filled with fantasy.
3. *Ibid.,* 72.
4. F. Bligh Bond, "Glastonbury Abbey," *SANH Proc.,* LV (1910), 115.
5. M. D. Knowles, *The Religious Orders in England* (Cambridge: At the University Press, 1959), III, 473.
6. Ian Keil, "London and Glastonbury Abbey in the Later Middle Ages," *London and Middlesex Archaeological Society,* XXI, pt. 2, 174.
7. *DNB,* IV, 323.

142 57	Glastonbury Somerset	St. John's: West Tower 4.23m x 4.30m

Historical Analysis:

No mention of the vaulting occurs in the extensive churchwardens' accounts, some of which are preserved.[1] R. P. Brereton dates the tower to 1485.[2] The same ridge stone jointing system is used here as in the tower vault at Ditcheat, which most likely dates to the last decades of the fifteenth century. The tower vault also shows the influence of Stillington's Chapel, Wells, which was built 1478-88. A date in the last years of the fifteenth century is appropriate for the vaulting.

General Description:

The vaulting springs from shafts and moulded capitals. Each vaulting quadrant is composed of four trefoil cusped panels. The horizontal bounding ribs are composed of straight segments. There are bosses at the rib intersections.

Technical Description:

Two-centered curves are employed. The construction is of ribs and panels with jointed masonry for the traceried parts.

1. "Churchwardens' Accounts, St. John's Glastonbury," *Somerset and Dorset Notes and Queries,* IV (1895), 89-96, 137-44, 188-92, 235-40, 281-88, 329-36, 379-84.
2. ". . . stated to have been built by Abbot John Selwood in 1485." BM Add. MS 37260, f. 14r.

18	Gloucester Gloucestershire	Cathedral: Cloister *East Walk:* Nine bays, each 3.40m x 3.74m (average) *East Walk:* One bay, 3.40m x 2.67m *North and South Walks:* Ten bays, each 3.58m x 3.43m (average) *Lavatorium (off North Walk):* Five bays, each 1.89m square *West Walk:* Ten bays, each 3.40m x 3.70m (average) *Corner Bays:* 3.40m x 3.40m (average)

Historical Analysis:

A documentary history of the abbey compiled in the fifteenth century, listing the benefactions of Abbot Walter Froucester (1381-1412), states that the cloister was begun and built up to the chapter house door in the time of Abbot Thomas Horton (1351-77), after which it was left unfinished for many years; Abbot Froucester, it then states, finished it at great expense.[1] Therefore, the cloister was built between 1351 and 1412. The documentary history does not indicate if Horton built the cloister from the chapter house door to the church, or from the chapter house to the northeast door of the cloister. Nor does it indicate if the cloister was vaulted from the beginning.

Leland and the *Monasticon* give sole credit to Froucester for the building of the cloister,[2] which confirms the fact that the majority of the cloister must have been built during Froucester's time. The *Monasticon* states that in one of the windows there were verses written by Froucester detailing the history of the convent.[3] J. T. D. Niblett saw no less than seven examples of the second badge of Richard II, the sprig of broom plant, on the old painted glass (now replaced) in the lavatorium off the north cloister walk.[4] This badge was first adopted by Richard II in 1393,[5] so the glass, and perhaps the completion of the cloister (at least the lavatorium), dates from after 1393.

General Description:

The moulding profiles of the walls along the whole of the east walk are uniform. A constant, but different profile occurs in the north, south, and west walks. This indicates at least two phases in the constructional sequence and supports the documentary evidence stating that the cloister was begun by Abbot Horton.

The vaulting is constant in its formal characteristics from the church to the chapter house along the east walk, except for bay II which is of different proportions (rectangular, with intersecting vaulting conoids that result in a different treatment of the central spandrel panel). Farther along the east walk numerous changes occur. From the door of the chapter house to the north door of the cloister, there are four different types (in terms of visual articulation) of tas-de-charge employed. The differences occur in the cusping patterns. In the rest of the cloister only one type is used. In the north part of the east walk, there are two different types of articulation of the lower horizontal banding, one with trefoil cusping on the bottom only, the other with trefoil cusping top and bottom. In the rest of the cloister, trefoil cusping is employed only on the bottom of this lower horizontal band. In addition, the central spandrel panels in bays VII to XII are different in one small detail in the articulation of their daggers. Finally, it has been previously stated, that the top horizontal banding in the east walk has trefoils, whereas the top band in the other parts of the cloister have quatrefoils.[6] This is not quite accurate; for the change occurs between bays XLIII and XLIV in the south walk.

From a formal consideration of the vaulting it is possible to point to two distinct phases in the construction pattern: bays VII to XII of the east walk on the one hand, and the rest of the cloister on the other. The minor change from trefoils to quatrefoils which occurs between bays XLIII and XLIV in the south walk probably does not represent a distinct time differential in the vaulting operations, for this change occurs in the same block of stone.

Technical Description:

The bays of the east walk are 3.40m x 3.74m, except bay II, which is 3.40m x 2.67m. The outside supports of the east walk tilt outward, while the window tracery is perpendicular to the floor. The result of this is a more square bay at the top than at the bottom. This building pattern may have been a fiddle used by the master mason to accommodate the proportions of a fan vault. Although it could be the result of building settlement (there are large stone arches above the vaulting at the bay divisions which suggest that the east walk of the cloister once had a second level and the outer wall would have carried a greater load), close investigation indicates that the walls were constructed in this way. The bays of the north and south walks (3.58m x 3.43m) are more square than those of the east walk. The bays of the west walk are not square (3.43m x 3.70m). The problem of fit there is solved by panels of different size. The bays of the lavatorium, which projects into the cloister's courtyard, are square. Evidently, by the time the lavatorium was built, the builders knew that a fan vault was easier to construct over a square bay. It seems possible that the cloister was laid out before a fan vault was decided upon.

145   Significant differences occur in the way in which the stones are cut. In bays VI to XII of the east walk the lower part of the vaulting is composed of irregular pieces of stonework. In those bays there is no standardized system of stone jointing. The rest of the east, north, south, and west walks have a standardized jointing system for both the central spandrel and the lower regions of the vaulting, and only minor **24**   variations occur to solve specific problems of fit. The lavatorium has a different stone jointing pattern because of its smaller size. Two-centered curves are employed in all the fan vaults of the cloister. The upper surface of the vaulting has mostly been plastered over, and there is rubble fill in the vaulting pockets. From what can **10**   be seen from above, the vaulting is completely of jointed masonry. (Some areas which **149**   are rib and panel appear to be restored work.) The stones of the wall ribs of the **150**   east walk are of uniform shape and size. Where the wall of the north transept juts in, the keystones are the same shape as those farther to the north, so it is evident that they were not specifically designed for the places they occupy but follow an already established pattern. This would indicate that construction proceeded from the north to the south along the east walk, or at least from the chapter house door to the south.

Conclusions:

It is apparent that two distinct phases of vault construction occurred: the north part of the east walk constituting one phase, the rest of the cloister the other. Probably, the north part of the east walk was built first, since it is technically less advanced than the rest of the vaulting. This section to the chapter house door may have been built in Abbot Horton's time–not the section from the chapter house door to the church. It is more plausible, however, that Abbot Horton did build the cloister from the chapter house door to the church, but that it was not immediately vaulted, nor was a fan vault initially intended, since the bays of the east walk are not square. The north part of the east walk was probably vaulted first, since it is more experimental in nature, followed by the rest of the east walk, then the south, west, and north walks. Thus a date of circa 1400 or thereafter is more reasonable for the vaulting than one of circa 1373, as has been suggested in the past.[7]

1. "... claustrum monasterii quod fuit in coeptum tempore Thomae Hortone abbatis et ad ostium capituli perductum et multis annis imperfectum ibidem relictum magnis expensis et sumptuosis honorifice construxit..." BM Cotton MS Dom. A viii, f.142b, printed in William Hart, editor, *Historia et Cartularium Monasterii Sancti Petre Gloucestriae* (3 vols.; London: Longman, etc., 1863-67), I, 55.
2. Leland, *Itin.,* II, 61; *Monasticon,* I, 535.
3. *Monasticon,* I, 535, 542.
4. W. Bazeley and J. Niblett, "Royal Badges in Gloucester Cathedral," *Records of Gloucester Cathedral,* I (for 1882-3), 114.
5. *Ibid.,* 115.
6. F. E. Howard, "Fan Vaults," *AJ,* LXVIII (1911), 5.
7. For example see Geoffrey Webb, *Architecture in Britain* (2nd edition; Harmondsworth: Penguin Books, Ltd., 1965), 143.

---

151   Gloucester   Cathedral: West Entrance to the Nave
         Gloucestershire   1.27m x 2.46m

Historical Analysis:

According to Leland, "Abbot Morwent newly erected the very west end of the church. . . ."[1] This would date the west entrance with its fan vault to the years 1420-37.[2]

General Description:

The vault is composed of two conoids. Cinquefoil cusping is employed along the upper horizontal band. The lower panels are not cusped. The central spandrel panel is composed of a quatrefoil in a circle, which encloses a shield (now blank) surrounded by three trefoil cusped daggers.

Technical Description:

Two-centered curves are employed. The vault is completely constructed of jointed masonry. The vertical joints run along the rib edges; that is, rib and panel are cut together from the same piece of stone, the rib being located at the edge of the stone. The beds are concave.

---

1. Leland, *Itin.,* II, 61.
2. *Monasticon,* I, 535.

<table>
<tr><td>2</td><td>Gloucester
Gloucestershire</td><td>Cathedral: East Entrance into the Cloister
from the North Side of the Church
2.09m x 0.96m</td></tr>
</table>

Historical Analysis:

No documentary evidence can be associated with this entrance way. Compared to the fan vaulting of the cloister, this one possibly was built later. Conceptually it is the same as the fan vault of the west entrance to the nave. Although there are formal as well as technical differences which separate them (type of cusping, stone jointing system used), these differences may be the result of difference in actual size and purpose. The west entrance fan vault is the larger and more elaborate one. Therefore, they both may have been built circa 1430.

General Description:

The vaulting is composed of two conoids. Each panel is trefoil cusped. The central spandrel panel is divided by a central ridge rib, with trefoils located on either side.

Technical Description:

Two-centered curves are employed. It is completely constructed of jointed masonry. The joints are all horizontal, since the space is spanned by one piece of stone. It was possible to construct it in this manner because of its short span.

<table>
<tr><td>3</td><td>Gloucester
Gloucestershire</td><td>Cathedral: Two Chantry Chapels off the Lady Chapel
4.19m x 2.50m</td></tr>
</table>

Historical Analysis:

No documentary evidence can be associated with the chantry chapels. However, according to Leland, "Abbot Hanley (1457-72) and Farley (1472-98) made our Lady Chappell, at the east end of the church."[1] A clue to the dating of the chantries may be found perhaps in the stained glass. The rose-en-soleil, the badge of Edward IV, is found in the glass of the south chantry;[2] this evidence indicates that the chantries may have been built during his reign. If so, they should be dated 1461-83.

General Description:

Both chapels are almost identical. The chapels are not rectangular in plan, as the west walls are not perpendicular to the north-south walls. They are both vaulted in two bays. Each vaulting quadrant is divided into two main panels. The subpanels are trefoil cusped. The central spandrel panel is articulated with a row of traceried wheels which run between two ridge ribs. Traceried wheels also run transversely to the center row and are located between the vaulting conoids. One difference between the chapels is in the articulation of the roses which are at the centers of the traceried wheels. The carving, especially in the south chantry, suggests a date closer to 1480 than 1460.

Technical Description:

Four-centered curves are employed. The construction is completely of jointed masonry. The central spandrel panel is flat.

1. Leland, *Itin.,* II, 61. For the dates of Hanley and Farley see *Monasticon,* I, 536.
2. W. Bazeley and J. Niblett, "Royal Badges in Gloucester Cathedral," *Records of Gloucester Cathedral,* I (for 1882-3), 114.

---

154   Great Malvern   Priory: Chantry Chapel in South Aisle of Chancel
            Worcestershire   Two bays, each 1.67m square

Historical Analysis:

No known documentary evidence can be positively associated with this chapel. It seems likely that the south aisle of the chancel, known as St. Anne's chapel, was finished by 1460.[1] Therefore, the chapel must date from circa 1460 or afterwards.

155 The stone jointing pattern and the general layout and treatment of the central spandrel panel are similar to the chantry chapel of Bishop Stanbury and the fan vault of the Vicars Cloister, both at Hereford and datable to the last quarter of the fifteenth century. However, the tracery pattern of the panels at Malvern is more mannered, and the rib profile is more developed. It could be dated as late as the chantry that Peter Hall of Sickley founded in the priory, 1496.[2]

General Description:

It was planned in two square bays with a panelled arch at the east end. Each vaulting quadrant is composed of three main panels. The central panels consist of four cinquefoil cusped circles framed by four cinquefoil cusped daggers.

Technical Description:

Four-centered curves are employed. The construction is completely of jointed masonry. The beds are concave.

1. Brian S. Smith, *A History of Malvern* (Leicester University Press, 1964), 65.
2. *Ibid.,* 82.

        Hampton Court   Palace: Ann Boleyn's Gateway
        Middlesex   5.20m square (approximately)

Historical Analysis:

The vaulting displays the badge of Ann Boleyn–the falcon and her initial A, entwined with an H in a true lover's knot.[1] Therefore, the vaulting must have been built circa 1533.

General Description:

The vaulting springs from moulded corbels. There are four panels per conoid. There are ridge ribs in both directions. The central spandrel panel is articulated with a boss at the center. The vaulting is similar to that of the north walk of St. Stephen's Cloister, Westminster.

Technical Description:

Four-centered curves are employed. The stonework is modern.[2]

---

1. Ernest Law, *The History of Hampton Court Palace* (3 vols.; London: George Bell and Sons, 1890), I, 164.
2. RCHM, *Middlesex* (1937), 34.

Hereford	Cathedral: Bishop Audley's Chapel
Herefordshire	4.11m (east-west span); 0.86m (radius of one conoid)

Historical Analysis:

Edmund Audley was Bishop of Hereford from 1492 until 1502, when he was transferred to Salisbury.[1] License to found a perpetual chantry in Hereford Cathedral and a mortmain licence to grant lands to the chaplain in Hereford Cathedral to the value of £10 per annum was granted to Bishop Audley in 1516.[2] It should also be noted that the arms of Bishop Mayew (1503-16) are painted on the chantry screen.[3] Audley's connections with St. George's, Windsor (Canon, 1474, Chancellor of the Garter, 1502)[4] explain the design of the chapel, for it is similar to the vaulting of John Shorne's Chapel at Windsor, built in the last decades of the fifteenth century.[5] Stylistically, a date of circa 1500 is more plausible than one of 1515 for the chapel. This is even more evident when this chapel is seen in relation to the chapel Audley built in Salisbury Cathedral, for which a licence was granted at the same time (1516).[6] Therefore, construction of the Hereford Chapel was most likely started, but not yet completed, when Audley left Hereford in 1502.

General Description:

The chapel is in two stories. The chapel in plan is composed of five sides of an octagon. The lower chapel has a stone ceiling upon which were painted ribs to resemble a fan vault between the main stone ribs. The upper chapel is vaulted with conoids which support a flat saucer dome. There is a boss depicting the Assumption of the Virgin in the center. The surrounding diagonal panels have bosses which depict (a) the deanery, (b and c) foliage, (d) fleur-de-lis, (e) Tudor rose, (f) see of Hereford, (g) shield with monogram "I. R.," and (h) St. Ethelbert.[7] The panels of the conoids are cinquefoil cusped.

Technical Description:

The lower chapel vaulting is rib and panel construction. The upper chapel vault is entirely built of jointed masonry. Presently the upper vault is suspended from the timbers above with iron rods, which may have been added when the chapel was restored (£770 was spent on it in 1858).[8] The vaulting of Shorne's Tower at Windsor displays basically the same stone jointing pattern and is self-supporting. There is no access to the roof space.

---

1. Emden, *Oxford*, I, 75.
2. *L & P Henry VIII*, II, pt. 1, 832.
3. George Marshall, *Hereford Cathedral* (Worcester: Littlebury and Company, Ltd., 1951), 161.
4. Emden, *Oxford*, I, 76.
5. W. H. St. John Hope, *Windsor Castle* (2 vols.; London: Country Life, 1913), II, 410-411.
6. *L & P Henry VIII*, II, pt. 1, 832.·
7. RCHM, *Herefordshire*, I (1931), 104.
8. Marshall, *op. cit.*, 162.

Analysis:

Mr. Norman Drinkwater has suggested that the Hereford Chapter House was fan vaulted.[1] His hypothesis is based on a drawing done in 1721 by Stukeley, who wrote that the ". . . chapter house . . . (was) destroyed in the Civil Wars . . . I saw its poor remains, whence I endeavoured to restore the whole in drawing as well as I could. . . . There are about four windows now standing, and the springing of the stone arches between, of fine rib work which composed the roof."[2] Therefore, very little of the chapter house was still standing when Stukeley saw it. The only parts of the vaulting that he could have seen in situ were the wall ribs and the tas-de-charge; and, there could have been little lying about on the ground because the building had been used as a quarry. In Stukeley's drawing the central column, which is articulated differently, must have occurred to Stukeley after the drawing was well under way. It is possible, though not probable, that the shadow at the foot of the drawing was the outline of the base of the central pulpit[3] that the chapter house was known to have had instead of the base of a central column. When looking at the side elevation of the vaulting fragment that Drinkwater has labeled as coming from the central conoid, it is clear that it came from one of the angles of the chapter house. This type of tas-de-charge is also common to lierne vaults (cf. Tewkesbury) and does not necessarily indicate a fan vault was employed.

A contract dated 1364 with Thomas of Cambridge for the completion of the chapter house indicates it was to be finished in seven years time–that is, by 1371.[4] This date seems plausible for two reasons: first, the window tracery (from Stukeley's drawing) belongs to the same family as the probable contemporary work in the east walk of the Gloucester cloister; and second, the way in which the cusping on the tas-de-charge stands clear of the panel behind suggests a date before the last quarter of the fourteenth century. (The Gloucester cloister cusping is different in concept–it lies directly on the surface of the back panel.) Considering the early date, 1371, for the chapter house, and the way in which the cusping is articulated, it seems more likely to have had a complex lierne vault than a fan vault. However, the possibility that it was fan vaulted cannot be ruled out.

1. For a complete history of the chapter house after its construction see Norman Drinkwater, "Hereford Cathedral: Chapter House," *AJ,* CXII (1955), 61-75.
2. William Stukeley, *Itinerarium Curiosum* (2nd edit.; London; Baker and Leigh, 1776), 71. The drawing is reproduced in Geoffrey Webb, *Architecture in Britain* (2nd edit., Harmondsworth, 1965), pl. 136(B).
3. Drinkwater, op. cit., 66.
4. William Capes, edit., *Charters and Records of Hereford Cathedral* (Hereford: Wilson and Philips, 1908), 231-32.

158   Hereford   Cathedral: Bishop Stanbury's Chapel

           Herefordshire   Two bays, each 2.49m square

Historical Analysis:

John Stanbury was bishop of Hereford from 1453 to 1474.[1] In his will, dated 25 February 1472,[2] he directed that he be buried on one side or the other of the high altar at the discretion of his executors.[3] Clearly, construction of his tomb and chantry chapel did not commence until after his death. The chapel was completed by 10 August 1492 (6 Henry VII), when Robert Geffrey and Hugh Ragoun, executors of Bishop Stanbury, made over in trust certain land and tenements, for the endowment of a chantry, "... in a chapell new bylded by us, the said Robert and Hugh, by the tombe of the late seyd bysshope in the northe syde of the cantedral churche of Hereforde."[4]

General Description:

It is vaulted in two square bays. Each vaulting quadrant is composed of four main panels. The subpanels at the uppermost level are divided into two ogee and trefoil cusped "lights" under a two-centered head with quatrefoils in the spandrels. The lower levels are also ogee-headed and trefoil cusped. The central spandrel is composed of four sexfoil cusped circles surrounded by four trefoil cusped daggers.

Technical Description:

Four-centered curves are employed. The construction is completely of jointed masonry. The keystone of the vault is square; its sides are placed parallel to the walls. A standard jointing system is employed, with joints that run along the centerlines of both transverse and longitudinal ridges.

1. John Le Neve, *Fasti Ecclesiae Anglicanae, 1300-1541, Hereford Diocese,* compiled by J. M. Horn (London: 1961), 2.
2. P.C.C. 16 Wattys, printed in Arthur T. Bannister, edit., *Registrum Johannis Stanbury, Canterbury and York Society,* XXV (1919), vii.
3. "... corpusque meum sepeliendum infra cancellum chore ecclesie nunc mee cathedralis herefordensis ex alterutra parte summi altaris ibidem juxta discrecionem executorum meorum...," *ibid.,* vii.
4. *Ibid.,* xi.

---

9   Hereford   Cathedral: Vicars' Cloister Porch
        Herefordshire   2.95m square

Historical Analysis:

On 18 October 1472 sanction was granted for the removal of the Vicars' College to its present site.[1] Construction of the new college most likely commenced before 1474, as Bishop Stanbury's arms appear in the cloister.[2] The porch was a later addition to the cloister; for the base mouldings of the two structures differ, and the vaulting of the porch cuts across the frames which surround the shields above the inner doorway. The fan vault is nearly identical in its formal and technical characteristics to the vaulting of Bishop Stanbury's Chapel, which was built circa 1474-92. A late fifteenth century date seems plausible for this vault.

General Description:

The vaulting springs from moulded capitals and shafts. The tracery pattern is the same as in Bishop Stanbury's Chapel, except that the four circles of the central spandrel panel here are cinquefoil cusped. Remains of a boss are located in the center of the vaulting.

Technical Description:

Four-centered curves are employed. The construction is completely of jointed masonry. The keystone of the vault is square; its sides are placed parallel to the walls. Vertical joints run down the centerlines of the ribs at the uppermost level.

1. P.R.O., *Calendar of the Patent Rolls,* Edward IV, 1467-1477, 365; George Marshall, "The Roof of the Vicars' Cloister at Hereford," *Woolhope Naturalists' Field Club Trans.,* for 1918, 1919, & 1920 (1921), 71.
2. Marshall, *op. cit.,* 80.

160   Highworth   St. Michael's: West Tower
            Wiltshire   4.57m x 4.07m

Historical Analysis:

No documentary evidence can be associated with this tower. The west arch of the tower having been remodeled, the tower not being square in plan, and the wall ribs of the vaulting being unevenly jointed to the walls, suggest that this fan vault was a later addition to an already extant tower. It is unique in the way in which the subpanels are treated and in the articulation of the central bell opening. The fact that the bell opening has a highly decorative character suggests a date in the early sixteenth century for this vault (cf. Fairford). The rib profile is not unlike that of the Poyntz Chapel, Bristol, thus confirming a sixteenth century date.

General Description:

The vaulting springs from moulded capitals and shafts. Each vaulting conoid is divided into four major panels. The subpanels are trefoil and cinquefoil cusped under two-centered heads. The central bell opening is articulated by a ring of panels, each enclosing a foliate boss. The areas left between the vaulting conoids and the central bell opening are articulated with trefoil cusped daggers east-west and cusped panels north-south.

Technical Description:

Two-centered curves are employed. The construction is of ribs and panels with jointed masonry employed for the traceried parts.

            Hillesden   All Saints Church: North Porch
            Buckinghamshire

Analysis:

The present vaulting was designed and presented to the church by Sir George Gilbert Scott.[1] In the nineteenth century, the springers of an earlier vault were in situ which Sir George thought to resemble the aisle vaults of Henry VII's Chapel, Westminster;[2] therefore, this porch may have been fan vaulted or was perhaps prepared for one.

1. George Gilbert Scott, "All Saints Church, Hillesden, Bucks," *Records of Buckinghamshire,* IV (1877?), 318.
2. *Ibid.,* 313.

---

161   Hilton   All Saints: South Porch
            Dorset   2.45m x 2.44m

Historical Analysis:

No documentary evidence can be associated with the porch. The vaulting is similar in style, material, and technology to the vaults of Milton Abbas, which is located only one and one-half miles away, suggesting a date late in the fifteenth century. The inclusion of a rose on the vaulting implies a date after 1485.

General Description:

The vaulting springs from corbels. Each vaulting conoid is divided into four panels which are trefoil cusped. The top horizontal bounding ribs are composed of straight segments. The central spandrel panel consists of four quatrefoil panels with bosses at the rib intersections. Two bosses display the arms of Milton and Abbotsbury Abbeys.[1] The others are foliate, one of which is a rose.

Technical Description:

Two-centered curves are employed. The construction is of ribs and panels with jointed masonry employed for the traceried parts. The central spandrel panel is flat. The material of construction is Ham Hill stone.

1. G. Dru Drury, "All Saints' Hilton," *Dorset Natural History and Archaeological Society Proc.,* LI (1930), 241.

4

Ile Abbots	St. Mary: South Porch
Somerset	3.20m x 3.20m

Historical Analysis:

No documentary evidence is known to exist. The porch itself is an early structure, the fan vault being a later addition.[1] The formal and constructive patterns of the vaulting are basically the same as the porch vaults of Kingston St. Mary, Curry Rivel, and North Curry. This would date the vaulting as circa 1500.

General Description:

The vaulting springs from moulded corbels. Each vaulting conoid is divided into four main panels which are further subdivided above the lower horizontal band, which is trefoil cusped top and bottom. The top horizontal band is also trefoil cusped. The central spandrel panel is articulated with a circle enclosing eight traceried panels which drop down to form a pendant. Not only is the bottom of the pendant articulated with a foliate boss, but there are also smaller foliate bosses along the ribs just before they drop down to form the pendant. The "corners" of the central spandrel panel are articulated with quatrefoils east-west and cinquefoil-cusped daggers north-south.

Technical Description:

Four-centered curves are employed. Rib and panel construction with jointed masonry for the traceried parts is employed. In some cases rib and panel look as if they are cut together. The central stone of the spandrel panel, which forms the pendant and acts as the keystone for the vaulting, is circular in plan.

1. J. Edwin Forbes, "Church of St. Mary the Virgin, Ile Abbots," *SANH Proc.,* LXXI (for 1925), xlix.

2

Ilminster	St. Mary: Crossing Tower
Somerset	3.83m x 3.83m

Historical Analysis:

According to tradition, Sir William Wadham (d. 1452) was responsible for the construction of the tower and St. Catherine's Chapel (n. transept), which houses his tomb.[1] Because the chapel and the tower are not bonded together, but just abut each other, they evidently were not constructed at the same time and do not belong to the same building campaign. The chapel was probably built first and adjoined an already extant crossing tower which was later rebuilt. On the basis of style the tower fan vault should be dated circa 1500. The tas-de-charge type is similar to those of the south porch at Crewkerne, and the use of larger bosses at the rib intersections typify later fan vaults, such as the towers at Wells, Muchelney, Shepton Beauchamp, and the north transept at Sherborne. The stone jointing pattern used here is the same as was used in the tower vaults at Ditcheat and Glastonbury, both of which are late fifteenth century. Thus, on stylistic and technical grounds, a date of circa

1500 is more reasonable for this vault than one of circa 1452.

General Description:

The vaulting springs from moulded capitals and shafts. The horizontal bounding rib is composed of circular segments. Large, and for the most part foliate, bosses are located at the rib intersections. The areas between the vaulting conoids and the central bell opening are articulated with quatrefoils in circles and daggers.

Technical Description:

Two-centered curves are employed. The construction is of ribs and panels with jointed masonry employed for the traceried parts. Although the vaulting module is square, the ribs are not equally spaced; this discrepancy is especially evident in the southwest and southeast conoids. The solution of fit indicates that the vaulting was originally planned for a slightly smaller span and was adjusted to fit this space. It is possible that the stones were cut at another site for later erection here. The pier bases look as if they might have been altered to accept the vaulting shafts.

1. James Street, *The Mynster of the Ile* (Taunton: H. Abraham, 1904), 54, 317.

---

163   Iron Acton   St. James the Less: West Tower
           Gloucestershire   3.50m (estimated)

Historical Analysis:

The inscription on the tomb of Robert Poyntz, located in the church, reads ". . . And thys stepyl here maked . . ."[1] Since Robert Poyntz died in 1439,[2] the tower must have been completed by that time. (Parts of it seem to have been completed earlier–perhaps Poyntz rebuilt it.) He also was responsible for the erection of the preaching cross in the churchyard,[3] which bears a similarity of detail to the tower. The facts that the cusping on the tower fan vault has foliate terminals and that the decoration is placed to the sides of the rib intersections make a date of circa 1439 plausible for this vault (cf. the west porch at Gloucester and the tower vault at Croscombe).

General Description:

The vaulting springs from sculptured corbels. The top horizontal bounding rib is composed of circular segments. Sculptured heads are placed at the apexes of the wall ribs. Trefoil cusping is employed throughout.

Technical Description:

Four-centered curves are employed. The vaulting is plastered and painted over. Nothing of the vaulting can be seen from above, so it is impossible to determine the type of construction.

1. Samuel Lysons, *A Collection of Gloucestershire Antiquities* (London, 1803), 1.
2. H. L. Thompson, "The Poyntz Family," *Bristol and Gloucestershire Archaeological Society,* IV (for 1879-80), 81.
3. *Ibid.*

           King's Lynn   Red Mount Chapel: Crossing Vault of the
           Norfolk   Upper Chapel
                                 2.17m square

Historical Analysis:

The Red Mount Chapel was most likely built as an oratory for pilgrims on the way to Walsingham.[1] Its date of construction is conjectural, although the Corporation Hall Books have a series of entries, 1482-85, in which Robert Curranunte on 23 April 1483 is first warned to build no chapel upon the common's ground and then on 25 January 1485 is given license ". . to build a chapel on the mount called Lady Hill."[2] On the basis of the Hall Book entries the date 1485 has often been assigned to the upper chapel.[3]

4   The chapel is octagonal in plan with a cruciform upper story. Close examination reveals that the brick and limestone octagonal structure is irregular in its layout; its corresponding sides are not parallel, and its buttresses are at variable angles to its sides. On the whole, precision is lacking. The cruciform stone upper chapel, on the other hand, is precisely set out. It is plainly visible that the sides of this upper chapel are not parallel to the sides of the octagonal lower structure.

The moulded brick handrail of an interior staircase, which leads from the west door to the upper chapel, is abruptly cut off where the stonework of the upper chapel begins. It is evident that this handrail once continued on. In addition, the upper chapel overhangs another staircase at the western end which connects the south door of the upper chapel with the northeast exterior entrance.

In the southwest corner of the lower chapel and in the corresponding position in the chamber above, a vertical shaft of about 5 cm in diameter is present. No trace of this shaft can be found in the upper chapel.[4]

The visual evidence supports the hypothesis that there were at least two distinct phases of building operations on the site, and the upper chapel should be seen as an addition to the octagonal structure.[5] The high quality of detailing of the upper chapel compared to the way in which it is integrated into the lower octagonal structure suggests that it was designed by a mason who was not on the site during the period of actual construction.

When Robert Curranunte was told to build no chapel, the octagonal structure might have already existed. However, the only evidence to suggest that this was the case, is found in the will of William March dated February 1480 in which he bequeathed 6s.8d. to the fabric of the Chapel of St. Mary the Virgin upon Guanock Hill;[6] this bequest may not refer to the same chapel, or, alternatively, the octagonal structure could already have been in the planning stages in 1480. The possibility exists that the octagonal structure was the one referred to in the Corporation Hall Book entries and, therefore, should be dated 1485. The upper chapel may have been built after 1504 when Sir John Gakenham reconfirmed the lease of the site as "to continue during the pleasure of the mayor and commons as appeared by the Resolution of the Hall of the 6th of May, 2nd Richard III."[7]

General Description:

5
6   It is a cruciform chapel in which the crossing is fan vaulted, and the arms have pointed tunnel vaults with applied tracery. The fan vault is square in plan. Each vaulting conoid springs from a moulded capital and shaft and is composed of four panels which are cinquefoil cusped. The horizontal bounding rib is composed of circular segments and is decorated with finialed cusps. Ridges rise on all four sides to a central boss (now destroyed). The ridge ribs are the same in section as the vertical radiating ribs of the vaulting conoids.

Technical Description:

Two-centered curves are employed. The construction is completely of jointed masonry. There are no stone joints along the centerlines of the ridges. The top part of the vault is composed of thirteen stones which abut each other but do not interlock. The beds are concave. The vaulting must have been precisely laid out, since no adjustments for fit are visible. It is not possible to view the vaulting from above.

177

1. William Taylor, *The Antiquities of King's Lynn* (Lynn: J. Thew, 1844), 116.
2. Corporation Hall Book No. 2, ff. 469, 470, 471, 507. Printed in Edward Milligen Beloe, *The Red Mount Chapel, King's Lynn* (Lynn: Faster and Bird, Ltd., 1897), 9-11.
3. *Engl. Med. Archit.*, 80.
4. Purcell, Miller and Tritton, "Report: The Red Mount Chapel–King's Lynn," 1969?, typescript. Copy in the King's Lynn Museum. Report on the structural condition with recommendations for restoration, etc.
5. Taylor, *op. cit.*, 112, suggested that the lower chapel within the mound was more ancient.
6. Beloe, *op. cit.*, 8.
7. H. Harrod, *Report on the Deeds and Records of the Borough of King's Lynn* (King's Lynn: Thew and Son, 1874), 51.

76	Kingston St. Mary	St. Mary's: South Porch
	Somerset	3.03m x 3.03m

Historical Analysis:

No known documentary evidence is available. The formal and constructive patterns of the vaulting are basically the same as the porch vaults of Curry Rivel, North Curry, and Ile Abbots. This would place the vaulting circa 1500. It was restored in 1875.[1]

General Description:

The vaulting springs from moulded capitals and shafts. The shaft in the northeast corner has been cut away. Each vaulting conoid is divided into four main panels which are further subdivided above the lower horizontal band, which is trefoil cusped top and bottom. The top horizontal band is also trefoil cusped. The central spandrel panel is articulated with a circle which encloses traceried panels. In the center of the vault is a foliate boss. The "corners" of the central spandrel panel are articulated with quatrefoils and trefoil cusped daggers north-south and trefoil cusped daggers alone east-west.

Technical Description:

Four-centered curves are employed. Rib and panel construction with jointed masonry for the traceried parts is employed. The central stone of the spandrel panel is circular in plan. The material used is Ham Hill stone.

1. I. S. Gale, *The Parish Church of Kingston St. Mary* (Taunton: Barnicott and Pearce. The Wessex Press, 1927), 16.

167	Lacock	St. Cyriac's: Present Lady Chapel
	Wiltshire	Two bays, each 3.02m square

Historical Analysis:

No known documentary evidence is available. The date 1427-37 can be associated with the chapel, however, since the arms of Robert Neville, Bishop of Salisbury, are located below a niche on the exterior above the east window of the chapel.[1] Analogies have been drawn between the northwest window of the chapel and the north windows of the north aisle, and between the east window of the chapel and the west window of the aisle.[2] The chapel was added after the north transept was built, because some of the respond of the pier was cut away to accommodate the west arch of the chapel.[3] The vaulting was most likely inspired by the cloister vaulting of Lacock Abbey, which probably dates to the first quarter of the fifteenth century. A record under the east window (parts of which are now missing) states that the chapel was repaired and the chancel rebuilt in 1777.[4] What changes, if any, were made at this time to the vaulting is not known, but apparently it was painted.

General Description:

It is vaulted in two square bays; the vaulting of each bay differs. The vaulting of the east bay is a combination of a lierne and a fan vault. The top horizontal bounding rib does not have the same section as the vertical and lierne ribs but is articulated with a band of foliage that may have been added after the vault was built. There is a hollowed out pendant boss in the middle of the bay, around which are placed bosses at the rib intersections, some of which depict chalices and the symbols of the passion; perhaps this was once a chantry chapel. A transverse arch divides the two bays. The west bay is definitely a fan vault. All of the ribs have the same section. No lierne ribs are present as in the east bay. The central spandrel panel and the conoids are treated as distinct entities, whereas in the east bay they were visually integrated. The central boss is similar to the one in the east bay. The panels are not cusped in either bay.

Technical Description:

Two-centered curves are employed. Rib and panel construction is used. Perhaps the east bay was built before the west bay, not only because of the differences in their vaults, but also because each bay has its own roof which runs north-south, rather than a single roof running east-west over both bays. Furthermore, the parapet along the north-south side is not well integrated with the center buttress.

1. C. H. Talbot, "Lacock Church," *British Archaeological Association. Journal* N.S., XI (1905), 260.
2. C. H. Talbot, "Notes on Lacock Church," *The Wiltshire Archaeological and Natural History Magazine,* XXVIII (1894-1896), 350 n.1.
3. *Ibid.,* 351.
4. *Ibid.,* 351 n.1.

3   Langport   All Saints: West Tower
         Somerset   3.70m x 3.70m

Historical Analysis:

Lady Margaret Beaufort held Langport until her death in 1509.[1] Since her badge, the portcullis, appears several times on the tower, it was probably erected between 1485-1509.[2] John Heron, surveyor to the king, may have been responsible for the rebuilding of the church.[3]

General Description:

The vaulting springs from moulded corbels. Each vaulting conoid is composed of four panels each of which is cinquefoil cusped. The top horizontal bounding rib is composed of circular segments. Between the central bell opening and the vaulting conoids are trefoil cusped daggers.

Technical Description:

Four-centered curves are employed. Rib and panel construction with jointed masonry for the traceried parts is employed. The beds are straight. The vaulting is built of Doulting stone.[4]

1. Melville Ross, "Historical Langport," *SANH Proc., Bath and District Branch,* 1934-38, 203.
2. W. Bond Paul, "The Church of Langport Eastover, County of Somerset," *SANH Proc.,* XL, pt. 2 (1894), 68.
3. Ross, *op. cit.,* 203; Thomas Gerard, *The Particular Description of the County of Somerset,* SRS, XV (1900), 132; E. H. Bates, "Langport Church Heraldry," *Notes and Queries for Somerset and Dorset,* VI (1899), 299-302.
4. Paul, *op. cit.,* 68.

Lavenham   Sts. Peter and Paul: South Porch
Suffolk

Analysis:

Arthur Oswald indicated that the fan vault was of the Wastell type.[1] But, it displays none of the traits characteristic of Wastell-type fan vaults, such as large center bosses, bratticing placed in the panels, and cinquefoil cusping, and it is clearly a modern addition to the structure. It was erected in 1865 when the church was restored.[2] No evidence is available to indicate that the porch was originally fan vaulted.

1. *Engl. Med. Archit.,* 282-3.
2. F. Lingard Ranson, *Lavenham Suffolk* (1947), 25.

Leigh-on-Mendip   St. Giles: West Tower (fragments)
Somerset   3.87m x 3.77m

Analysis:

Pevsner has noted the remains of springers of an uncompleted vault in the tower and has indicated that they were intended for a fan vault.[1] He may well be right, but a lierne vault such as was built in the west tower at Cheddar (Somerset) has the exact same type of springer. Therefore, it is impossible to tell exactly what type of vault was to be built.

1. Pevsner, *BE, North Somerset and Bristol* (1958), 217.

168   Littlebury   Holy Trinity: North and South Porches (fragments)
Essex   Each porch is 3.66m square

Historical Analysis:

Wills dated 1504 and 1505 make bequests for the construction of a new porch on the south side of the church.[1] As both porches are identical, they both can be dated to the first decade of the sixteenth century.

General Description:

Only the springers and wall ribs remain. As each springer has seven ribs, each vaulting conoid would have had six panels. The panels would have been cinquefoil cusped. It is not certain that a fan vault was originally intended; for almost identical wall ribs and springers at Burwell (Cambridgeshire) result in a vault that only approximates a fan vault. (The Burwell springers only have five ribs, resulting in four panels, but the vaulting is smaller, being 3.05m square.)

Technical Description:

Four-centered curves are employed. The construction is of ribs and panels with jointed masonry for the traceried parts. The ribs were rebated to receive the panels. No evidence is present that indicates the use of dowels.

1. Wills noted in *The Parish Church of Holy Trinity Littlebury* (4th edit., Hull: Tranbe Printers Ltd., 1969), n.p.; for the will of Reignolde Hasylbeche, vicar of Littlebury, who died 4 July 1504, leaving £20 toward the making of the new south porch, see J. C. Challenor Smith, "Some Additions to Newcourt's Repertorium," *Essex Archaeological Society Trans.,* VII (1900), 45.

Maids Moreton	St. Edmund's
Buckinghamshire	*North Porch:* Two bays, each 2.12m x 1.35m
	South Porch: 2.12m x 2.10m
	Tower: 3.74m square
	Vestry: 1.98m square

Historical Analysis:

The church is said to have been built circa 1450 by two ladies of the Peyvre family.[1] Perhaps, a seventeenth century inscription in the nave of the church is the source of this tradition.[2] No documentary evidence can be associated with the building of the church.

The church was apparently built in at least two stages, for the chancel employs different window tracery and hood mouldings, and has a continuous moulding running at the sill level which does not occur in the nave. The same design module in plan was used for both the nave and chancel, so the whole church was probably laid out at the same time. The design of the chancel with its window recesses carried down to form window seats suggests a date in the first half of the fifteenth century. This feature was employed in the chancel at Adderbury (1408-18), the Oxford Divinity School (ca. 1430), and in the Wilcote Chapel, North Leigh.[3] This window solution occurs also in the nave, thus lending credence to the theory that the whole church was laid out at the same time.

Sir Thomas Peyvre, leaving no direct heir, died in 1429[4] (and not as has been previously stated in 1449).[5] At his death, patronage of the parish passed to the Broughtons.[6] If tradition is correct insofar as connecting the present structure to the Peyvre family, it is possible on the architectural evidence to suggest that the structure was started before Sir Thomas's death instead of circa 1450–the traditional date assigned to it.[7]

The fan vaults at Maids Moreton apparently are unique. The south porch and vestry fan vaults are almost identical in both their technical and formal characteristics. The vestry fan vault may be a later addition to an already extant structure since it does not spring from shafts as does the fan vault of the south porch. The fact that the fan vault in the south porch springs from shafts which have round moulded bases in the northern corners and octagonal bases in the southern corners suggests a change of plan had taken place during the period of construction.

The fan vault of the north porch utilizes two and four-centered curves to solve the problem of how to fan vault a rectangular module. This solution for fan vaulting a rectangular bay suggests a date of circa 1500, rather than a date in the first half of the fifteenth century (cf. south porch at Saffron Walden).

A particular characteristic of the tower fan vault is the flattened, half circular heads of the panels. This characteristic–along with the use of a bold rib profile–is found in the south porch vault of St. Stephen's, Bristol, which can be dated 1480.[8] This fact, when seen in conjunction with the use of rosettes to decorate the vaulting corbels, suggests a late fifteenth century date for the tower fan vault. Also, the type of tas-de-charge is similar to that at Fotheringhay, which can be dated 1529.[9]

Therefore, while the rebuilding of this church may have begun circa 1430, it most likely continued into at least the last quarter of the fifteenth century. It was at this time that the fan vaults were most likely built.

General Description:

Vestry and South Porch: The panels of the vaulting conoids are trefoil cusped under two-centered heads. The horizontal bounding ribs are composed of circular segments. The central spandrel panel is articulated with a large multifoiled circle with floriated cusping. In the center of the circle is a large sculptured flower. In the areas left between the circle and the vaulting conoids are cinquefoil cusped daggers.

172 North Porch: It is fan vaulted in two rectangular bays. The vaulting springs from moulded capitals and shafts. The center shafts along the east and west walls bisect windows. There are external buttresses at these locations that appear to have been constructed at the same time as the rest of the porch, thus indicating one building campaign for both the porch and the vaulting. The panels of the vaulting conoids are trefoil cusped under two-centered heads. The vaulting conoids intersect in the east-west direction and just meet in the north-south direction. The horizontal bounding ribs are composed of circular segments. A large, low-relief, sculptured boss articulates the center of each bay.

173 Tower: The fan vault springs from large sculptured corbels. The panels are trefoil cusped under flattened, half circular heads. The horizontal bounding ribs are composed of circular segments. The same type of carved rosette which appears on the vaulting corbels also appears along the canopy parapet located over the west doorway. Therefore, the fan vault of the tower was built about the same time as the canopy over the west doorway.

Technical Description:

Vestry and South Porch: Four-centered curves are employed. The construction is completely of jointed masonry. Some joints bisect the vertical radiating ribs by running along their centerlines.

North Porch: Two and four-centered curves are employed. The construction is completely of jointed masonry. No joints occur on rib centerlines.

Tower: Two-centered curves are employed. The construction is of ribs, panels, and jointed masonry.

1. Browne Willis, *The History and Antiquities of the Town, Hundred, and Deanry of Buckingham* (London: Printed for the Author, 1755), 227; VCH, *Buckinghamshire,* IV (1927), 198.
2. Charles E. Keyser, "A Monograph on the Church of St. Edmund's, Maids Moreton," *Records of Buckinghamshire,* VI (n.d.), 422.
3. For a more complete analysis of this feature and the dating of the particular monuments see F. E. Howard, "Richard Winchombe's Work at the Divinity School and Elsewhere," in T. F. Hobson, edit., *Adderbury Rectoria,* Oxford Record Society, VIII (1926), 34-41.
4. P.R.O., Chan. Ing. p.m. 8 Henry VI, no. 21. Cited in VCH, *Buckinghamshire,* IV (1927), 198n.2, 361-362. Peyvre was buried in Toddington. For the inscription on his tomb, "Hic jacet Thomas Peyvre qui obiit Ao. Dni. MCCCCXXIX cuius anime propitiatur deus" see BM Cotton MS Cleopatra C. III, f.8, "Notes taken by Francis Thynne in 1582-1583," printed in part in *Bedforshire Notes and Queries,* I (1886), 63.
5. Willis, *op. cit.,* 234; George Lipscomb, *History and Antiquities of the County of Buckinghamshire* (1847), IV, 210.
6. John L. Myres, "The Parish and Church of Maids Moreton, County of Bucks.," *Records of Buckinghamshire,* VI (n.d.), 416; VCH, *Buckinghamshire,* IV (1927), 361-2.
7. Willis, *op. cit.,* 227.
8. This porch was under construction in 1480 when William Worcestre visited it. See John H. Harvey, edit., *William Worcestre Itineraries* (Oxford: At the Clarendon Press, 1969), 315, 317.
9. VCH, *Northampton,* II, 575.

---

174 Malmesbury   Abbey: Cloisters (fragments)
    Wiltshire   *Bay:* 3.25m square (approximately)[1]
             Fan Vault of Doorway from Church: 2.24m x 1.12m

Historical Analysis:

No documentary evidence can be associated with this cloister. The use of four-centered curves, moulded octagonal bases and capitals, trefoil cusped panels under two-centered heads, and gridiron tracery in the windows, suggests a date toward the middle of the fifteenth century (cf. All Souls College, Oxford). Tiles found in the cloister walks having the initials "W. C.," "W. W.," and "T. B.," probably stand for the following abbots of Malmesbury: Walter de Camme (1362-96). William (1423), and Thomas Bristow (1434-56).[2] If the tiles are commemorative in character, the cloister probably dates from Bristow's time, 1434-56. The cloisters were complete by 1480 when William of Worcestre visited and found the cloister to be 62 or 64 paces long in each direction.[3] If one pace equals 21 inches, then the cloister was 106 or 112 feet in each direction;[4] excavations carried out by Harold Brakspear found the cloister to be 112 feet in each direction.[5]

General Description:

The cloisters are entered through a processional doorway (porch) from the church which is fan vaulted in one rectangular bay. This small fan vault is similar to the vaulting at Gloucester (cf. west porch, ca. 1420-37), but is more developed. The panels are cinquefoil cusped, the central spandrel panel is articulated with quatrefoils in circles, and the curve employed is four-centered (Gloucester is two-centered). The main bays of the cloister are square. Each vaulting quadrant had four ribs which start from the capital and were doubled halfway up. Each panel was trefoil cusped. The central spandrel panels are articulated with large circles which contain large quatrefoils with foliated terminals, subdivided by smaller cusps.

Technical Description:

Four-centered curves were employed, as evidenced by the curve of the vaulting which shows up against the church wall. The fan vault of the doorway (porch) is also four-centered. From Harold Brakspear's reconstruction drawing of the cloister, it appears to have been built entirely of jointed masonry.[6]

1. Reconstruction drawing in Harold Brakspear, "Malmesbury Abbey," *The Wiltshire Archaeological and Natural History Magazine,* XXXVIII (1913-14), 458-497; reprinted from *Archaeologia* LXIV, 399, with additions.
2. *Ibid.,* 489, and VCH *Wiltshire,* III, 223, 228.
3. "Longitudo claustri ex omni parte continet quodlibet claustrum .62 vel .64 gressus." Corpus Christi College, Cambridge, MS. 210, fo.210, printed in *William Worcestre Itineraries,* edited by John Harvey (Oxford: At the Clarendon Press, 1969), 286.
4. Harvey, *ibid.,* xvii-xviii, for a discussion of Worcestre's dimensions.
5. Brakspear, *op. cit.,* 487.
6. Brakspear, *op. cit.*

60 Mells   St. Andrew's: South Porch
       Somerset   3.10m x 3.65m

Historical Analysis:

No known documentary evidence is available. This fan vault is almost identical to the one at Doulting. Leland described the church as being built "yn time of mine."[1] The porch vault was probably built circa 1500.

General Description:

The porch is rectangular in plan; the vaulting springs from sculptured capitals and shafts on the east and west walls and from sculptured corbels in the middle of the north and south walls. The design module for the vaulting is one quarter of the east-west span, that is, 75 cm. This dimension is the radius of each vaulting conoid and of the circular central spandrel. Between this spandrel (in the center of which was once a pendant), and the vaulting conoids, are four smaller circles, each of which enclose quatrefoils with large foliate cusp ends. This vaulting solves the problem of how to fan vault a rectangular plan without having intersecting conoids, and shows the ingenuity of the designer.

Technical Description:

Two-centered curves are employed throughout. The construction is completely of jointed masonry.

---

1. Leland, *Itin.,* V, 105.

---

175 Mells   St. Andrew's: West Tower
  Somerset   4.77m x 4.87m (at ground level)

Historical Analysis:

The present tower was begun in the fifteenth century, and continued being built well into the sixteenth century. John Sammell, Senior, bequeathed "To the building of the tower of the church of Mells £3" in 1446.[1] Leland stated that "The church is faire and buidid yn tyme of mynde *ex lapide quadrato . . ."*[2] The sixteenth century building was supported by bequests in the will of John Robyns (1524): "To the church of Mells £20 with the £7 that I gave to the making of the vestrye there."[3] Evidently, the tower was not intended to have been fan vaulted from the start, since the wide wall ribs were built out from the walls to achieve a square vaulting module to accommodate the proportions of a fan vault.

General Description:

The vaulting springs from moulded capitals and shafts. Each vaulting conoid is composed of four panels which are articulated at the top by a band of trefoils in ovals. The other panels are trefoil cusped under two-centered heads. There are ridge ribs up to the central bell opening. These characteristics suggest a date in the second half of the fifteenth century (cf. Cardinal Beaufort's Chapel, Winchester Cathedral) rather than a date well into the sixteenth century.

Technical Description:

Two-centered curves are employed. The construction is of ribs and panels with jointed masonry for the traceried parts.

---

1. F. W. Weaver, edit.,*Somerset Medieval Wills 1501-1530,* 2nd Series, SRS, XIX (1903), 345.
2. Leland, *Itin.,* V, 105.
3. Weaver, *op. cit.,* 225.

---

176 Mildenhall   St. Mary's: West Tower Gallery
  Suffolk   5.27m x 5.26m;
    Vaulted in three bays, each 1.76m x 5.26m

Historical Analysis:

No known documentary evidence can be associated with the building of the tower gallery. There was a tower standing in 1464 when William Chapman bequeathed 10 marks "... ad reparacione magne campane pendente in campanile ecclesie de Myldenhall."[1] The interior archway of the west door, which does not follow that of the exterior, and the wall ribs of the gallery vaulting, which are four-centered whereas the windows of the tower are two-centered, are strong evidence that the gallery was a later addition to an already extant structure. The use of arches of two different curvatures (one for the wall ribs along the north and south sides, another for the vaulting span north-south), in conjunction with a vault which is constructed completely of jointed masonry, suggests a date in the sixteenth century. In 1530 Henry Pope bequethed "towarde the makynge of the grett belle iij. £. x. s. to be payde by the hands of the sayde Thomas Larke whansoever the towne doo go abowgnt the makynge thereof."[2] This evidence may indicate that the tower was in the process of being remodelled or that a remodelling was being planned at that time. Entries in the churchwarden's accounts for 1555 indicate that work on the steeple was just being completed.[3] Thus, the fan vault probably dates to the period 1530-55. Furthermore, it is possible that Thomas Larke could be identical with the chaplain to Henry VII, surveyor at Cambridge and Bridewell Palace, and could have been the man responsible for the idea of putting a fan vault in a commemorative context at Mildenhall. (Note the shields in barbed quatrefoils on the east end of the gallery.)[4]

General Description:

There are stone benches along the north and south sides. Around the east archway inside are a series of canopied niches for statues. In addition, the font originally stood directly in front of the gallery in the nave.[5] This gallery apparently served the functions of a porch, and it has been suggested that it was a baptistery.[6] The gallery is vaulted in three rectangular bays. The vaulting ribs are all of the same section and spring from shafts without capitals. Cinquefoil cusping is employed in the majority of the panels. The horizontal bounding ribs are composed of circular segments. The simultaneous use of two-centered, four-centered, and ogee curves in the tracery patterning makes the vault visually exciting.

Technical Description:

Four-centered curves are employed. The vault is completely constructed of jointed masonry. No joints occur along the north-south ridges, but they do occur in the middle stone of each bay along the east-west ridge. The vault is constructed of a very hard local chalk, similar to clunch but of a different geological horizon.[7]

1. Samuel Tymms, "Mildenhall Church," *Bury and West Suffolk Archaeological Institute Proc.,* I (1853), 269.
2. *Ibid.,* 270.
3. "1554. Itm. payd to Joons the carpenter, for his work in the steple, for makyng of the lattes wyndowe and the iiij lyght closen, and the mendyng of ye weste wyndow and plancheryng of ye belsoller and stoppyng of the well and mending of the soller . . . Item pyd. for iij hundred of bord for to close the lettes windows, and the iiij lyghts and the west window and the soller in the steple . . . xij s."
   "1555. Itm. payd. to wyllym darbe for nayle for the lattys windows, and the dore in the steple . . . iiij s." Printed in "Extracts from Churchwardens Books No. 2, Mildenhall, Suffolk," *The East Anglian,* I, no. XIV (January, 1862), 187.
4. For information on Thomas Larke see Arthur Oswald, "Stephen Gardiner and Bury St. Edmunds," *Suffolk Institute of Archaeology, Proc.,,* XXVI (1955), 54.
5. Tymms, *op. cit.,* 272.
6. Tymms, *op. cit.,* 272.
7. Alfred E. Lee, "St. Mary's Church, Mildenhall," *Norfolk Archaeology.* XXIV (1932), lxx.

9 | Milton Abbas | Abbey: Crossing Tower
Dorset | 7.29m x 7.62m

Historical Analysis:

No known documentary evidence can be associated with the vaulting. The north and south transepts were vaulted by Abbot William Middleton (1481-1525), as evidenced by his initials and devices on the bosses.[1] The crossing vault is similar in its use of material, but it is more elaborate in terms of design and execution than the vaulting of the transepts. It seems likely that the transepts were vaulted first, followed by the crossing. Therefore, a date of circa 1500 is plausible. The vaulting was most likely patterned on the vaulting of Sherborne Abbey.

General Description:

The vaulting springs from moulded capitals and shafts. The top horizontal bounding rib is composed of straight segments. The panels are trefoil cusped above and below, and the upper regions of the trefoils are subcusped. Bosses occur at rib intersections; most of the bosses are foliate, while others display the arms of King Athelstan, the abbeys of Milton and Cerne, the families of Bingham, Coker, Latimer, and Morton, and other benefactors of the abbey.[2]

Technical Description:

Two-centered curves are employed. The construction is of ribs (Ham Hill stone) and panels (chalk) with jointed masonry for the traceried parts.[3] Adjustments were made in the vaulting to accommodate a slightly rectangular plan; the ridge ribs are not lined up in a straight line.

1. RCHM, *Dorset,* III, pt. 2 (1970), 186, 187.
2. Herbert Pentin, "The Bosses in Milton Abbey, Dorset," *The Antiquary,* XLIV (1908), 14.
3. R. H. Carpenter, "On the Benedictine Abbey of S. Mary, Sherborne . . ." *RIBA Sessional Papers 1876-77* (1877), 145n.

---

39   Minster Lovell   St. Kenelm: Crossing Tower
           Oxfordshire   3.65m x 3.65m

Historical Analysis:

The church was most likely rebuilt by William Lovell at the same time he was rebuilding the adjoining manor house, circa 1431-42.[1] The window tracery of the Great Hall of the manor house was identical to that of the church.[2] Lovell died in 1455.[3] In the nineteenth century his tomb was under the southern arch of the tower.[4] Masons' marks are present on the tower, as is the name Bedwell.[5] A "Thomas Bedell" occurs in the Merton College (Oxford) accounts among the masons for the building of the tower there in 1448.[6] In 1453 Lovell contributed stone and timber to the building of the Divinity School, which suggests that his building operations were complete and he was disposing of surplus material.[7] This fan vault should be dated between 1430 and 1450.

General Description:

The vaulting springs from moulded capitals and shafts. Each vaulting quadrant is composed of two main panels and subpanels. Only the lower subpanel is trefoil cusped. The horizontal bounding rib is composed of straight segments. There are foliate bosses at the rib intersections.

Technical Description:

Two-centered curves are employed. The construction is of ribs and panels with jointed masonry for the traceried parts. The top horizontal rib is cut to include part of the adjoining panel.

1. A. J. Taylor, *Minster Lovell Hall* (2nd edit.; London: HMSO, 1958), 6.
2. See Buck's print of 1729 of Manor House in *ibid.,* 10-11.
3. *Ibid.,* 7.
4. John Prichard, *Views, Elevations, and Sections of Minster Lovell Church* (Oxford: Published by John Henry Parker, 1850), n.p.
5. E. A. Greening Lamborn, "The Lovell Tomb at Minster," *Oxfordshire Archaeological Society, Report* 83 (1937), 19.
6. *Ibid.,* 19.
7. *Ibid.,* 20.

186

Muchelney
Somerset

Abbey: Cloister (fragments)
2.87m x 2.64m

Analysis:

No documentary evidence can be associated with the cloister. The greater part of the south walk is still standing; the vaulting is no longer in situ and only a few fragments remain. Each vaulting quadrant was most likely composed of four trefoil cusped panels. The horizontal bounding ribs were composed of straight segments. The central spandrel panel was a square (about 94 cm on a side) which was articulated with four quatrefoils in panels. There were bosses (some foliate, some heads) at the main rib intersections. The vaulting was two-centered as evidenced by the wall ribs which are still in situ. The construction was of ribs and panels with jointed masonry used for the traceried parts. There is no evidence that dowels were used. The ribs are rebated to receive the panels which have an average thickness of 10 cm. The vaulting on stylistic and technical grounds is similar to the later vaults at Sherborne Abbey, the south porch at Hilton (Dorset), and the tower vault at Ilminster (Somerset). Therefore, it was probably built in the latter part of the fifteenth century.

Muchelney
Somerset

Sts. Peter and Paul: West Tower
3.37m x 3.34m

Historical Analysis:

No documentary evidence is available. One of the bosses of the vault is carved with a shield encircled by a garter; it is carved with the Daubeney arms and with their badge of bat's wings above. This probably refers to Gils, Lord Daubney, who became a Knight of the Garter in 1487 and died in 1507.[1] The date of the tower vault, therefore, is probably between 1487 and 1507. It should be noted that this vault is similar to the one at Shepton Beauchamp (Somerset).

General Description:

The vaulting springs from sculptured corbels. Each vaulting quadrant is composed of four main trefoil cusped panels. The top horizontal bounding rib is composed of straight segments. There are bosses at the rib intersections, four of which are larger than the others.

Technical Description:

Two-centered curves are employed. The construction is of ribs and panels with jointed masonry for the traceried parts. The ridges to the bell opening are composed of only two large stones. Since the curve of the vaulting does not follow that of the tower arch, the vault may have been a later insertion into an already extant tower.

1. E. Buckle, "Shepton Beauchamp Church," *SANH Proc.,* XXXVIII (1891), 42.

North Curry
Somerset

Sts. Peter and Paul: South Porch
3.66m x 3.69m

Historical Analysis:

No known documentary evidence can be associated with this porch. However, since the parapet of the chancel was under construction circa 1506,[1] and it is the same as that of the porch, the porch may have been constructed at the same time. The basic formal and constructive patterns of its vault are the same as the porch vaults of Kingston St. Mary, Curry Rivel, and Ile Abbots, which helps to substantiate a date in the first decade of the sixteenth century for it. The vaulting was restored in 1881.[2]

General Description:

The vaulting springs from moulded capitals and shafts. Each vaulting conoid is divided into four main panels. The subpanels are trefoil cusped. The central spandrel panel is articulated with a circle enclosing eight traceried panels which drop down to form a pendant. The bottom of the pendant is articulated with a foliate boss, and there are smaller foliate bosses along the ribs just before they drop down to form the pendant. The "corners" of the central spandrel panel are articulated with quatrefoils north-south and cinquefoil cusped daggers east-west.

Technical Description:

Four-centered curves are employed. The construction is of ribs and panels with jointed masonry for the traceried parts. The center stone of the vault, which forms the pendant, is square in plan. The material of construction is Ham Hill stone.

---

1. Great Britain, Royal Commission on Historical Manuscripts, *Calendar of the Manuscripts of the Dean and Chapter of Wells,* II (1914), 169, 174, 195, 230.
2. Hugh P. Olivey, *North Curry: Ancient Manor and Hundred* (Taunton: Barnicott & Pearce, Athenaeum Press, 1901), 90.

---

1 North Leigh St. Mary's: Wilcote Chapel
  Oxfordshire 5.10m x 2.50m
   Two bays, each 2.54m x 2.50m

Historical Analysis:

License to endow a chantry in North Leigh Church was granted to Elizabeth, the widow of Sir William Wilcote, in 1438,[1] twenty-seven years after the death of her husband.[2] Stone has suggested that the type of architecture, which strongly suggests Richard Winchombe's work, and the costume and armour of the effigies, make it certain that the tomb and chapel were erected by 1425 at the latest.[3] However, when this fan vault is compared to other fan vaults, a date of 1438 is more reasonable than one of 1425; because four-centered fan vaults were just beginning to be constructed circa 1440 (cf. All Souls College, Oxford; Chantry Chapel of Henry IV, Canterbury), and while there are differences between this vault and the one at All Souls College, Oxford, the similarities are more important. In both vaults, for example, the subpanelling rises directly from the capitals, the capitals in both vaults are similar, and the central spandrel panels are both articulated with four quatrefoils in circles. The Wilcote fan vault is far more ornate and has a greater span which might account for some of the differences between them. Both vaults are built completely of jointed masonry.

General Description:

It is fan vaulted in two bays. The vaulting springs from moulded capitals and shafts, except in the center of the south wall where it springs from a moulded corbel. The subpanels rise directly from the corbel level and the top row of subpanelling is trefoil cusped. The central spandrel panel in each bay is composed of quatrefoils in circles which are separated from each other by trefoil cusped lozenges which radiate out from the center. The quatrefoils in the west bay contain foliate bosses, while those in the east bay contain blocklike bosses.

Technical Description:

Four-centered curves are employed. The construction is completely of jointed masonry.

1. P.R.O., *Calendar of the Patent Rolls,* Henry VI, III, 306.
2. J. M. Davenport, *Lords Lieutenant and High Sheriffs of Oxfordshire, 1086-1868,* 22a.
3. Lawrence Stone, *Sculpture in Britain: The Middle Ages* (Harmondsworth: Penguin Books, 1955), 265n.17.

| 9 | North Petherton | St. Mary: West Tower |
| | Somerset | 4.00m square (approximately) |

Historical Analysis:

No documentary evidence can be associated with the tower. It is strikingly similar to the tower of Probus in Cornwall, which can be dated circa 1517 on documentary evidence.[1] The North Petherton tower should be dated to the first two decades of the sixteenth century, because the Probus tower was probably patterned after it, and it would seem unlikely for Cornishmen to copy anything that was not the latest vogue. The vaulting is similar in size and style to that of Batcombe (Somerset), which is more elaborate and refined (cf. rib profile).

General Description:

The vaulting springs from moulded capitals and shafts. Each vaulting conoid is composed of four panels, the subpanels of which are trefoil cusped. The horizontal bounding rib is composed of circular segments. The spaces between the central bell opening and the vaulting conoids are articulated with quatrefoils in circles.

Technical Description:

Four-centered curves are employed. The construction is of ribs and panels with jointed masonry for the traceried parts.

1. Great Britain, Star Chamber Proceedings, P.R.O., Bundle 17, no. 209, a bill of complaint relating to the building of the tower, cited in H. Michell Whitley, "Probus Church and Tower," *Journal of the Royal Institution of Cornwall,* IX (1889), 486, 488.

| 8 | Norwich | St. Giles: South Porch |
| | Norfolk | 3.20m x 3.27m (fan vault only) |

Historical Analysis:

No documentary evidence can be associated with this fan vault. The south porch was extant in 1459 because Christian, relict of John Brosyard, was buried in it by her husband.[1] Since the porch is rectangular in plan, tunnel vaults, which are decorated with shields, were inserted at each end of the porch to obtain a square vaulting module. The fan vault appears to be a later addition to the porch. Perhaps the top exterior frieze (now restored) was added to the porch at the same time. While in concept this fan vault is similar to dated examples which range from 1450 to 1540 (cf. Lady Chapel, Canterbury, Chewton Mendip), its complex rib profile suggests a date close to 1450 (cf. north porch, St. Peter Mancroft, Norwich).

General Description:

Each vaulting conoid is divided into four main panels. The subpanels are trefoil cusped under two-centered heads. The middle horizontal bounding rib is composed of straight segments, while the one at the top is composed of circular segments. The central spandrel panel is articulated with a large circle that encloses four smaller circles which contain sub-cusped quatrefoils. In the areas left between the large circle and the vaulting conoids are placed quatrefoils in circles.

189

Technical Description:

Two-centered curves are employed. The construction appears to be completely of jointed masonry.

1. Francis Blomefield, *An Essay Toward a Topographical History of the County of Norfolk* (Fersfield, 1739), II, 657.

32   Ottery St. Mary   St. Mary: Dorset Aisle
           Devonshire   *Dorset Aisle:* 5.80m (approximately)
                                   North Porch: 2.90m square

Historical Analysis:

There is no record that this chapel was consecrated, nor that it was ever a chantry chapel. The arms of Bishop Oldham (1504-19) appear on the southwest pier facing the nave and below the battlements directly above the west window of the aisle.[1] The arms of Bishop Voysey (1519-51) are on the southeast vaulting corbel.[2] The Lady Cicely, Marchioness of Dorset, and holder of the manor of Knyghtestone, married Henry Lord Stafford in 1503.[3] The Stafford Knot appears below the battlements above the west window of the aisle and on the attached north porch.[4] Lord Stafford died in 1523, Lady Cicely in 1530; no mention of the Dorset Aisle is made in her will, written in 1527.[5] Therefore, the aisle was probably constructed between 1504 and 1527. Since the vaulting does not quite fit into the chapel, it is possible that it was not planned from the start. Perhaps it was inserted after the aisle was finished or nearly so; for while Voysey's arms appear on one of the vaulting corbels, Oldham's do not (however, four are obliterated). It would seem likely that the chapel was started shortly before 1520 and finished by 1530.[6] A similar aisle with an attached north porch and the same window tracery, also displaying the Stafford Knot, was built at Axminster, circa 1525-30.[7]

General Description:

It is vaulted in five rectangular bays. The vaulting springs from sculptured corbels. Each vaulting quadrant is composed of four main panels which are further subdivided. The vertical radiating ribs intersect the transverse and longitudinal ridge ribs. The vaulting conoids are bounded by only a middle horizontal rib which is composed of straight segments. The sub-panels are cusped. In the center of each bay is an openwork pendant boss, at the bottom of which is carved a Tudor rose. The boss in the middle bay, while similar to the others, is twisted into a spirallike shape.

179   The fan vault of the north porch has been rebuilt. The vaulting springs from moulded capitals and shafts. Each vaulting quadrant is composed of four panels which are cinquefoil cusped. The horizontal bounding rib is composed of circular segments. The vault has a sculptured boss at its center (recut). This vault is similar to the vault of the Founder's Oratory, Magdalen College Chapel, Oxford.

Technical Description:

Two-centered curves are employed. The construction is of ribs and panels with jointed masonry for the traceried parts. The wall rib of the vaulting is cut off in places along the south wall. Mr. Reed noticed in 1927 some ninety-eight perforations of the vaulting with lead tubes.[8] The reason for these remains unknown. The fan vault of the north porch is similar to the aisle except that four-centered curves are employed.

1. John Neale Dalton, *The Collegiate Church of Ottery St. Mary* (Cambridge: At the University Press, 1917), 22, 28.
2. *Ibid.,* 22.

3. *Ibid.*, 25.
4. *Ibid.*, 27, 29.
5. *Ibid.*, 25, 26n.
6. Perhaps construction even began after Oldham's death (i.e. after 1519), for there is reference in his will instructing the Warden and College of Ottery to contribute five marks yearly to the support of his obit in the cathedral. This was still being paid in 1544, see F. Rose Troup, "Bishop Oldham and Ottery St. Mary," *Devon and Cornwall Notes and Queries,* XVII (1933), 152-157. Therefore, his arms may have had a commemorative character and may have been included in the building program after his death.
7. Pevsner, *BE, South Devon* (1952), 44; Dalton, *op. cit.,* 26-7.
8. Harbottle Reed, "Architectural Notes on Some Churches Visited During the Congress," *British Archaeological Association. Journal,* N.S., XXXIII (1927), 176.

---

7 Oxford All Souls College: Vestibule to the Chapel
Oxfordshire Lobby in the East Range
Vestibule to the Chapel: Four bays, each 2.11m x 1.97m
Lobby in the East Range: One bay, 2.09m x 2.11m

Historical Analysis:

All Souls College was founded by Archbishop Chichele.[1] Three sides of the quadrangle and the base of the chapel up to the 1.07m course were the first parts to be built in 1439-40.[2] In January 1442, John Massyngham, a sculptor, was paid for the great stone figures over the altar and later for other decorative work in the chapel.[3] The chapel was complete or nearly so by 1 June 1442 when the first mass was said in it.[4] A deed of 1443 mentions the property on which the college is built. It seems likely that the fan vaults were built between 1439 and 1442.

The masons worked in two groups, one at Oxford, the other at Burford. The largest number worked on Taynton stone in the yard at Burford under the *magister lathomorum,* Richard Chevynton.[6] At Oxford Robert Jannyns was in charge. Jannyns was the lower paid mason and was under the direction of Chevynton.[7] It is probable that the fan vaults were prefabricated at Burford for later erection at Oxford.

General Description:

The fan vaults of the vestibule and the east lobby will be considered together as they are virtually identical in size and have the same formal and technical characteristics. The vestibule is fan vaulted in four almost square bays. The vaulting springs in most cases from moulded shafts and capitals and in a few instances from sculptured corbels. The lobby is fan vaulted in one bay; there the vaulting springs from corbels. In both vaults each vaulting conoid is composed of two main panels which are each subdivided. The subpanels are cinquefoil cusped under two-centered heads. The central spandrel panel is articulated with four quatrefoils in circles.

Technical Description:

Four-centered curves are employed. The construction is completely of jointed masonry. The vertical stone joints run on centerlines between the ribs. The keystone of the vault is square.

1. E. F. Jacob, "The Building of All Souls College, 1438-1443," in *Historical Essays in Honour of James Tait* (Manchester: Printed for the Subscribers, 1933), 121.
2. *Ibid.,* 125.
3. *Ibid.,* 130; For information on Massynham see *Engl. Med. Archit.,* 182.
4. Jacob, *op. cit.,* 132.
5. Jacob, *op. cit.,* 124.
6. Jacob, *op. cit.,* 128; Chevynton may have come from Somerset see E. A. Gee, "Oxford Masons, 1370-1540," *AJ,* CIX (1952), 65.
7. Jacob, *op. cit.,* 128.

| 181 | Oxford | Christchurch: Chantry Chapel |
| | Oxfordshire | Two bays, each 1.45m x 1.42m |

Historical Analysis:

No documentary evidence can be associated with this chapel. On stylistic grounds the chapel should be dated to the end of the fifteenth century; the central spandrel panel is handled in much the same manner as that of the Founder's Oratory (built ca. 1480) in Magdalen College Chapel, Oxford and in the Bradford-on-Avon Porch now located at Corsham House (Wiltshire). Along the exterior above the doorway level is a cornice of running vine ornament and a cresting of Tudor flowers.[1]

General Description:

It was built in two stories. The lower story is fan vaulted in two bays and serves as a canopy over the tomb of an unidentified man and woman (indents of brass figures of a man and woman are present on top of the altarlike stone slab). The vaulting springs from moulded capitals and shafts. Each vaulting quadrant is divided into four cinquefoil cusped panels. The horizontal bounding ribs are composed of circular segments. The central spandrel panel is articulated with intersecting diagonal ribs which form four cinquefoil cusped panels. Foliate bosses are placed at the intersections of the diagonal ribs and horizontal bounding ribs of the vaulting conoids.

Technical Description:

Relatively flat four-centered curves are employed. The construction is completely of jointed masonry. The vaulting of each bay is composed of four stones. The joints run along the transverse and longitudinal axes.

1. RCHM, *City of Oxford* (1939), 43.

| | Oxford | Corpus Christi College: Gatehall |
| | Oxfordshire | |

Analysis:

It is a modern or very restored fan vault.[1] The present construction may follow an original design from the second decade of the sixteenth century. William Est and William Vertue were joint master masons at that time.[2]

1. RCHM, *City of Oxford* (1939), 50.
2. Thomas Fowler, *The History of Corpus Christi College,* Oxfordshire Historical Society, XXV (Oxford: At the Clarendon Press, 1893), 61ff.

| 182 | Oxford | Magdalen College Chapel: Founder's Oratory |
| | Oxfordshire | Two bays, each 1.83m square (approximately) |

Historical Analysis:

Bishop Waynflete (d. 1486), the founder of Magdalen College paid William Orchard £10 for a "clausura." The chapel itself was finished circa 1480.[1] This date probably marks the completion date for the oratory.

General Description:[2]

The vaulting springs from moulded corbels. Each vaulting conoid is divided into four cinquefoil cusped panels. The horizontal bounding ribs are composed of circular segments. The diagonal ribs are carried across the bays. There are ridge ribs in both directions. Foliate bosses are placed at the rib intersections.

Technical Description:
Four-centered curves are employed.

1. E. A. Gee, "Oxford Masons, 1370-1530," *AJ,* CIX (1952), 76.
2. RCHM, City of Oxford (1939), 71, and Joseph Skelton, *Oxonia Antiqua Restaurata* (2nd Edit.; London: J. B. Nichols and Son, 1843), 39ff.

---

33 Oxford   Queens College: Former Gateway (now destroyed)
       Oxfordshire

Historical Analysis:
The former gateway of Queens College was fan vaulted as evidenced by a drawing made circa 1720 by James Green.[1] The gateway itself was built in the fourteenth century and was demolished when the college was rebuilt between the years 1672 and 1760.[2] The fan vault must have been a later addition to the original structure and most probably was inserted between the years 1504 and 1516 inclusively; for the long rolls for those years are missing[3] and no payments for the vaulting of the gateway are noted in the long rolls which are extant for the other years. Also, as evidenced by Green's drawing, this fan vault was similar in conception to the vaulting of the gateway of St. John's College, Cambridge, which was constructed in the second decade of the sixteenth century.[4] Therefore, a date in the early sixteenth century is plausible for it.

1. Aymer Vallance, *The Old Colleges in Oxford* (London: B. T. Batsford, 1912), 31. The drawing was engraved and published in Joseph Skelton, *Oxonia Antiqua Restaurata* (2nd Edit.; London: J. B. Nichols and Son, 1843), pl. 39.
2. RCHM, *City of Oxford* (1939), 97.
3. John Richard Magrath, *The Queens College* (2 vols.; Oxford: At the Clarendon Press, 1921), I, 165.
4. Edward Miller, *Portrait of a College; A History of the College of St. John the Evangelist* Cambridge (Cambridge: At the University Press, 1961), 6-8.

Oxford   St. Mary the Virgin: South Porch (fragments)
Oxfordshire

Analysis:
The south porch was rebuilt in 1637, the ceiling of which was apparently constructed of recycled parts from an earlier structure.[1] The present fan vaulted ceiling had to be greatly adapted to fit in its present location.[2] The church itself was rebuilt in the late fifteenth century, construction ending around 1492.[3] The ceiling, therefore, could well have been recycled from an earlier porch on the site.

1. R. H., "Remarks on the Church of St. Mary the Virgin, Oxford," *AJ,* VIII (1851), 141.
2. For a plan of the ceiling see *Ibid.,* 142.
3. For a history of the church see T. G. Jackson, *The Church of St. Mary the Virgin, Oxford,* (Oxford: At the Clarendon Press, 1897).

Peterborough   Cathedral: "New Building"
Northamptonshire   Small bays, each 4.82m x 4.92m
                           Large bays, each 7.99m x 4.85m

Historical Analysis:
The rebus and initials of Abbot Robert Kirton appear on this structure in many

places,[1] and summary building accounts for the work are preserved in transcription from Kirton's Register (now lost)[2] to prove that the "New Building" was constructed during his abbacy, that is, between 1496 and 1528.[3] The cost of the work was 3,000 marks.[4] Unfortunately, the summary building accounts are not dated. Arthur Oswald has suggested that the vaulting dates from before 1509 and cites as his evidence the presence of Prince of Wales's feathers amongst the carved ornaments of the chapel.[5] The Prince of Wales's feathers, however, do not occur on the vaulting,[6] and furthermore, they were often included in sculptural programs even when there was no Prince of Wales. For example, they are carved on the interior gateway of St. John's College, Cambridge, which was built circa 1511-20.[7] The *Monasticon* gives the date of completion of the "New Building" as about 1518.[8] If so, this building should be seen as leading away from King's College Chapel, Cambridge instead of leading up to it as it has been interpreted in the past. Oswald attributes the design to John Wastell on the basis of its visual similarity to the vaulting of King's College Chapel, Cambridge.[9] However, there are conceptual and technical differences which separate them.

General Description:

In plan the structure is U-shaped and wraps around the eastern end of the cathedral. It is divided into nine bays. Five large rectangular ones are located along the eastern end and two small bays are located at both the north and south to form extensions of the north and south aisles of the cathedral. There are twelve exterior buttresses, each of which is topped with a sculptured figure, possibly of the apostles. The corners between the "New Building" and the feretory are squared off, and the remaining triangular area is articulated with a flat ceiling ornamented with applied tracery. There were originally five entrances to the "New Building," two from the aisles and three from the feretory which are now closed. Three altars were originally located opposite these entrances from the feretory, the dedications of which are not known.[10]

The vaulting springs from moulded capitals and shafts. Each vaulting quadrant is composed of six panels. There is one horizontal bounding rib per conoid in the small bays, while the large bays have three; these bounding ribs are continuous from bay to bay and are articulated with bratticing. The panels in each case are cinquefoil cusped. The transverse and longitudinal ridges rise up in each bay to the center, which displays a sculptured boss.[11] The crown of the vaulting over the large bays is higher than that over the small bays.

Technical Description:

Two-centered curves are employed in the small bays, while two and four-centered curves are used in the large bays. The ribs are not in all cases placed equidistantly, for example, when the vaulting turns the corner. The construction is of ribs and panels with jointed masonry used for the traceried parts. The beds are concave. The depth of panel is 9 cm. Mutton bones are used as dowels.[12] The stones which comprise the transverse ridges are cut to interlock, forming rigid connections. No joints fall on the centerlines of the vaulting ridges. In the large bays the ribs are rebated to receive the panels, while in the small bays the panels are placed directly on top of the ribs. Stiffening walls are utilized in the middle of each vaulting conoid along the eastern end of the structure. The pockets of the vaulting have rubble fill to two-thirds their height.

184
185
186
187
188

95

---

1. VCH, *Northamptonshire,* II, 437; W. D. Sweeting, *The Cathedral Church of Peterborough* (London: George Bell and Sons, 1898), 76.
2. Transcription made by John Bridges. Oxford, Bodleian Library, MS Top. Northants. C.5, f.174. I am thankful to Dr. Richard Marks, who told me the location of this transcription.

3. *Monasticon,* I, 363; VCH, *Northamptonshire,* II, 92.
4. Oxford, Bodleian Library, MS Top. Northants. C.5, f.174, cited in John Bridges and Peter Whalley, *The History and Antiquities of Northamptonshire* (2 vols.; Oxford, 1791), II, 558.
5. *Engl. Med. Archit.,* 283.
6. For description of the bosses see C. J. P. Cave, "The Roof Bosses in the Cathedral and in the Church of St. John the Baptist at Peterborough and in the Cathedral at Ripon," *Archaeologia,* LXXXVIII (1940), 276-7.
7. Edward Miller, *Portrait of a College; A History of the College of St. John the Evangelist Cambridge* (Cambridge: At the University Press, 1961), 6-8.
8. *Monasticon,* I, 363.
9. *Engl. Med. Archit.,* 283.
10. S. Gunton, *The History of the Church of Peterborough* (London: Richard Chiswell, 1686), 56; VCH, *Northamptonshire,* II, 444
11. For description see Cave, *op. cit.,* 276-7.
12. Information from Mr. G. G. Pace.

16	Putney	St. Mary the Virgin: Bishop West's Chapel
	Surrey	Two bays, each 2.26m x 2.99m

Historical Analysis:

When Putney Church was rebuilt in 1836, this chapel was preserved and moved to its present location.[1] Bishop Nicholas West of Ely, the alleged son of a Putney baker,[2] was most likely responsible for the erection of the chapel, for his arms appear on the vaulting.[3] The arms of the see of Ely also appear on the vaulting.[4] Therefore, this chapel was built after 1515, the year in which West became bishop of Ely,[5] and was probably completed before his death in 1533.[6] The design of the fan vault suggests a date closer to 1515 than to 1533, because the panel treatment of the vaulting conoids is identical to that of the nave aisle fan vaults of St. George's Chapel, Windsor. In addition, if the chapel had been built close to 1533, the design probably would have been similar to the chapel West erected for himself in Ely Cathedral, 1525-33.[7]

General Description:[8]

It is fan vaulted in two rectangular bays. The vaulting springs from moulded capitals and shafts. Each vaulting quadrant is composed of four panels. The sub-panels are cinquefoil cusped. The vaulting conoids intersect in the north-south direction and just meet in the east-west direction. The central spandrel panel in each bay is articulated with a quatrefoil and sub-cusped circular panel containing a shield of arms. In the panels to the east and west of the circles are carved rosettes with the letter "W" superimposed.

Technical Description:

Four-centered curves are employed throughout. The construction appears to be completely of jointed masonry (there is a heavy coat of paint on it).

1. Edward Wedlake Brayley, et al., *A Topographical History of Surrey* (5 vols.; London: G. Willis, 1850), III, 477.
2. VCH, *Surrey,* IV (1912), 81.
3. RCHM, *London,* II (1925), 93.
4. *Ibid.*
5. *DNB,* LX, 337.
6. Emden, *Cambridge,* 629.
7. VCH, *Cambridgeshire,* IV (1953), 73.
8. For plans see J. G. Jackson and G. T. Andrews, *Illustrations of Bishop West's Chapel in Putney Church,* Surrey (London: Carpenter and Son, 1825).

Saffron Walden   St. Mary the Virgin: South Porch
Essex   4.47m x 4.82m
                        Two bays, each 4.47m x 2.41m

Historical Analysis:

A building contract was probably drawn up by Thomas Clyff in 1485 between two churchwardens of Saffron Walden on the one hand and Simon Clerk and John Wastell on the other.[1] Incomplete churchwarden's accounts are also preserved from this period,[2] but there is no direct reference to the south porch.[3] In 1485, £7 was paid for forty-five tons of stone and in 1488 reference was made to the "Resceyuors for the new works of the south Ile."[4] The rebuilding of the nave and clerestory began between 1497 and 1499 and was still going on in 1526.[5] The capitals of the south porch are far simpler in design than are those of the nave. If the vaulting of the south porch was constructed at the same time as the nave and clerestory, their details should bear greater similarity. Furthermore, the exterior moulding of the south porch, although not at the same level, is consistent with that of the south aisle. It seems likely, therefore, that the south porch was constructed during the period 1485-97.

General Description:

It is fan vaulted in two rectangular bays. The vaulting springs from moulded capitals and shafts. Intersecting diagonal ribs as well as a transverse rib between the two bays, all of the same section, emphasize the rectangularity of the bays. The north-south ridge is horizontal, while the ridges going east-west rise to the center. The center of each bay is articulated with a large foliate boss. Each vaulting conoid is composed of three panels. The main panel is subdivided into two tiers, the lower of which is cinquefoil cusped in one panel. The upper tier is divided into two panels each of which is cinquefoil cusped. The junction of the intersecting conoids is articulated only by a simple rib. If the date 1485-1497 is accepted, this design should be seen as one of the first experiments leading up to the vaulting of both the Bell Harry Tower at Canterbury Cathedral and King's College Chapel, Cambridge.

Technical Description:

Two and four-centered curves are employed. The construction is of ribs and panels with jointed masonry used for the traceried parts. No joints occur along the centerlines of the ridges.

1. Cambridge, King's College Muniments, College Accs., vol. v, cited in *Engl. Med. Archit.,* 64.
2. Preserved in the Essex County Record Office, Chelmsford. Extracts published in Richard Lord Braybrooke, *The History of Audley End* (London: Samuel Bentley, 1836), and in *Engl. Med. Archit.,* 64.
3. It should be noted that in 1466 William Glanford and John Pollard contracted to build a new porch at Saffron Walden (Churchwarden's Accounts, ff. 73-75, cited in *Engl. Med. Archit.,* 133). It is uncertain to which porch this refers. This is not as significant as it may seem, because the fan vaulting of the south porch may be a later addition; for the curve of the vaulting does not follow that of the exterior door.
4. *Engl. Med. Archit.,* 64.
5. From will bequests see (H. W. King), "Saffron Walden," *Essex Archaeological Society Trans.,* N.S., II (1884), 298-300; H. W. King, "Excerpts from Ancient Wills," *ibid.,* 359-369; J. C. Challenor Smith, "Some Additions to Newcourts' Repertorium," *ibid.,* N.S., VII (1900), 281; G. Montagu Benton, "Essex Wills at Canterbury," *ibid.,* N.S., XXI (1937), 246.

| St. Albans | Cathedral: Monument to Humphrey, |
| Hertfordshire | Duke of Gloucester (decorative detail only) |

Historical Analysis:

The monument was most likely set up by Abbot John Stoke before 1450.[1]

General Description:

The monument consists of a triple arch. The two end bays are articulated with fan vault conoids and openwork pendants.

Technical Description:

Two-centered curves are employed. It is completely constructed of jointed masonry. Part of the vaulting is suspended from above.

1. VCH, *Hertfordshire* (1908), II, 493; BM Cotton MS Nero, D, vii, f.36.

---

9 St. Albans   Cathedral: Ramryge Chapel
     Hertfordshire   3.64m x 2.13m
     Four bays, each 0.91m x 2.13m

Historical Analysis:

Thomas Ramryge became abbot in 1492 and died in 1519.[1] The records of his abbacy have disappeared.[2] On the floor of the chapel is an incised slab of Abbot Ramryge,[3] and his initials and rebus occur in several places on the chapel.[4] The use of tracery panels that are divided by the vertical ribs, combined with the delicate bratticing placed in the panels, indicate a date in the second decade of the sixteenth century.

General Description:

The vaulting springs from sculptured capitals and shafts. The central spandrel panel takes on a distinctly more visual importance than the vaulting conoids, and is articulated with circles, quatrefoils, and ogee tracery forms. The openwork pendants, which are the focal points of the vaulting, are located along the bay divisions. This helps to unify the interior space.

Technical Description:

Four-centered curves are employed. The construction is completely of jointed masonry which is suspended from iron rods from above and from the sides.[5] The material of construction is clunch.[6]

1. Ernest Woolley, "The Ramryge Chantry in St. Alban's Abbey Church," *St. Albans and Hertfordshire Architectural and Archaeological Society Trans.,* for 1930 (1931), 31, and L. F. R. Williams, *History of the Abbey of St. Albans* (London, 1917), 230.
2. Woolley, *op. cit.,* 31.
3. Woolley, *op. cit.,* 34 and VCH, *Hertfordshire* (1908), 446.
4. For complete description of heraldry see Woolley, *op. cit.,* 31ff.
5. For structural drawings see *The Builders Journal and Architectural Record,* Feb. 3, 1897. Some structural details of the vaulting may be related to the vaulting of the chapter house which was recently excavated. Dr. Richard Morris's report (Warwick University), when published, promises to add greatly to our knowledge.
6. VCH, *Hertfordshire* , II (1908), 496.

---

7 St. David's   Cathedral: Trinity Chapel
     Pembrokeshire   4.88m x 10.97m (approximately)

Historical Analysis:

In his will dated 20 May 1521 Bishop Edward Vaughan (1509-22) requested to be buried in the Trinity Chapel and bequeathed £20 for the completion of its vaulting.[1] Therefore, it can be assumed that the vaulting was under construction at that time.

General Description:[2]

The vaulting is composed of two square bays of fan vaulting, which run north-south, with small pointed and panelled tunnel vaults at each end. The vaulting springs from moulded capitals and shafts; the center ones along the east and west walls are corbelled. Each vaulting conoid is composed of four main panels. The subpanels are cusped and are articulated with intersecting tracery. There are transverse and longitudinal ridge ribs which meet at a central boss in each bay.

Technical Description:

Four-centered curves are employed. The construction is of rib and panels with jointed masonry employed for the traceried parts. No joints occur along the ridges.

1. Prerogative Court of Canterbury, 2 Bodfelde, proved 27 Jan. 1523. Cited in Emden, *Cambridge*, 607.
2. For a complete description of the chapel and its heraldry see William Basil Jones and Edward A. Freedman, *The History and Antiquities of St. David's* (London: J. H. Parker, etc., 1856), 70ff.; J. Oldrid Scott, "Discovery of Windows in St. David's Cathedral," *Archaeologia Cambrensis,* 5th Series, XIV (1897), 332-334; W. H. St. John Hope, "St. David's Cathedral," *AJ,* LXVIII (1911), 416-419.

---

45   Salisbury   Cathedral: Bishop Audley's Chantry Chapel
            Wiltshire   4.24m x 2.14m
                                         Two bays, each 2.12m x 2.14m

Historical Analysis:

License was granted in 1516 to Bishop Edmund Audley to found a perpetual chantry in Salisbury cathedral.[1] He died in 1524 and was buried in this chapel.[2] Construction of the chapel, therefore, may have just been completed or just started circa 1516.

General Description:

Fan vaulted in two square bays. Each vaulting quadrant is composed of four cinquefoil cusped panels with heads composed of straight segments. The horizontal bounding rib is articulated with bratticing. The central spandrel panel in each bay is composed of a large sculptured boss which is surrounded by four quatrefoils in circles. There are transverse and longitudinal ridge ribs. The vaulting was originally painted and gilded, some of which remains.

Technical Description:

190   Four-centered curves are employed. The construction is completely of jointed masonry.

1. *L & P Henry VIII,* II, pt. I, 832.
2. Emden, *Oxford,* I, 76.

---

191   Salisbury   King's House: Porch
            Wiltshire   2.73m square

Historical Analysis:

The King's House was the prebendal mansion of the abbots of Sherborne (Dorset).[1] No known documentary evidence can be associated with the porch. The porch vault and the grotesque gargoyles above are carried out in Ham Hill stone –also employed at Sherborne–and not in Chilmark stone like the earlier work.[2] The east archway to the porch, which is panelled with a quatrefoil at its apex, more closely resembles the clerestory panelling of the nave of Sherborne Abbey (1475-1504)[3] than the choir which does not have quatrefoils at the apex. The north archway was added to the porch in the nineteenth century.[4] The type of tas-de-charge employed is similar to those at Sherborne. Most likely, the craftsmen from Sherborne Abbey were employed in the building of this porch in the last quarter of the fifteenth century.

General Description:

The vaulting springs from sculptured corbels. Each vaulting conoid is composed of four main panels. Cusping is placed on the inside of the panels along the top bounding rib. The central spandrel panel is composed of four subcusped quatrefoils in circles. There are sculptured bosses at the rib intersections and at the apexes of the wall ribs.

Technical Description:

Two-centered curves are employed. The construction is of ribs and panels with jointed masonry for the traceried parts. The central spandrel panel along with parts of the horizontal bounding rib and cusping, is composed of one stone, which explains the unusual cusping pattern.

---

1. Dora H. Robertson, "Reformation in Salisbury, 1535-1660," in Hugh Shortt, editor, *City of Salisbury* (London: Phoenix House Ltd., 1957), 64.
2. C. R. Everett, "Notes on the Prebendal Mansion of Sherborne Monastery Commonly Known as the King's House . . . ," *Wiltshire Archaeological and Natural History Magazine,* XLVII (1937), 400.
3. Leland, Itin., I, 153.
4. This door does not appear in early nineteenth century prints. For example, pl. XX in Peter Hall, *Picturesque Memorials of Salisbury* (Salisbury: W. B. Brodie and Co., 1834).

---

34 35 36	Shelton Norfolk	St. Mary: South Porch (fragments) 2.73m x 2.64m

Historical Analysis:

The church was being rebuilt in the last decade of the fifteenth century. In his will, dated 21 March 1497 and proved in May 1498, Sir Raufe Shelton directed his executors to ". . . perform and make up completely the church of Shelton aforesaid, in masonry, tymber, iron, and leede, according to the form as I have begunne it in as shorte a tyme as conveniently it maie be done of my owne goods if God dispose that I may not see the performance of the same."[1] The south porch, which bears the Shelton arms over its entrance,[2] was most likely built circa 1498. The fan vault retains only its wall ribs. There is no record that it was ever completed.

General Description:

From the vaulting fragments still in situ, it is clear that each vaulting quadrant was to have been composed of two tiers; the lower tier was to be composed of four panels, while the upper tier was to have eight panels. The panels in both tiers were to have half circular heads. Delicate bratticing was placed along the tops of the horizontal bounding ribs. Since this detail was used in Henry VII's Chapel, Westminster, the design for the porch may have been updated to reflect the latest court style. If so, actual construction probably dates to the early years of the sixteenth century.

Technical Description:

Two-centered curves are employed. The construction is of ribs and panels with jointed masonry for the traceried parts. The ribs were rebated to receive the panels.

1. William Harvey, *The Visitation of Norfolk in the Year 1563* (Norwich: Agas H. Goose, 1895), II, 395.
2. Pevsner, *BE, North-West and South Norfolk* (1962), 309.

---

65   Shepton Beauchamp   St. Michael: West Tower
             Somerset   4.00m square

Historical Analysis:

On one of the bosses is carved a shield encircled by a garter. A similar boss is found in the tower at Muchelney which has the Daubeney arms carved below the garter. The Muchelney boss undoubtedly refers to Giles, Lord Daubeney, who became Knight of the Garter in 1487 and died in 1507.[1] It seems probable that the Shepton Beauchamp boss had the same signification. If so, the date of the tower may be fixed to 1487-1507. The vaulting of the Muchelney tower is almost identical to this one and may have been built by the same workshop.

General Description:

The vaulting springs from sculptured corbels. Each vaulting quadrant is composed of four main trefoil cusped panels. The top horizontal bounding rib is composed of straight segments. There are bosses at the rib intersections, four of which are larger than the others. There are transverse and longitudinal ridge ribs.

Technical Description:

Two-centered curves are employed. The construction is of ribs and panels with **192** jointed masonry used for the traceried parts. The ridges to the bell opening are composed of only two large stones.

1. E. Buckle, "Shepton Beauchamp Church," *SANH Proc.,* XXXVIII (1891), 42.

---

72   Shepton Mallet   Sts. Peter and Paul: West Tower
             Somerset   4.34m x 4.38m

Historical Analysis:

No documentary evidence is known to exist. The tower itself probably dates to the period 1380-1440.[1] The way in which the east and west sides of the vaulting are altered to fit into the space and the way the wall ribs are handled along the north and south walls indicate that the vault was a later addition to the structure. Stylistically, this vault is similar in conception and size to the one at Chewton Mendip (Somerset); it was most likely added to the tower around the same time that Chewton Mendip was built, circa 1540.

General Description:

The vaulting springs from corbels. Each vaulting conoid is composed of six main panels. The subpanels are trefoil cusped under two-centered heads. Located around the central bell opening are four quatrefoils in circles with foliate bosses at their centers.

Technical Description:

Two-centered curves are employed. The construction is of ribs and panels with jointed masonry used for the traceried parts.

1. A. K. Wickham, *Churches of Somerset* (New Edit.; London: MacDonald, 1965), 42.

Sherborne	Abbey
Dorset	*Chancel:* 7.48m (north-south span)
	Nave: 7.92m (north-south span)
	North Transept: 7.96m (east-west span)
	St. Katherine's Chapel: 4.85m x 4.00m
	Wykeham Chapel: 3.05m x 3.40m

Historical Analysis:

Only scant documentary evidence is preserved for the establishment of the construction sequence of the fifteenth century work in the abbey. Leland states "Al the est parte of S. Mary chirch was reedified yn Abbate Bradefordes tyme (1436-59), saving a chapelle of our Lady an old peace of work that the fier came not to, by reason that it was of an older building. Peter Ramesunne next abbate saving one to Bradeford buildid *à fundamentis* al the west part of S. Marie chirch . . . Ramesunne abbate sette a chapelle caullid our Lady of Bow hard to the southe side of the old Lady Chapelle."[1] About the fire of circa 1436[2] Leland reported ". . . a preste of Al-Hawlois shot a shaft with fier into the toppe of that part of S. Marye chirch that devidid the est part that the monkes usid from the townesmen usid: and this partition chauncing at that tyme to be thakkid yn, the rofe was sette a fier, and consequently al the hole chirch, the lede and belles melted, was defacid."[3] Leland's report has been interpreted to mean that the roof at the time of the fire was a temporary one, so the rebuilding of the abbey commenced earlier in Abbot Brunyng's time, between 1415 and 1436.[4] It is clear that the roof was leaded and bells hung, therefore part of the structure was already permanent. Marks from the fire on the vaulting shafts, springers, and walls of the crossing, chancel and its aisles, have been cited as additional evidence that the rebuilding program started before the fire.[5] In fact, construction might have already progressed to the point that the vaulting of the chancel was to be built next.

In 1446 a license was granted on the petition of the abbot and convent. It showed that the choir, bell tower and the bells therein, and other buildings were burned by a sudden fire, and they were to acquire in mortmain lands and rents up to the value of £10 per year.[6] It seems that the rebuilding of the choir and crossing after the fire were under way in 1446. If Leland's testimony is accurate, this work was finished during Abbot Bradford's time, that is, by 1459. There is no reason to disagree with this dating.

The question remains whether fan vaulting was intended before the fire, for springers with equally spaced ribs were also common in lierne vaults. If the time lapse between the fire and the rebuilding after it was long enough, perhaps a new master mason was in charge of the operation and redesigned the vault.

Leland's placing of the rebuilding of the nave to Abbot Ramsam's time, 1475-1504, is substantiated by the fact that Ramsam's initials and rebus are found on many parts of it.[7] As Tudor roses and portcullises appear on the bosses of the vaulting,[8] if not designed after 1485, the vaulting of the nave was constructed when the Tudors came to power.

The dating of the north transept fan vault is conjectural. John Harvey suggested that it was built before that of the nave, and in any case between 1475 and 1504.[9] His hypothesis seems unlikely for several reasons. While the chancel and nave fan vaults are both similar and different from the technical point of view, the north transept fan vault represents a distinct break in workshop methodology, thereby indicating that it was constructed after the nave vaulting. Furthermore, the type and carving of the roof bosses in the north transept differ from those in the nave. The north transept bosses are relatively larger and foliate (one displays a rose), while the bosses in the nave are small and tend to be heraldic. In addition, the rebus and initials of Abbot Ramsam appear in the nave and in the Chapel of St. Mary-le-Bow,[10] but they do not appear in the north transept. If the north transept vaulting was built during Ramsam's time, he probably would have included his initials or rebus on it as he did in the other parts of the church he is known to have rebuilt. Therefore, on the basis of the formal and technological evidence, the vaulting of the north transept most likely dates from after 1504.

According to Leland, Canon Doggett (d. 1501) built a chapel on the south side of the church;[11] it has been suggested that this chapel may correspond to St. Katherine's Chapel, which is located between the south transept and the south aisle of the nave.[12] It is impossible to determine if this is the case, but St. Katherine's Chapel was most likely vaulted in the late fifteenth century, because it displays similar formal and technical characteristics to the vaulting of the nave.

The fan vault of the Wykeham Chapel is completely different in conception to the other fan vaults in the abbey; the central spandrel panel and the vaulting conoids are treated as distinctly different parts, the horizontal bounding ribs are composed of circular segments, and there are no bosses at the rib intersections. These differences indicate that the design was provided for it by someone who was outside the abbey workshop. Since no documentary evidence can be associated with the chapel, and the fact that it is so different from the other vaults in the abbey makes it impossible to establish a date for it based on the internal evidence. It would seem likely that it was built circa 1500, as the type of tas-de-charge is similar in type to the tower vault at Ilminster (Somerset). If the vaulting of the Wykeham Chapel were earlier or were designed by someone in the abbey workshop, it might have employed a tas-de-charge similar to the type in St. Katherine's Chapel. It is plausible that this chapel may have been intended to be a chantry chapel and that a patron, rather than the abbey, was responsible for its erection, thus explaining its differences to the other fan vaults in the abbey.

General Descriptions:

27
28 Chancel: The vaulting springs from sculptured capitals and shafts. Each vaulting conoid is divided into four main panels, the sub-panels of which are trefoil or multifoil cusped. The horizontal bounding ribs are composed of straight segments. The panels between the vaulting conoids are lozenge-shaped, subdivided, and cusped. A longitudinal ridge rib is present. Foliate bosses are placed at the rib intersections, except for the middle boss in each bay, which bears a shield of arms of Stafford of Hooke.[13] The chancel vault has at least five visual characteristics which imply a unified spatial conception: (1) the vaulting conoids were conceived of as ruled surfaces of rotation, thereby tying one bay to the next; (2) the horizontal bounding rib near the top serves the same function and leads the eye from one bay to the next; (3) there are quartered, lozenge-shaped, subdivided and cusped panels placed between vaulting conoids which contribute to the breakdown of distinct bay divisions; (4) the longitudinal ridge rib is horizontal, i.e. parallel to the floor; (5) the transverse ridges commence with lozenges, which further visually break down transverse divisions.

193 Crossing: It is separated from the choir vault by a panelled tunnel vault which replaced the eastern arch of the tower. The crossing vault displays the same basic formal characteristics as the choir vault, except there is a central bell opening.

194
195 Nave: The vaulting springs from shafts and sculptured capitals, which differ from those in the chancel. Each vaulting conoid is composed of four main panels, with trefoil cusped subpanels. The horizontal bounding ribs, like those of the choir,

are composed of straight segments. There are lozenge shaped cusped panels between the vaulting conoids. Bosses are placed at rib intersections.[14] At first glance both chancel and nave vaults are composed of similar visual elements, but careful analysis points to fundamentally different spatial concepts. To summarize it simply, the lozenges in the chancel are placed in the A, A,′ A rhythm; those in the nave are placed in an A, B, A rhythm. There are no lozenges at the ends of the transverse ridges. In addition, the longitudinal ridge is not horizontal, but rises up toward the center of each bay. Therefore, the designer of the nave vault emphasized to a greater degree the visual integrity of the individual bay.

North Transept: The vaulting springs from shafts and sculptured capitals, which are similar to those in the nave. Each vaulting conoid is divided into four main panels, the subpanels of which are trefoil cusped or trefoil subcusped. Large foliate bosses are located at the rib intersections. The horizontal bounding ribs are composed of straight segments. The central spandrel panel is articulated with an octagon, which is composed of eight radiating trefoil cusped panels with a large foliate boss at their center. There are ridge ribs in both directions.

St. Katherine's Chapel: The vaulting springs from sculptured capitals and shafts. Each vaulting conoid is composed of four main panels, the subpanels of which are trefoil cusped. The central spandrel panel is composed of four quatrefoil cusped panels and is domical in shape. There are foliate bosses at the rib intersections.

Wykeham Chapel: The vaulting was probably a later addition to an already extant structure because it springs from sculptured corbels, and is best suited to a square vaulting module, which this chapel does not have. Each vaulting conoid is composed of four trefoil cusped panels. The horizontal bounding ribs are composed of circular segments. The central spandrel panel is composed of four multifoil cusped circles with foliate bosses. The central boss is modern.[15]

Technical Descriptions:

Chancel: The transverse section is a continuous curve, thus the central spandrel panel has a domical feeling. The construction is of ribs and panels with jointed masonry for the traceried parts. The ridges are a combination of jointed, and rib and panel construction. The ribs and jointed masonry are of Ham Hill stone, while the panels were originally of tufa (now replaced).[16]

Crossing: It is identical with the choir vault in height, curvature, and materials of construction.

Nave: Two-centered curves are employed. The transverse ribs rise considerably, giving a domical effect. The construction is of ribs and panels with jointed masonry for the traceried parts. The ridges are a combination of rib and panel, and jointed masonry construction.

North Transept: Two-centered curves are employed. The construction is of ribs and panels with jointed masonry for the traceried parts. In contrast to the choir, crossing, and nave vaults, the ridges are entirely composed of jointed masonry until the central octagon is reached. The octagon is formed by a wedge-shaped outer ring of stones, which forms a compression ring. As a result, the center of the octagon composed of ribs and panels, is not necessary for the stability of the vaulting and could have been omitted. The stones used for the large foliate bosses of the ridges are hollowed out from above. The same kind of stone is used for all parts of the vault. Four vertical series of wedge stones were inserted into this vault when it was restored in the nineteenth century.[17] This was necessary because the vault was spreading out as a result of outward movement of the walls. This also explains the present distortion in the traceried pattern.

St. Katherine's Chapel: Two-centered curves are employed. The construction is of ribs and panels with jointed masonry for the traceried parts.

Wykeham Chapel: Two-centered curves are employed. Construction is of ribs and panels with jointed masonry employed for the traceried parts.

1. Leland, *Itin.,* I, 152-153. See also, for further details and description of structure J. F. Petit, "Sherborne, Dorsetshire," *Memoirs Illustrative of the History and Antiquities of Bristol . . . Archaeological Institute of Great Britain and Ireland* (for 1851, pub. 1853) and R. Willis, "Sherborne Minster," *AJ,* XXII (1865), 182.
2. For the date see the Ordinance of Bishop Roger Neville, 12 November 1436, printed in John Hutchins, *The History and Antiquities of the County of Dorset,* (4 vols.; 1870), IV, 257-8.
3. Leland, *Itin.,* I, 152.
4. RCHM, *An Inventory of the Historical Monuments in Dorset,* I (1952), 200.
5. *Ibid.,* 200, and J. H. P. Gibb, *Fan Vaults and Medieval Sculpture of Sherborne Abbey* (Sherborne: Friends of Sherborne Abbey, 1979), 3. This publication contains excellent color photographs of the vaults, which show scorch marks left by the fire.
6. P.R.O., *Calendar of the Patent Rolls,* Henry VI, IV (1441-46), 416.
7. RCHM, *op. cit.,* 204.
8. RCHM, *op. cit.,* 204.
9. *Engl. Med. Archit.,* 246.
10. Joseph Fowler, *Medieval Sherborne* (Dorchester: Longmans, Ltd., 1951), 267.
11. Leland, *Itin.*
12. Fowler, *op. cit.,* 269.
13. RCHM, *op. cit.,* 202.
14. For complete description see RCHM, *op. cit.,* 204.
15. RCHM, *op. cit.,* 204.
16. F. H. Carpenter, "On the Benedictine Abbey of S. Mary, Sherborne with notes on the Restoration of Its Church," *Royal Institute of British Architects Sessional Papers,* 1876-77 (1877), 145; for description of the tufa see J. F., "Calcareous Tufa in Medieval Buildings," *Somerset and Dorset Notes and Queries,* XXII (1938), 114-5.
17. J. H. P. Gibb, "Restoring Sherborne Abbey," *Country Life,* 16 August 1979, 473-474.

Silton	St. Nicholas: North Chapel
Dorset	2.70m (approximately)

Historical Analysis:
Dated to circa 1500 on the basis of style.[1]
General Description:
While the chapel is rectangular, the fan vault is square and is continued east in the form of a four-centered arch with a ribbed and panelled soffit. Each conoid springs from corbels carved with angels bearing shields, and has two tiers with trefoil cusped panels. The central spandrel panel is circular and contains four roundels with quatrefoil cusping.
Technical Description:
Four-centered curves are employed.

1. RCHM, Dorset, IV (1972), 77.

---

202 | Spalding | St. Mary and St. Nicolas: North Porch |
|---|---|
| Lincoln | 3.35m square |

Historical Analysis:
No documentary evidence can be associated with the north porch. It has been suggested that it was built by Prior Robert II after 1496.[1] This date seems likely because of the unusual tracery pattern of the vaulting conoids, which can be seen

later, for example, in the Salisbury Chantry, Christchurch. The tracery pattern of the central spandrel panel is similar to the pattern employed in the openwork arches of Henry VII's Chapel, Westminster, thus suggesting a date of circa 1500.

General Description:

The vaulting springs from moulded capitals and shafts. Each vaulting conoid is composed of two major panels. Subpanels with ogee curved heads are developed. The horizontal bounding ribs are composed of circular segments. The central spandrel panel consists of a series of interlocking ogee quatrefoils.

Technical Description:

Two-centered curves are employed. The construction is of ribs and panels with jointed masonry for the traceried parts.

---

1. J. P. Hoskins, *The Story of the Parish Church of S. Mary and S. Nicolas, Spalding* (Gloucester: The British Publishing Co., Ltd., n.d.), 29.

Stavordale	Priory: Jesus Chapel
Somerset	4.72m x 3.05m (approximately)

Historical Analysis:

The chapel was built by John Lord Zouche; in his will, dated 8 October 1525 and proved 26 March 1526, he requested to be ". . . buried . . . in the chapell of the chauntrie of Jesus . . . by me late ordeyned and founded," and Lord Zouche provided ". . . two prestes to synge in the chapell of Jesus by me newe buylded in the Priory of Staverdell . . ."[1] Therefore, this chapel was built shortly before 1525.

General Description:[2]

Vaulted in one and one-half bays. The basic vaulting module is square. The vaulting springs from sculptured corbels. Each vaulting quadrant is composed of four panels. The subpanels are trefoil cusped. The horizontal bounding ribs are composed of circular segments. There are foliate bosses at the main rib intersections. The central spandrel panel is articulated with a traceried wheel. The areas left between the central traceried wheel and the vaulting conoids are articulated with trefoil cusped daggers. The chapel is lavishly decorated with animals, shields, and angels.

Technical Description:

Four-centered curves are employed. The construction is of ribs and panels with jointed masonry for the traceried parts.

---

1. F. W. Weaver, edit., *Somerset Medieval Wills, 1501-1530* (SRS, XIX, 1903), 241-2.
2. For complete physical description of the chapel see Harry Clifford, "Architectural Notes on Stavordale Priory, Somerset," *The Antiquary,* XLIX (1913), 51-2.

58

Taunton	St. James: West Tower
Somerset	4.34m (north-south)

Historical Analysis:

No documentary evidence is known to exist. The tower is almost identical to the one at Bishop's Lydeard, which has been dated circa 1440-50.[1] The tower was rebuilt with some alterations in 1871-73, at which time the fan vaulting of the original tower was reused. However, the angel corbels from which the vaulting springs, are nineteenth century.[2] Although the tower may be dated circa 1450, the fan vaulting may have been added later, because the tracery forms employ four-centered curves, a characteristic more common in fan vaults built circa 1500 (cf. Wrington).

The vaulting springs from corbels. Each vaulting quadrant is composed of four main panels. The subpanels are trefoil cusped under four-centered heads. Between the central bell opening and the vaulting conoids are four quatrefoils in circles.

Technical Description:

203   Two-centered curves are employed. The construction is of ribs and panels with jointed masonry for the traceried parts.

1. A. K. Wickham, *Churches of Somerset* (New Edit.; London: MacDonald, 1965), 45.
2. C. J. Lane, *A History of the Parish Church of St. James' Taunton* (Gloucester: British Publishing Company, Ltd., n.d.), 7, 8, 17.

---

67   Taunton   St. Mary Magdalene: West Tower
          Somerset   5.20m (north-south)

Historical Analysis:

Evidence from will bequests indicates that the tower was being rebuilt 1488-1514.[1] The fan vault probably was built during that period. It is difficult to determine if it was a later addition to an already extant tower, since the tower was rebuilt in 1862.[2] The fan vaulting was one of the few things that was saved from the original tower and was reinstalled in the restored one.[3] The angel corbels may not be original.

General Description:

The vaulting springs from corbels. Each vaulting quadrant is composed of six main panels. The subpanels are trefoil cusped under two-centered heads. Between the vaulting conoids and the central bell opening are four quatrefoils in circles, each of which contains foliate bosses.

Technical Description:

Two-centered curves are employed. The construction is of ribs and panels with jointed masonry for the traceried parts.

1. Summarized in (E. H. Bates) "St. Mary's Church, Taunton," *SANH Proc.,* LIV (for 1908), 30-31.
2. W. H. Ashwith, *The Church of St. Mary Magdalene, Taunton, 1508-1908* (Taunton: Alfred E. Goodman, The Phoenix Press, 1908), 69.
3. Joshua Toulmin, greatly enlarged by James Savage, further enlarged by Charles George Webb, *The History of Taunton* (Taunton: C. G. Webb, 1874), supplement, 28.

---

34   Tewkesbury   Abbey: Beauchamp Chapel
          Gloucestershire   1.68m x 2.24m (fan vault only)
                                      0.84m x 0.56m (vaulting module)

Historical Analysis:

The chapel was erected by Isabel Despencer after the death of her husband, Richard Beauchamp, Earl of Worcester (who died in 1421 at the siege of Meaux), and was dedicated on 2 August 1438.[1] The earl's arms appear on the floor tiles,[2] and a statue of Isabel may have originally been intended to be placed in one of the niches in the upper level of the chapel.[3] An inscription on the chapel recalls the death in 1439 of Isabel in London.[4] Therefore, the chapel was built between 1421 and 1439.

General Description:[5]

It is divided into two stories, the lower covers only the two western bays, and is fan vaulted. Each vaulting quadrant is composed of four cinquefoil cusped panels. The central spandrel between the vaulting conoids is articulated with a large subcusped quatrefoil in a circle and small quatrefoils in circles. Traces of paint and gilding remain on the vaulting.

Technical Description:

Two-centered curves are employed. The construction is completely of jointed masonry. The vault is more decorative than structural, since it is constructed of flat slabs of stone.

1. "... ubi postea domina Isabella uxor ejus ordinavit pulchram capellam arte mirifice fabricatam, quam consecrari fecit in honorem beatae dilectricis Domini nostri Jesu Christi, Mariae Magdalenae, sanctae Barbarae virginis, et sancti Leonardi abbatis. Quae capella dedicata est ij die mensis Augusti anno Domini mccccxxxviij." BM, Cotton MS Cleopatra C. III, f.220a, printed in *Monasticon,* II, 63. Details of the Earl's life summarized in John H. Blunt, *Tewkesbury Abbey and its Associations* (London, 1875), 75.
2. A. S. Porter, "Some Notes on the Ancient Encaustic Tiles in Tewkesbury Abbey," *AJ,* XLVIII (1891), 83.
3. C. H. Bickerton Hudson, "The Founders' Book of Tewkesbury Abbey," *Bristol and Gloucestershire Archaeological Society Trans.,* XXXIII (for 1910), 60-66. See also her will, dated 1 December 1439 in which she directs a statue of her to be made according to the design and model by Thomas Porchalion, in N. H. Nicholas, *Testamenta Vetusta* (2 vols.; London: Nichols and Son, 1826), I, 239-40.
4. For the inscription see John Gough Nichols, *Description of the Church of St. Mary, Warwick, and of the Beauchamp Chapel, . . . the Chantry of Isabella, Countess of Warwick in Tewkesbury Abbey* (London: J. B. Nichols and Son, 1838), 27.
5. For drawings of plan, elevation and section see *Vetusta Monumenta,* V (London, 1825), pls. XLIII-XLV.

04
05

Tewkesbury   Abbey: Cloister (fragments)
Gloucestershire

Analysis:

The cloisters were pulled down by the king's commissioners in 1541.[1] One bay was restored in 1875-79.[2] The restoration was based on the vaulting of the Gloucester cloister. Only one tas-de-charge was in situ, and there were no vaulting fragments found, so the evidence for a fan vault is indeed slim. The construction of the cloister probably began in the fifteenth century, because the wall mouldings are similar to those used in phase two of the building operations of the cloister at Gloucester. However, some of the subpanels of the wall panelling at Tewkesbury (parts are still in situ) employ four-centered heads, while two-centered heads are used for the corresponding detail at Gloucester, which indicates a later date for Tewkesbury. Construction apparently was still going on in 1503, as evidenced by a bequest in the will of William Wade: "I will that my Lord Abbot of Tewkesbury have and receive of the prior of Deerhurst XLIs. toward the building of the cloyster, which the prior oweth me."[3]

1. Ernest F. Smith, *A New Handbook and Guide to Tewkesbury Abbey* (Tewkesbury: R. A. Newman, n.d.), 21.
2. *Ibid.*
3. C. E. Woodruff, *Sede Vacante Wills* (Kent Archaeological Society, Records Branch, III, 1914), 43.

22

Tewkesbury   Abbey: Founder's Chapel
Gloucestershire   1.66m (north-south) (approximately)

Historical Analysis:

The chapel was built in 1397 by Abbot Thomas Parker to commemorate the founder of the abbey, Robert FitzHamon, who died in 1107.[1]

General Description:

Vaulted in two slightly rectangular bays, the vaulting springs from shafts in the corners of the chapel and from pendants between the bays. Each vaulting quadrant is composed of four main panels and one minor one, which abuts on the window side. The subpanels along the top horizontal bounding rib are cinquefoil cusped with foliated cusp ends under two-centered heads. The subpanels located along the lower horizontal band, on the other hand, are trefoil cusped with foliate cusp ends under ogee heads. The central spandrel panel is composed of four quatrefoils in circles.

Technical Description:

Two-centered curves are employed. The construction is completely of jointed masonry.

1. "Super quo successu temporum dominus Thomas Parkarus abbas octodecimus capellam erigi fecit ex lapide satis mirifice tabulatam, sub anno gratiae mcccxcvij." BM, Cotton MS, Cleopatra C.III, f.220a, printed in *Monasticon,* II, 60.

21	Tewkesbury	Abbey: Trinity Chapel
	Gloucestershire	1.66m (north-south span)

Historical Analysis:

Edward Lord Despencer died in 1375; the Trinity Chapel was later erected by his wife.[1] While this chapel is similar to the Founder's Chapel (1397), the panels which comprise the lower horizontal band of the vaulting conoids have two-centered heads; those of the Founder's Chapel have ogee heads. This, when seen in conjunction with the way in which the vaulting cuts across the window tracery compared to the way the detail is handled on the Founder's Chapel, indicates an earlier date of circa 1380 for its construction.

General Description:

It is vaulted in two slightly rectangular bays. The vaulting springs from shafts in the corners of the chapel and from pendants between the two bays. By using the pendants the designer created a square vaulting compartment which readily accommodated the proportions of a fan vault. (The idea for pendants in combination with a fan vault reached its ultimate development in Henry VII's Chapel, Westminster.) Each vaulting quadrant is composed of four main panels and one minor one which abuts on the window side. Each subpanel is cinquefoil cusped under a two-centered head. The central spandrel panel is articulated with four quatrefoils in circles.

Technical Description:

Two-centered curves are employed. The construction is completely of jointed masonry. The extrados of the vault follow the intrados.

1. "Et praedictus Edwardus secundus obiit in Cambria, apud Lanblethian in die sancti Martini, anno mccclxxv et sepultus est apud Theokes ante ostium vestiarii juxta presbiterium, ubi uxor ejus aedificavit capellam ex lapidibus arte mirifica constructam, quae dedicata est in honore Sanctae Trinitatis." BM, Cotton MS, Cleopatra C.III, f.220a, printed in *Monasticon,* II, 62.

	Thorncombe	Forde Abbey: Hall Porch
	Dorset	

Analysis:

It was built by Abbot Thomas Charde circa 1528 as evidenced by the inscription on the superstructure of the porch: "An'o D'ni millesimo quinquesimo VICmo octo° A D'no factum est Thomas Chard abb."[1] The work is similar to Cerne, Muchelney and Milton Abbas in appearance and character.[2] The central boss of the vaulting is uncut.[3]

1. J. S. Udal, "Notes on the History of Ford Abbey," *Dorset Natural History and Antiquarian Field Club,* IX (1888), 139.
2. Alfred Clapham and A. R. Dufty, "Forde Abbey," *AJ,* CVII (1950), 119.
3. "Ford Abbey," *Dorset Natural History and Antiquarian Field Club,* XXVIII (1907), lxxxii.

48	Tong	St. Bartholomew: Vernon Chapel
	Shropshire	5.18m x 2.84m (approximately)

Historical Analysis:

Sir Henry Vernon in his will, dated 18 January 1515 and proved on 5 May 1515, directed his ". . . body to be buryed in the place at Tonge where I haue assigned my selfe to lye . . . I wyell that my said tombe and chappell be made wtin ij yeres next aftar my deceasse . . . I bequeth and gyff for Makyng of the sayde tombe and Chappell Cli . . ."[1] The will continues with instructions for the establishment of a chantry. License to found the chantry was given on 10 February 1519 (10 Henry VIII).[2] Construction of the chapel most likely started in 1515 and completed when the license was granted.

General Description:

It is fan vaulted in two bays. The vaulting springs in the middle from a pendant along the north side. Each vaulting quadrant is composed of four main panels. The subpanels are trefoil cusped. The central spandrel panel is articulated with a pendant composed of eight radiating cinquefoil cusped panels. The eastern pendant terminates in a foliate boss, while the western one displays the Vernon arms.[3] Between the central pendant and the vaulting conoids are trefoil cusped daggers. Remains of gilding can be seen on the western pendant.[4]

Technical Description:

Four-centered curves are employed. The construction is completely of jointed masonry.

1. W. A. Carrington, "Will of Sir Henry Vernon of Haddon," *Journal of the Derbyshire Archaeological and Natural History Society,* XVIII (Jan., 1896), 81-93.
2. *L & P Henry VIII,* III, no. 102(5). Instructions for the chantry priest, etc., in Reg. Geoffrey Blyth (Coventry and Lichfield), f.29, extracts printed in K. L. Wood-Legh, *Perpetual Chantries in Britain* (Cambridge: At the University Press, 1965), 65, n.2, 3; further information on the chantry in A. Hamilton Thompson, "Certificates of the Shropshire Chantries," *Shropshire Archaeological and Natural History Society,* 4th Series, I (1911), 148.
3. George Griffiths, *A History of Tong, Shropshire* (2nd edit.; London: Simpkin, Marshall, Hamilton, Kent, & Co., Ltd., 1894), 53; D. H. S. Cranage, *An Architectural Account of the Churches of Shropshire* (2 vols.; Wellington: Hobsen & Co., 1901), I, 50.
4. J. L. Petit, "Tong Church, Salop," *AJ,* II (1845), 8; Cranage, *op. cit.,* I, 50.

6	Torbryan	Holy Trinity: South Porch
	Devonshire	2.59m x 3.05m

Historical Analysis:

The church itself is an early fifteenth century structure.[1] Since the porch is rectangular in plan, a tunnel vault was inserted at one end to provide a square vaulting module to accommodate the proportions of a fan vault. This solution suggests that the fan vault was a later insertion into an already extant porch. It would seem likely that it was added after 1488 when the neighboring manor was held by the Petre family, who had strong connections with the court.[2] Sir William Petre, who was principal secretary of state in 1544,[3] was born in the parish in 1505-06.[4]

General Description:

The top tier of each vaulting conoid is composed of four panels. The panels of each tier are cinquefoil cusped. The central spandrel panel is composed of four quatrefoils in circles. The areas left between the central spandrel panel and the vaulting conoids are articulated with trefoil cusped daggers. Demi-angels bearing shields of arms appear on the central rib of each vaulting conoid.

Technical Description:

The construction is completely of jointed masonry. The central spandrel panel is composed of four stones, the joints of which run perpendicular to the walls.

1. Robert Duins Cooke, *Notes on the Churches and Parishes of Ipplepen and Torbryan* (2nd Edit.; Newton Abbot: "Advertiser," 1937), 24.
2. *Ibid.,* 23; For information about the manor see J. J. Alexander, "Early Owners of Torbryan Manor," *Devonshire Association Trans.,* LXVIII (1936), 197-214.
3. J. D. Mackie, *The Earlier Tudors* (Oxford: At the Clarendon Press, 1966), 648.
4. Lawrence Snell, *The Suppression of the Religious Foundations of Devon and Cornwall* (Marazion: Wordens of Cornwall, 1967), 62.

---

25   Wardour Castle   Entrance Passage (fragments)
         Wiltshire   7.85m x 2.60m

Historical Analysis:

The present building belongs to the period after 1393, when in that year John, 5th Lord Lovel of Titchmarsh, obtained a license to build a castle.[1] The whole concept of the plan owes much to France, especially to the Château de Concressault in the Department of Cher.[2] Lord Lovel campaigned in France during the Hundred Years War, which may explain the use of the unusual plan (hexagonal) in England.[3] It is implied in the license of 1393 that the stone walls of the castle were not up as yet;[4] therefore, construction and perhaps planning commenced after that time.

General Description:

It is vaulted in three square bays. The vaulting springs from capitals and shafts; the ribs were bent to disappear into the capitals. From a study of the remaining fragments, it appears that the upper tier of each vaulting quadrant was composed of four panels, and that the top horizontal bounding rib was made up of circular segments. The panels do not appear to have been cusped. It is not known how the central spandrel panels were articulated.

Technical Description:

Two-centered curves are employed. The remaining fragments suggest that construction was completely of jointed masonry. The disparity in geometry of the arches of the doorways with the wall arches of the vaulting, and the fact that the stonework of the walls directly over the wall arches of the vaulting looks as if it may have been remodelled, suggest that the vaulting may have been inserted later. The other vaults in the castle are all of rib and panel construction and not nearly so grand.

1. Laurence Keen, "Excavations at Old Wardour Castle, Wiltshire," *The Wiltshire Archaeological and Natural History Magazine,* LXII (1967), 67.
2. *Ibid.,* 67.
3. R. B. Pugh and A. D. Saunders, *Old Wardour Castle* (London: HMSO, 1968), 15.
4. "conessimus . . . quod ipse quoddam manerium suum de Werdour . . . cum muris de petra et

calce includere, firmare, kernellare et batellare et castrum inde facere et castrum illud sic factum tenere possit." P.R.O., C.66/337, m.17, cited in Keen, *op. cit.,* 67.

35	Warwick	St. Mary's: Chantry Chapel off the Beauchamp Chapel
	Warwickshire	4.57m x 2.25m (approximately)

Historical Analysis:

On 11 May 1437, Richard Beauchamp obtained a license to found a chantry in Warwick.[1] In his will, dated 8 August 1437, he instructed that a chapel of our Lady be built in ". . . the place as I have devised."[2] His executors on 11 September 1439 received a license to grant in mortmain to the Dean and Chapter of St. Mary's, lands, etc., to the value of £40 a year.[3] On 17 July 1441 commission was granted to John Mayell of Warrewyk, Thomas Kerver of Warrewyk, and John Skynner of Warrewyk to pay carpenters, masons, workmen and laborers from money out of the goods of Richard, late Earl of Warwick, to build a chapel within the College of Warwick.[4]

Extant summary building accounts cover the period from 1442 to 1464.[5] Contracts let for the fittings (1449-54), suggest that the actual structure was complete or nearly so by that time.[6] This is confirmed by the fact that £1754.0s.1d. out of a total cost for the chapel of £2481.4s.7½d. was expended by 1449-50.[7] Therefore, the chantry chapel was most likely planned circa 1441 and completed by circa 1449. The main chapel was not consecrated until 1475.[8]

Mr. Philip Chatwin has suggested that Thomas Kerver was the mason in charge,[9] but there is no documentary evidence to support this. Judging from the renown of the other artisans employed on the chapel, such as John Massyngham and John Prudde,[10] and the unique design of the chapel, most likely a well-known mason-designer would have been employed. Alternatively, Thomas Kerver may have been in charge of the daily operations on the site, with another mason responsible for the design of the chapel.

General Description:

This chantry chapel is located off the north side of the main chapel and is separated from it by a screen. It contained an altar of unknown dedication.[11] The vaulting springs from moulded capitals and shafts and is composed of ten compartments. The basic vaulting module is square. The vaulting is characterized by rows of pendants, each of which drops down from a traceried wheel. The subpanels are trefoil cusped. The panels were originally painted blue.[12]

Technical Description:

Irregular curves, which approach four-centered curves, are employed. The vaulting is completely constructed of jointed masonry.

1. P.R.O., *Calendar of the Patent Rolls,* Henry VI, III (1436-41), 429.
2. For the will of Richard Beauchamp see Thomas Hearne, *Historia Vitae et Regni Richard II,* (Oxford, 1729), 240-9.
3. P.R.O., *Calendar of the Patent Rolls,* Henry VI, III (1436-41), 429.
4. *Ibid.,* 574.
5. These are the yearly accounts of Thomas Heggeford, Nicholas Rodye, and William Barkeswell, executors of the Earl. Printed in John Gough Nichols, *Description of Church of St. Mary Warwick and of the Beauchamp Chapel* (London: J. B. Nichols and Son, 1838), 33-36.
6. For the contracts see Nichols, *ibid.,* 29-33.
7. Computed from the accounts printed in Nichols, *op. cit.,* 33-36.
8. William Dugdale, edited and enlarged by William Thomas, *The Antiquities of Warwickshire* (2nd Edit.; 2 vols.; London: Osborn and Longman, 1730), I, 447.
9. Philip B. Chatwin, "Recent Discoveries in the Beauchamp Chapel, Warwick," *Birmingham*

Archaeological Society Trans., LIII (for 1928, pub. 1931), 146.

10. Nichols, *op. cit.*, 29-33; *Engl. Med. Archit.*, 182.

11. VCH, *Warwickshire*, VIII (1969), 524.

12. Chatwin, *op. cit.*, 149.

---

66   Wedmore   St. Mary Magdalene: Crossing Tower
           Somerset   4.10m x 4.17m

Historical Analysis:

No documentary evidence can be associated with the tower. According to Buckle, the tower had two changes of plan; the belfry story appears to be a later addition.[1] The use of cinquefoil cusping, ridge ribs, and foliate bosses (fragments only remain) at some rib intersections, suggest a date of circa 1500 for this vault. It apparently was inserted into an already extant tower.

General Description:

The vaulting springs from moulded corbels. Each vaulting quadrant is divided into four panels, each of which is cinquefoil cusped under a two-centered head. Remains of foliate bosses are present at some rib intersections. Ridge ribs are present in both directions.

Technical Description:

Two-centered curves are employed. The construction is of ribs and panels with jointed masonry for the traceried parts. The ridges in both directions are composed of only two stones.

1. E. Buckle, "Wedmore Church," *SANH Proc.*, XLVIII, pt. 1 (for 1902), 46.

---

31   Wells   Cathedral: Crossing Tower
           Somerset   8.84m x 8.88m

Historical Analysis:

No documentary evidence can be associated with the tower vaulting. Stylistic evidence suggests a date of circa 1500 (cf. the tower vault at Milton Abbas and the north transept vault at Sherborne Abbey). Based on the assumption that the construction of the tower vaulting coincided with the construction of the Cloister Lady Chapel, John Harvey has suggested that William Smyth was its designer. Smyth was master mason *(lathamus)* to Wells Cathedral in 1480.[1]

General Description:

The vaulting springs from moulded corbels. Each vaulting quadrant is composed of four major panels which are divided into two major and one minor tier. The uppermost tier is composed of panels which are trefoil cusped with sub-cusps under two-centered heads on the top and bottom. The panels of the lower tiers are only trefoil cusped. Therefore, the vaulting is richer at the top than at the bottom in terms of its decorative quality. The horizontal bounding ribs consist of straight segments. There are foliate bosses at the rib intersections. The vaulting quadrants intersect to form ridges which are articulated with ridge ribs. A star pattern is developed around the central bell opening.

Technical Description:

207
208 Two-centered curves are employed. The construction is of ribs and panels with
209 jointed masonry for the traceried parts. The ribs (12 cm wide) are rebated to receive the panels. The ridges are constructed of jointed and rib and panel masonry. The

beds are straight. The same material, Doulting stone, is used for all parts.

1. *Engl. Med. Arch.,* 246, citing the Wells Cathedral Fabric Roll for 1480-81.

<table>
<tr><td>Wells</td><td>Cathedral: Cloister Lady Chapel (Stillington's Chapel)</td></tr>
<tr><td>Somerset</td><td>*Nave and Choir:* 4.95m x 6.70m (bay size)[1]</td></tr>
<tr><td></td><td>*Crossing:* 6.70m x 6.70m</td></tr>
<tr><td></td><td>*Transepts:* 6.70m x 5.56m</td></tr>
</table>

Historical Analysis:

Hugh Sugar, treasurer of the cathedral and vicar general of the bishop, reported on 15 October 1476, during the only visit of Bishop Stillington to Wells,[2] that the old Lady Chapel by the cloister was *ruinosa et defectiva*.[3] Owing to the rebuilding of the Lady Chapel by the cloister, it was ordered on 28 January 1478 that the Consistory Court was in the future to be held in the Chapel of the Holy Rood at the end of the nave.[4] On 1 October 1487 collations were made to chantries at the altar of St. Nicholas in the new chapel.[5] On 22 September 1488, it was noted that the Consistory Court met in the Chapel of the Holy Rood for the last time on the Monday after St. Matthew's Day,[6] and the next Consistory Court was held in the new Cloister Lady Chapel on 25 October 1488.[7] Thus, the Cloister Lady Chapel was constructed between 1478 and 1488. Bishop Stillington, the donor of the chapel, was buried in it during May 1491.[8] The chapel was destroyed in 1552.[9]

General Description:

Fragments found during the nineteenth century indicate that the vaulting conoids were polygonal in shape. The horizontal bounding ribs, therefore, were composed of straight segments. In contrast, the central spandrel panel in each bay was articulated with a circular pendant. The areas left between the vaulting conoids and the central pendant were articulated with traceried panels. Trefoil cusping seems to have been employed throughout. Bosses, for the most part foliate, were located at the major rib intersections. One boss found during the excavation depicted an angel holding a shield.[10]

Technical Description:

The construction is of ribs and panels with jointed masonry for the traceried parts. The ribs were cut out of long stones and were rebated to receive the panels. The panels were made out of a light porous material, possibly tufa or artificial stone.[11] Almost every stone found during the excavation had rough axed joints.[12] The beds were straight. Thickness varied considerably from stone to stone as can be seen from the fragments preserved in the present cloister. The panel thickness was at least 15 cm. Rib and panel taken together reached a depth of at least 30 cm, some stones being in part considerably thicker (up to 50-60 cm).

1. For sizes and the report on the nineteenth century excavation see Edmund Buckle, "On the Lady Chapel by the Cloister of Wells," *SANH Proc.,* XL (1894), 13.
2. H. C. Maxwell-Lyte, edit., *The Registers of Robert Stillington and Richard Fox,* SRS, LII (1937), xv, 108-09.
3. Aelfred Watkin, edit., *Dean Cosyn and Wells Cathedral Miscellanea,* SRS, LVI (1941), 91-2.
4. *Ibid.,* 155.
5. Wells Cathedral Library, MS Rii.2, f.15. Cited in Royal Commission on Historical Manuscripts, *Calender of the Manuscripts of the Dean and Chapter of Wells,* II, (1914), 107.
6. Watkin, *op. cit.,* 155.
7. Watkin, *op. cit.,* 155.
8. Royal Commission on Historical Manuscripts, *op. cit.,* II, 107.
9. For full account of its destruction see Wells Cathedral Charter 773 cited in Royal Commission on Historical Manuscripts, *op. cit.,* II, 105, and printed in *SANH Proc.,* XL, pt. II (1894), 29-31.

10. Buckle, *op. cit.,* 18.
11. Buckle, *op. cit.,* 18. Unfortunately, none of these panels from the excavation are preserved.
12. Buckle, *op. cit.,* 21.

---

211   Wells   Cathedral: Sugar's Chantry Chapel
           Somerset   1.08m x 2.41m (vaulting only)

Historical Analysis:

Hugh Sugar (d. 1489) in his will dated 18 October 1488 and proved 5 May 1489 requested to be buried in the nave of Wells Cathedral or Glastonbury Abbey.[1] No provision was made in his will for the construction of this chapel. On 22 June 1489 Canon William Bocat, *nomine ac vice executorum Magistri Hugonis Sugar,* asked to pull down and take away a wooden chapel in the nave of the church (Wells) and to build it again; the dean and chapter granted permission.[2] This wooden chapel may have contained the altar of St. Edmund which is known to have been close to Sugar's chantry for two reasons: the tomb of Bishop Erghum is partly covered by Knight's Pulpit which is attached to Sugar's chapel,[3] and Bishop Erghum willed to be buried ". . . in the body of the church in the place where I have placed my stone, near the altar of St. Edmund."[4] It seems plausible that Sugar's chapel may have replaced the wooden chapel referred to by Bocat. If so, it was built shortly after his death in 1489.

General Description:

The vaulting forms a canopy over the altar. There are no horizontal bounding ribs which establish the limits for the vaulting conoids. Instead, the ridge ribs serve this function. Each vaulting conoid is composed of five major panels, the subpanels of which are trefoil cusped. Straight ribs, which are continuations of the vertical ribs, divide the top spandrel panel into subpanels which contain quatrefoils in circles and trefoil cusped daggers.

Technical Description:

Two-centered curves, which are slightly flattened, are employed. The construction is completely of jointed masonry. The top of the vaulting is flat when looked at from above.

1. F. W. Weaver, edit., Somerset Medieval Wills, 1383-1500, SRS, XVI, (1901), 275.
2. Herbert Edward Reynolds, *Wells Cathedral: Its Foundation, Constitutional History and Statues* (Leeds: M'Corquodale and Co. Ltd., 1881), 175.
3. Arthur B. Connor, "Monumental Brasses in Somerset," *SANH Proc.,* LXXXIII (for 1936), 196.
4. F. W. Weaver, edit., *Somerset Medieval Wills, 1501-1530,* SRS, XIX, (1903), 294-7.

Westminster   Abbey: Henry VII's Chapel
Middlesex   *Nave:* Four bays, each 4.26m x 10.58m
                         Side Aisles: Four bays, each 3.50m square
                         Eastern Chapels: Each 3.30m x 4.06m

Historical Analysis:

At least four papal bulls, 1494-98, indicated Henry VII's intention to be buried in St. George's Chapel, Windsor.[1] An indenture, dated 28 July 1498, between the king and the abbot of Westminster mentions Henry VII's intention to alter his place of burial, along with that of Henry VI, to Westminster and to rebuild the Lady Chapel there.[2] Numerous papal bulls and other indentures, which sorted out the financial and other arrangements for the endowment and establishment of chantries, etc., followed.[3] Therefore, the new Lady Chapel at Westminster was conceived to be a vast chantry chapel. About 1502 work began on the new chapel by pulling down the old one built by Henry III, and razing a nearby tavern called the White Rose.[4] According to John Stowe, the foundation stone was laid on 24 January 1503 (18 Henry VII).[5] The building accounts are not known to survive.[6]

Entries in the chamber accounts for the years 1502 to 1509 indicate that at least £14,856 was spent on the construction of the chapel.[7] Just before his death Henry VII turned over an additional £5,000 for completion of the project.[8]

In his will Henry VII mentioned that the ". . . Chapell be desked, and the windowes of our said Chapell be glased, with stores, ymagies, armes, bagies and cognoisants, as is by us redily divised, and in picture delivered to the Priour of Sainct Bartilmews besids Smythfeld, maistre of the works of our said Chapell."[9] He goes on to instruct ". . . that the walles, doores, windows, archies and vaults, and ymagies of the same our Chapell, within and without, be painted, garnished and adorned, with our armes, bagies, cognoisants, and other convenient painteng, as in goodly and riche maner as suche a work requireth, and as to a Kings werk apperteigneth."[10] Since Henry VII left instructions for the fitting and decoration of the chapel and the greater part of the money for its construction had already been spent before his death, it seems likely that the vaulting was structurally complete by 1509.

W. R. Lethaby, writing in 1906 and again in 1925, attributed the design of the chapel to Robert Vertue.[11] More recently, Webb and Harvey have suggested that the vaulting was designed by William Vertue, circa 1510.[12] Robert Vertue was the first named in a list of the king's three masons who gave an estimate for a proposed tomb for Henry VII in 1506,[13] and he was known to be working at the Tower of London in 1501-02[14] and at Greenwich at least from October 1499 to October 1503[15] when Henry VII's Chapel was already under construction. Furthermore, William and Robert Vertue were consulted together for the building of Bath Abbey.[16] However, there is no known documentary evidence that connects either Robert or William Vertue to the actual design or construction of Henry VII's Chapel or to any part of it–Robert Vertue only gave an estimate for the tomb which was designed by someone else.[17] Therefore, the attribution of Henry VII's Chapel to the Vertues is conjectural.[18]

General Description:[19]

The nave of the chapel consists of four rectangular bays. The east end is formed from five sides of a rectangular octagon. There are five radiating eastern chapels. The openwork main vaulting ribs of the apse, which spring from moulded capitals and shafts, are cusped and feathered and terminate in panelled pendants. In the center of the vault is another panelled pendant. Surrounding this central pendant are cusped panels which enclose four portcullises, two fleur-de-lis, and two roses. The side pendants are articulated with a horizontal band of bratticing. The vaulting of the nave follows the same basic pattern as that of the apse. A panelled tunnel vault separates the nave from the apse.

The side aisle fan vaults spring from moulded capitals and shafts. Each vaulting conoid is divided into four panels, each of which develops complex subpanels. The central spandrel panel is articulated with a pendant. In the areas left between the central pendant and the vaulting conoids are placed two portcullises, a rose, and a fleur-de-lis.

The eastern chapels, being rectangular in plan, have vaulting conoids which intersect in one direction and just meet in the other. The panels of the vaulting conoids develop complex subpanels. The central spandrel panel is flat and is articulated with a large circle which encloses eight subcusped quatrefoils in circles. At the center of this large circle is a lozenge-shaped panel which contains a portcullis.

215

Technical Description:

215
216
217
Two and four-centered curves are employed in the nave and apse. The large transverse arches of the nave support the main pendants along the sides, for the bottom stone of each pendant also functions as one of the voussoirs of the transverse arch. The jointed stone courses of each pendant are built upon this stone and from this point upwards run independently beneath the transverse arch. Consequently, almost the total load is transmitted to the transverse arch at this point, which in turn carries it to the abutment system (walls, piers, flying buttresses). The additional rib which runs from the main transverse arch (it is almost at right angles to it) to the wall prevents the transverse arch from buckling. The vaulting conoids of

218
the side pendants function as shell structures. The central pendant in each bay func-

219
tions as a keystone for this vaulting. The main radial ribs of the apse rise up and through the vault and run along the top of it to help support the central pendant. The vaulting pockets of both nave and apse are empty. The average panel thickness is 10 cm. Panel with attached rib reaches a depth of 27 cm. The beds for the most part are concave. A somewhat standardized jointing system is employed.

220
The fan vaults of the nave side aisles have intersecting diagonal arches which run along the top of the vaulting conoids. The keystone of these arches drops down to form the pendant. However, the vaulting conoids function independently as shell structures and are constructed of jointed masonry. It is only in the area of the pendant that the two structural systems work together. Four-centered curves are employed. The vaulting pockets are empty. The beds are concave.

The fan vaults of the eastern chapels are completely of jointed masonry. Four-centered curves are employed. The vaulting pockets are empty.

1. T. Rymer, *Foedera,* XII, 565, 591, 644, 672.
2. Indenture between the king and abbot of Westminster respecting the removal of the body of King Henry VI from Windsor, and its burial in the abbey of Westminster, and the expenses to be incurred thereby: ". . . the said King begon to make and bilde of new the Chapell of Our Lady within the Collegiat Church of Wyndsore, intending to have translated the body of his said uncle into the same, and nigh unto him within the said Chapell to have be buried himself; *sed, ita sentiente regio concilo,* hath fynally determyned to convey and bring the said holy body from the said Collegiat Church of Wyndsore to the said monastery of Westminster, and there to be commytted to perpetuall sepulture in the Chapell of Our Lady within the church of said Monastery, the which Chapell oure said souverain Lord entendeth to make and bilde of new and in the same, not farre from be said uncle, to be buried himself." Noted in *Royal Commission on Historical Manuscripts, 4th Report* (1874), pt. I, 179, col. I, no. 7b, printed in P. Grosjean, edit., *Henrici VI Angliae Regis Miracula Postuma,* Subsidia Hagiographia, XXII, 1935, 200*-201.*
3. Bull, Pope Alexander VI (1499) see T. Rymer, *Foedera,* XII, 739. Indulgence from Pope Alexander VI to those who should visit or of their goods contribute to the Chapel see Oxford, Corpus Christi College Library, Cantab. MS 170, f.56. For Papal Bulls of Julius II (1504) see T. Rymer, *Foedera,* XIII, 97, 100, 102. For Indentures between the King and Convent of Westminister see BM MS Harl. 1498 and P.R.O., *Calendar of the Close Rolls,* Henry VII, vol. II (1500-09), 138-57.
4. John Stoew, *The Survey of London* (London: Elizabeth Pvrslow, 1633), 499.
5. *Ibid.,* the inscription reads "Illustrisimus Henricus Septimus, rex Angliae et Franciae, et dominus Hiberniae, posuit hanc petram, in honore beatae virginis Mariae XXIIII die Januarij anno Domini MCCCCCII et anno dicti regio Henrici septimi, decimo octavo."
6. *Engl. Med. Archit.,* 233.
7. Philips MS 4104 (1502-5) and P.R.O. E.36/214 (1505-9). Cited in H. M. Colvin, et. al., *History of the King's Works,* III, pt. 1 (1975), 213.
8. For details see Colvin, *ibid.,* 213n.2.
9. Thomas Astle, *The Will of King Henry VII* (London, 1775).
10. *Ibid.*
11. W. R. Lethaby, *Westminster Abbey and the King's Craftsmen* (London: Duckworth and Co., 1906), 226; W. R. Lethaby, *Westminster Abbey Re-Examined* (London: Duckworth and Co., 1925), 163-6.
12. G. Webb, *Architecture in Britain* (2nd edit., Harmondsworth, 1965), 200, and John Harvey, *The*

Mediaeval Architect (London: Wayland Publishers, 1972), 164.

13. *L & P Henry VIII,* I, 142.
14. BM ADD.MS 7099, ff. 70, 71, 77b, from Philips MS 4104.
15. *Ibid.,* f. 77b, 177; P.R.O. E101/415/3, ff. 13r, 20r, 30r, 38, 45, 60, 63r, 101, and E101/517/4.
    For Greenwich see P. Dixon, *Excavations at Greenwich Palace, 1970-71* (1972).
16. ". . . Robt and William Vertu have been here . . ." Westminster Abbey Muniment 16,040, printed in J. Armitage Robinson, "Correspondence of Bishop Oliver King and Sir Reginald Bray," *SANH Proc.,* LX, pt. II (for 1914), 4.
17. ". . . after the manner of the moulding of the patrone that Master Pageny got made . . ." *L & P Henry VIII,* I, 142.
18. For further discussion of this problem see Colvin, *op. cit.,* 214 and W. Leedy, "The Design of the Vaulting of Henry VII's Chapel, Westminster: A Reappraisal," *Architectural History,* XVIII, (1975), 5-11.
19. See also J. P. Neale and E. W. Brayley, *History of the Abbey Church of Westminster* (1818), L.N. Cottingham, *Plans, Elevations, Sections and Details of Henry VII's Chapel, Westminster,* 2 vols. (1822-29), J. Britton, *The Architectural Antiquities of Great Britain,* II (1835), and RCHM, *London,* I (1924).

Westminster	Abbey: Jesus Chapel
Middlesex	4.00m square (approximately)

Historical Analysis:

It was built as a chantry chapel by Abbot Islip (d. 1532).[1] The sub-sacrist noted the provision of pound tapers to be burned in the chapel at Christmas in 1523.[2] Payments are recorded in the *Novum Opus* rolls from 1525 to 1530 for the decoration of the chapel. In 1525-26 Thomas Nele, "hardehewer," was paid 13s.4d. for work in the Jesus Chapel.[3] The decoration of the chapel must have been complete by 1530 when Master Humphrey received the last installment of the money owing him for ". . . payntyng uppon the wall in IhS chappell."[4] Therefore, it seems likely that the basic structure of the chapel was complete or nearly so by the end of 1523 and the decoration of it was completed later, possibly by 1530.

General Description:

It was a two story chapel. The lower story is covered with a combination lierne and fan vault. The central spandrel panel is articulated with an eight point star, the cells of which are filled in with carved devices.[5] Most of the panels are cusped. The horizontal bounding ribs are composed of straight segments.

Technical Description:

Four-centered curves are employed. The construction is completely of jointed masonry. The beds are straight.

---

1. Jocelyn Perkins, *Westminster Abbey: Its Worship and Ornaments,* 3 vols., Alcuin Club Collections No. XXXVII (1952), III, 8-9.
2. H. F. Westlake, *Westminster Abbey, The Last Days of the Monastery* (London: Philip Allan and Co., 1921), 109.
3. R. B. Rackham, "The Nave of Westminster Abbey," *British Academy Proc.,* IV (1909-10), 81.
4. Westlake, *op. cit.,* 109.
5. For complete description see RCHM, London, I (1924), 75.

Westminster	St. Stephen's Cloister
Middlesex	*North and South Walks:* Five bays, each 3.05 square
	East and West Walks: Six bays, each 3.12m x 3.28m
	Chapel: 5.03m x 3.35m

Historical Analysis:

The cloisters were built by Dean John Chambers, circa 1526 to 1529.[1] The cost was 11,000 marks.[2] The design of the cloisters has been attributed to William Vertue and their completion to Henry Redman.[3] This hypothesis is based on the assumption that Henry VIII funded the cloister, and if so, the £18.5s.0d. that was paid to Vertue from the royal purse in 1526 might have been his fee for this work,[4] but no known document connects this work with either Vertue or Redman.

General Description:

The cloister is rectangular in plan.[5] The corner bays are vaulted with complex lierne vaults, each of which develops a complex starlike pattern. The fan vaults of the north and south walks differ from those of the east and west walks. Those of the north and south walks have an extra horizontal rib which is articulated with bratticing placed within the panels; their central spandrel panels differ; and they are articulated with a large circle in which quatrefoils in circles and a large central boss are placed. The fan vaults in the east and west walks do not have this large enclosing circle, and their central bosses are relatively smaller. The vaulting in all the walks springs from triple grouped shafts with moulded capitals and bases. However, the vaulting in the chapel, which is located off the west walk, springs from single shafts with moulded capitals and bases. The fact that the chapel vaulting has bratticing placed in the panels like the vaulting of the north and south walks suggests that they were vaulted about the same time. Also, the mouldings and other details, such as the treatment of the exterior buttresses of the chapel, differ from those in the west walk, and the chapel is poorly integrated into the west walk. This evidence suggests the chapel was planned after the west walk was laid out. While the differences in vaulting between the north and south and east and west walks may be accounted for by the proportions of the different bays (rectangular versus square), it is more plausible to suggest that the east and west walks were vaulted first, followed by the north and south walks and the chapel.

Technical Description:

Four-centered curves are employed throughout the cloister walks, while two-centered and four-centered curves are employed in the chapel. All the vaults are completely constructed of jointed masonry.

1. RCHM, *London*, II (1925), 123.
2. *Monasticon*, VI, 1349.
3. *Engl. Med. Archit.*, 220, 273.
4. *L & P Hen. VIII*, IV, 869.
5. See the plans published in E. W. Brayley and John Britton, *The History of the Ancient Palace and Late Houses of Parliament at Westminster* (London: John Weale, 1836), pls. XVII-XXIII.

70   Weston Zoyland   St. Mary's: West Tower
          Somerset   4.01m x 4.01m

Historical Analysis:

No documentary evidence can be associated with this tower. The vaulting is nearly identical in size, and formal and technical characteristics to the vaulting of the west tower of St. Mary's, North Petherton (Somerset), which on circumstantial evidence can be dated to the first quarter of the sixteenth century. Therefore, this fan vault can be dated to the first quarter of the sixteenth century.

General Description:

The vaulting springs from moulded capitals and shafts. Each vaulting conoid is divided into four major panels, the subpanels of which are trefoil cusped under two-centered heads. The top horizontal bounding rib is composed of circular segments. In the areas left between the vaulting conoids and the central bell opening are placed quatrefoils in circles.

Technical Description:

Four-centered curves are employed. The construction is of ribs and panels with jointed masonry for the traceried parts. In the second stone course out from the walls, a stone joint is present along the centerline of the ridges.

---

25   Winchester   Cathedral: Cardinal Beaufort's Chapel
           Hampshire   3.35m (north-south) (approximately)

Historical Analysis:

In his will, Cardinal Henry Beaufort (d. 1447) desired to be buried in the cathedral "in eo videl't loco quem pro sepultura mea elegi & assignavi," and provided for the establishment of a chantry in his chapel.[1] The second volume of Beaufort's register does not survive, and there is no mention in any of the medieval accounts of Beaufort's Chapel. It has been suggested that this chapel was not completed until after his death in 1447.[2] The chapel was heavily restored in 1819.[3]

General Description:

The chapel is vaulted with two end bays and a larger and higher central bay. Each end bay is divided into two square vaulting modules, the vaulting quadrants of which are composed of five trefoil cusped panels. Along the horizontal bounding rib is a row of quatrefoils in circles. The central spandrel is panelled and has ridge ribs in both directions. Each vaulting quadrant of the center bay is composed of seven panels, the subpanels of which are trefoil cusped. The uppermost level of the panels is articulated with a row of quatrefoils in circles which have foliate bosses at their centers. In the center of the bay is a demi-angel holding the shield of arms of Cardinal Beaufort.[4]

Technical Description:

Four-centered curves are employed. The construction is completely of jointed masonry. The chapel itself up to the springing of the canopy is of Purbeck marble with leaded joints.[5] The canopy is of different stone.

---

1. J. Nichols, *A Collection of All The Wills, Now Known to Be Extant of the Kings and Queens of England, etc. . . .* , (London: J. Nichols, 1780), 321.
2. R. N. Quink, "The Tomb of Cardinal Beaufort," *Winchester Cathedral Record,* No. 23 (1954), 9.
3. Quink, *ibid.,* 7.
4. *Vetusta Monumenta,* II (1789), 1.
5. VCH, *Hampshire and the Isle of Wight,* V, 55.

---

26   Winchester   Cathedral: Bishop Waynflete's Chapel
           Hampshire   One bay, 2.90m x 2.67m
                               Two bays, each 1.45m x 2.67m

Historical Analysis:

This chapel was built as a chantry chapel dedicated to St. Mary Magdalene by Bishop William Waynflete (d. 1486). It was most likely completed in his lifetime, as he willed to be buried ". . . in quadam capella beate Marie Magdalene in parte orientali ejusdem ecclesie mee in qua tumulus preparatus est."[1]

General Description:

The chapel is vaulted in two end bays and a larger and higher center bay. In the end bays, fan vault details are applied to a deformed tunnel vault. In the center of each end vault is a traceried wheel with a gilt foliate boss at its center. The center vaulting compartment is domical in form. A large boss located at its center, depicts a demi-angel holding a shield of the bishop's arms.[2] The tracery pattern around the boss is starlike; the pattern is emphasized by the use of blue and gold paint.

Technical Description:

Irregular four-centered curves are employed, so the vaults do not develop regular geometric forms. The construction is completely of jointed masonry.

1. From his will dated in 1486, printed in Richard Chandler, *The Life of William Waynflete* (London: Printed for White and Cochrane, 1811), 379-80.
2. W. H. St. John Hope, "Report on Bishop Waynflete's Chapel in Winchester Cathedral" (22 January 1898, Copy in Tract 237,* Society of Antiquaries, London), 5-6.

26	Winchester	College Chapel
	Hampshire	9.15m (north-south span)

Historical Analysis:

Winchester College was founded in 1382 by William of Wykeham and was conceived to be a chantry to pray for the founder's soul.[1] Construction started in 1387 and continued until shortly after 1400.[2] William Wynford was master mason, and the designer of the wooden vault was most likely Hugh Herland.[3]

General Description:

It is vaulted in six rectangular bays. The wooden vault springs from moulded and sculptured stone corbels. The vault is unique in the way the rectangular bays and the central spandrel panels are treated. Although the ribs are of the same curvature, they are placed at variable angles to each other. The vaulting conoids are terminated at the central spandrel level by an oblique rather than a horizontal section. Therefore, the outline of the vaulting conoids is not the usual semicircle that is obtained by cutting a conoid horizontally, but is an oval curve. Each vaulting quadrant is composed of four cinquefoil cusped panels. The central spandrel panel is an octagon which is composed of eight cinquefoil cusped panels. There are bosses at the rib intersections. The original color scheme was scarlet for the mouldings set against a white ground.[4]

Technical Description:

Two-centered curves are employed. The vault is constructed of oak.[5]

1. Arthur F. Leach, *A History of Winchester College* (London: Duckworth & Co., 1899), 135.
2. W. F. Oakeshott and John H. Harvey, *Winchester College* (1954), 3.
3. *Engl. Med. Archit.,* 127-131; John H. Harvey, "The King's Chief Carpenters," *British Archaeological Association Journal,* 3rd Series, XI (1948), 25.
4. John H. Harvey, "Winchester College," *British Archaeological Association Journal,* 3rd Series, XXVIII (1965), 118-19, 119 n.3.
5. *Ibid.,* 118-19.

	Windsor	St. George's Chapel
	Berkshire	*Choir Aisle Bays:* 3.64m x 3.94m
		Nave Aisle Bays (excepting westernmost):
		3.70m x 3.80m
		Crossing: 8.22m x 11.02m
		Polygonal Chantry Chapels: 4.13m (east-west)

Historical Analysis:

Actual construction of the chapel began in 1476-77,[1] but planning for it goes back to 1472-73.[2] The chapel was conceived by Edward IV (d. 1483) to be a vast chantry chapel.[3] In his will, dated 20 June 1475, he requested burial in St. George's and gave instructions for his tomb: ". . . we wol that overe the same sepulture ther bee made a vawte of convenient height as the place wil suffre it, and that upon the said vawte ther bee a Chapell or closet with an Autre convenient and a Tombe to be made and selt there . . ."[4] In 1483-84 the body of Henry VI, by order of Richard III, was moved from Chertsey Abbey to Windsor.[5] The tomb of Henry VI was located on the south side of the choir in the second bay.[6] It was the original intention of Henry VII to be buried in St. George's; for this project he procured no fewer than four papal bulls of indulgence between 1494 and 1498, and payments are recorded for the construction of a tomb for him there.[7] In 1517 at the Chapter of the Order of the Garter, Henry VIII announced Windsor to be his intended burial place.[8]

In 1480 a payment of £66.13s.4d. was recorded for Teynton stone called "vow-tyngstone."[9] Hope proposed that the stone was for the eastern bays of the choir aisles.[10] And he considered that the first part of the vaulting to be finished, circa 1480, was the north choir aisle westward of Edward IV's chantry; because he thought the boss of the third bay bore the arms of Thomas FitzAlan as Lord Maltravers.[11] Cave and London disagree with this identification and have proposed that the arms belonged to Thomas, the 10th Earl of Arundel, thus suggesting a date of after 1487 for this boss.[12] The heraldry on the vaulting in the fourth bay of the north choir aisle, which displays the arms of William Lord Hastings (d. 1483), may be post-humous like the Bray heraldry in the nave.[13] Hope cited evidence to suggest this; for in the account of the treasurer of the college for 1498-99 are payments recorded to ". . . Johanni Freman carpentario pro factura unius Schaffold pro ly peynting Armorum domini de Hastynges per diem vjd.: Et solut. Nicholao Deryk pro ly peyn-ting Armorum domini de Hastynges ex mandato magistri decani xiijs., iijd.," which might refer to the decoration of this boss and thereby give a clue to its exact date.[14] The bosses of the fifth, sixth, and seventh bays bear the arms of St. George, etc.[15] and cannot be used for dating. The evidence, although not conclusive, indicates that the bays west of Edward IV's chantry in the north choir aisle were vaulted after 1487 and probably close to 1500.

7   The first two bays of the north choir aisle are occupied by the Chantry Chapel of Edward IV. John Harvey proposed that it was an afterthought, as the exterior windows look as if they have been altered and that the central spandrel panels of the vaults are the same as those employed in the nave aisle vaults.[16] However, Edward IV indicated his desire for the chantry and described it in his will of 1475, which was written when actual construction was just commencing; therefore, it seems likely that it was planned from the start. Furthermore, the central spandrel panels of the
8   vaulting differ from those in the nave aisle vaults. First, while both are articulated with quatrefoils in circles, those in the nave are set in panels, which is not the case in the vaulting of Edward VI's chantry. Second, they both employ different stone jointing patterns. Both formal and technical archaeological evidence, therefore, points to two different construction periods–one for the Chantry Chapel of Edward IV, the other for the nave aisle vaults.

In 1478 Sixtus IV authorized the removal of John Shorne's bones to Windsor.[17] The making of the enclosure for Shorne's Chapel appears in the accounts for 1480-
9   81.[18] The boss in the south bay of the ambulatory, which is directly in front of Shorne's Chapel, depicts Edward IV and Bishop Beauchamp, who was surveyor of St. George's, kneeling on either side of a tall Celtic cross.[19] It seems plausible, there-fore, that the vaulting of Shorne's Chapel and the bay immediately in front of it were built circa 1480. Since the vaulting of the south bay of the ambulatory and

the vaulting of Edward IV's chantry display the same formal and technical characteristics, they may have been built at the same time. If so, the stone referred to in the accounts of 1480-81 as "vowtyngstone" might have been intended for the vaulting of Edward IV's chantry, the ambulatory, and Shorne's Chapel.[20] These vaults may have been the first to have been completed, instead of–as has been previously suggested by Hope[21] and later by Harvey[22]–the western bays of the north choir aisle.

Heraldic evidence indicates that the south choir aisle was vaulted *temp*. Henry VII (1485-1509).[23] It seems likely that it would have been finished by 1506 when the contract was let for the main choir vault.[24]

Major construction did not begin on the nave until after 1503 and may have been completed by 1511.[25] Therefore, the nave aisle vaults should be dated circa 1505.

A chantry was founded in 1506 in the Beaufort Chapel[26] and another in the
230 Urswick Chapel in 1507.[27] These chapels are most likely contemporaneous and should be dated 1506.

231 In the middle of the fan vault of the crossing is a boss which depicts the arms of Henry VIII within a garter. A scroll across the base of the boss is inscribed "Anno Regis XX."[28] This dates the vault to 1528. The actual idea to vault the crossing goes back at least to 1523 when ". . . Vertu fremason . . ." is mentioned in connection with it.[29] It seems likely that William Vertue may have been the designer or builder of the vault.[30] However, construction of the vault commenced after 1526 since the arms of Sir Henry Gildeford, who was elected Knight of the Garter in that year, are on the vault.[31]

Henry Janyns was master mason circa 1475-83.[32] The fan vaults of the ambulatory, the Chantry Chapel of Edward IV, and John Shorne's Chapel should be attributed to him. The choir aisle fan vaults, which if built circa 1500 as has been suggested, may have been constructed to an already envisioned design of Henry Janyns by Robert Janyns or Richard Nymes who were the masons employed at Windsor at that time.[33] The nave aisle fan vaults and the fan vaults of the Beaufort and Urswick chapels are heavily dependent in both design and conception to the vaults built in St. George's circa 1480. It seems possible that Robert Janyns was following the basic plan–with minor variations–set circa 1475 for the chapel.[34] In contrast, the main vaults of the nave and choir are poorly integrated into the shell and definitely show the hand of a different and less articulate designer, who was perhaps William Vertue.[35] The fan vaults of circa 1480 are conceived of as shells, while the nave and choir vaults are conceived of as frames (ribs) with shells between them (panels).

General Description:
227 Chantry Chapel of Edward IV and the North and South Bays of the Ambulatory: The vaulting springs from moulded capitals and shafts. Each vaulting quadrant is composed of four main panels, the subpanels of which are trefoil cusped. The horizontal bounding ribs are composed of circular segments. The central spandrel panel is articulated with a circle which contains eight quatrefoils in circles. The areas left between the large central circle and the vaulting conoids are articulated with quatrefoils in circles.

40 North and South Choir Aisles: The vaulting springs from moulded capitals and shafts. Each vaulting quadrant is composed of four main panels, the subpanels of which are cinquefoil cusped. The horizontal bounding ribs are composed of circular segments. The central spandrel panel is articulated with an octagon which contains a central boss surrounded by eight quatrefoils in circles that are enclosed in panels. A foliate boss is at the center of each quatrefoil within the octagon. The areas left between the octagon and the vaulting conoids are articulated with cinquefoil cusped daggers.

28   Nave Aisle Vaults: The vaulting springs from moulded capitals and shafts. Each vaulting quadrant is composed of four main panels, the subpanels of which are trefoil cusped. The horizontal bounding ribs are composed of circular segments. The central spandrel panel is articulated with a large circle which contains a central boss surrounded by eight quatrefoils in circles that are enclosed in panels. A boss is at the center of each quatrefoil within the large central circle. The areas left between the central circle and the vaulting conoids are articulated with cinquefoil cusped daggers, excepting in the westernmost bay of each aisle where in the north-south direction quatrefoils in circles are employed because of the greater east-west dimension of that bay.

43   Polygonal Chantry Chapels: The plan of each utilizes five sides of an octagon. The chapels are vaulted by using conoids in the angles which in turn support a rather flat saucer dome. In the central part of the vault a starlike pattern is developed which is surrounded by a ring of quatrefoils in circles. The panels and subpanels are cusped. The conoids which support this central area are articulated with trefoil cusped panels.

31   Crossing Tower: The vaulting springs from moulded capitals and shafts. Each vaulting conoid is composed of seven panels and is divided vertically into two main tiers by a horizontal band of bratticing. Directly below this band is a row of subcusped quatrefoils in circles, only some of which contain heraldic bosses, and above it is a row of diamond-shaped cusped and subcusped panels which contain heraldic bosses. The central spandrel panel is articulated with a large circle with a boss at its center, which is surrounded by ten cinquefoil cusped panels. In the areas left between the vaulting conoids and the large central circles are placed daggers, each of which is divided into two subpanels which are cinquefoil cusped.

Technical Description:

Chantry Chapel of Edward IV and the North and South Bays of the Ambulatory: Four-centered curves are employed. The construction is completely of jointed masonry. The central boss, which is one circular stone, is surrounded by eight wedged-shaped stones, the centerlines of which are placed so as to line up with the central axes and diagonals of the vaulting module.

32
33   North and South Choir Aisles: Four-centered curves are employed. The construction is completely of jointed masonry. The central boss, which is one stone, is surrounded by eight wedged-shaped stones, the joints of which fall on the central axes and diagonals of the vaulting module. The panel thickness is 7½ cm. The vaulting pockets are empty. The foundations of the north choir aisle go down to chalk, while those of the south choir aisle from the west side of John Shorne's Chapel to the south transept rested on a bed of clay, varying in thickness from 30 to 60 cm, which had been left between the footings and the chalk below.[36] This suggests that the whole of the north choir aisle might have been laid out during the period 1475-83, and the south choir aisle from Shorne's Chapel to the south transept belongs, as has been suggested earlier, to the period circa 1500.

34
35   Nave Aisle Vaults: Four-centered curves are employed. The construction is completely of jointed masonry. The central boss, which is one circular stone, is surrounded by eight separate stones, the joints of which fall on the central axes and diagonals of the vaulting module. The vaulting pockets are empty. The bosses were not originally painted.[37]

36
37
38   Polygonal Chantry Chapels: The wall ribs are two-centered. The construction is completely of jointed masonry. The vaulting pockets are empty.
39
40   Crossing Tower: Four-centered curves are employed. The construction is of

ribs and panels with jointed masonry employed for the traceried parts. The panel thickness is 10 cm. There is rubble fill in the vaulting pockets. The vault was rebuilt by Brakspear in the 1920s.[38]

1. W. H. St. John Hope, *Windsor Castle* (2 vols.; London: Country Life, 1913), II, 375.
2. *Ibid.,* II, 377.
3. Maurice Bond, "Burial Places of the English Monarchs," *RSG,* 1970, 33.
4. Hope, *op. cit.,* II, 376, 419. Hope suggests the vaulting of Edward IV's Chantry is *temp.* Henry VII.
5. Hope, *op. cit.,* II, 383.
6. Bond, *op. cit.,* 34.
7. T. Rymer, *Foedera,* XII, 565, 591, 644, 672. For tomb payments see BM ADD MS 7099 (transcriptions from Philips MS 4104), ff. 70, 71, 72, 73, 79. The last entry of 20 January 18 Henry VII (1503-4) is a payment to ". . . Mast. Estfeld for conveying the King's Tombe from Windsor to Westminster."
8. Bond, *op. cit.,* 35.
9. Hope, *op. cit.,* II, 401.
10. Hope, *op. cit.,* II, 382.
11. Hope, *op. cit.,* II, 384.
12. C. J. P. Cave and H. Stanford London, "The Roof-bosses in St. George's Chapel Windsor," *Archaeologia,* XCV (1953), 107.
13. Hope, *op. cit.,* II, 384; Cave and London, *op. cit.,* 107. The foundation of Hasting's Chantry took place twenty years after his death, see Hope, *op. cit.,* II, 420, although the chapel may have been constructed earlier, see Hope, *op. cit.,* II, 385.
14. Hope, *op. cit.,* II, 486 n.45.
15. For description see Hope, *op. cit.,* II, 420.
16. John Harvey, "The Architects of St. George's Chapel, Part II, The Fifteenth and Sixteenth Centuries," *RSG,* 1962, 95.
17. Hope, *op. cit.,* II, 411, 466 n.16.
18. Hope, *op. cit.,* II, 411.
19. Hope, *op. cit.,* II, 410.
20. Hope, *op. cit.,* II, 382, recognizes that these vaults are early.
21. Hope, *op. cit.,* II, 384.
22. Harvey, *op. cit.,* 94.
23. For complete discussion of the iconographic problem see Hope, *op. cit.,* II, 412, and Cave and London, *op. cit.,* 110.
24. Harvey, *op. cit.,* 94.
25. Harvey, *op. cit.,* 90.
26. Hope, *op. cit.,* II, 457.
27. Hope, *op. cit.,* II, 385.
28. Hope, *op. cit.,* II, 463.
29. Hope, *op. cit.,* II, 462.
30. Hope, *op. cit.,* II, 463.
31. Cave and London, *op. cit.,* 118.
32. Hope, *op. cit.,* II, 378, 379.
33. BM ADD MS 7099, ff.55, 64. Richard Nymes and Robert Janyns worked on Henry VII's Tower at Windsor, see Hope, *op. cit.,* II, 586, and P.R.O., E101/415/3, ff. 23r, 28r.
34. The major design change was to lengthen the nave by the addition of one bay to the west which is about 60 cm wider than the bays to the east, as evidenced by the foundations for a wall which are still in place under the present floor of the nave, see St. George's Windsor, Archives, MS IV B. 25, 43 (H. Brakspear's Report for 1927).
35. William Vertue on 5 June 1506 signed a contract for the construction of the choir vault. It has been suggested that he designed the west front, see Harvey, *op. cit.,* 88, 90.
36. St. George's Windsor, Archives, MS XVIII.59.2. Notes dealing with the Foundations of the South Side of the Choir by R. B. Robertson (1923), n.p.
37. St. George's Windsor, Archives, MS IV B.25, 63 (H. Brakspear's Report for 1930).
38. St. George's Windsor, Archives, MS IV B.25, 29 (H. Brakspear's Report for 1926).

Woodspring Priory   Crossing Tower
Somerset

Analysis:
The fan vault is a modern addition, for John Rutter in 1829 wrote: "the interior (of the tower) has been completely extracted, and the shell of the tower left even without a roof until the present proprietor had it leaded."[1]

1. John Rutter, *Delineations of the North Western Division of the County of Somerset* (London: Longman, Rees and Co., 1829), 61.

---

41   Wrington   All Saints: West Tower
Somerset   4.33m x 4.43m

Historical Analysis:
No documentary evidence can be associated with this tower. The exterior of the tower has an ornament known as Henry VII's label,[1] which might place its construction between the years 1485 and 1509. This dating seems probable when the vaulting is compared to the chancel aisle vaults of St. George's Chapel, Windsor, and Bishop Alcock's Chapel, Ely, which have panels that are similar in conception.

General Description:
The vaulting springs from moulded capitals and shafts. Each vaulting conoid is divided into four major panels which have four-centered heads. The subpanels are trefoil cusped. In the areas between the vaulting conoids and the central bell opening are placed quatrefoils in circles and uncusped daggers.

Technical Description:
Two-centered curves are employed. The construction is of ribs and panels with jointed masonry employed for the traceried parts. The material of construction is Downside stone,[2] which might have been quarried at Felton.[3]

1. "Walks and Excursions," *Bath Natural History and Antiquarian Field Club,* VIII (1897), 181.
2. Scarth, "Wrington: A Sketch of Parochial History," *SANH Proc.,* XXXIII, pt. 2 (1887), 14.
3. John Rutter, *Delineations of the North Division of the County of Somerset* (London: Longman, Rees and Co., 1829), 61.

Glossary

arch   A structure of wedge-shaped stones, usually curved in profile.

bay   A principal compartment, as marked off by some sort of architectural boundaries. Normally a square or rectangular area defined by opposite pairs of piers.

bed   (of a stone course) In masonry, the surface on which the stones are laid. In stone arches and vaults the beds are inclined at greater or lesser angles to the horizontal.

centering   The temporary supports on which an arch or vault is constructed. Usually of wood, but sometimes other materials were used, such as earth.

compressive stress   The stress resulting from the contraction, or pushing together of material.

conoid   The expanding masonry funnel whose shape is defined by ribs as they rise from their common springing and diverge in arcs.

dead load   The weight of the structure itself.

dowel   A peg used to unite two members, sometimes used to prevent lateral displacement.

extrados   The upper, usually convex, surface of an arch or vault.

flying buttress   An exposed arch which carries the thrust of the vaulting over the roof of the aisle to an external buttressing pier.

intrados   The inner, usually concave, surface of an arch or vault.

jointed masonry   A vault, or part of one, of solid masonry in which the stones are closely jointed, and for decorative reasons, the ribs and panels are merely carved out of the lower, inner, surface.

rib   An arch which visually divides a vault into compartments.

springer   The first stone in an arch or vault whose lower bed is horizontal and upper bed is inclined.

stress   Force per unit of area.

tas-de-charge   In vaulting, the lower courses of stone, whose beds are horizontal.

tensile stress   The stress resulting from the elongation of an elastic body. Tensile stress tends to crack or separate material.

thrust	A compressive structural action. More specifically, the action exerted by an arch on its supports.
242 vault	An arched covering, usually in brick or stone. *Lierne Vault:* A vault which has tertiary ribs, liernes, which do not spring from one of the main springers or from the central boss. Used to create mesh patterns. *Rib Vault:* A vault with diagonal ribs projecting along the groins. *Ridge Rib:* Rib along the longitudinal or transverse ridge of a vault. *Quadripartite Vault:* A bay of vaulting which is divided into four parts. *Tierceron Vault:* A vault which has secondary ribs, tiercerons, which issue from one of the main springers and lead to a place on the ridge rib.
voussoir	One of the wedge-shaped blocks that make up an arch.
web	The shell of a vault rather than the ribs.

List of Abbreviations

AJ	*Archaeological Journal*
BGAS	*Bristol and Gloucestershire Archaeological Society Transactions*
BM	British Museum, London
DNB	*Dictionary of National Biography*
Emden, *Cambridge*	Emden, A. B. *A Biographical Register of the University of Cambridge to 1500.* Cambridge, 1963.
Emden, *Oxford*	Emden, A. B. *A Biographical Register of the University of Oxford to A.D. 1500.* 3 vols. Oxford, 1957-1959.
Engl. Med. Archit.	Harvey, John, et al. *English Mediaeval Architects: A Biographical Dictionary Down to 1540.* London, 1954.
L & P Henry VIII	*Letters and Papers, Foreign and Domestic, of the Reign of Henry VIII.* London, 1862-1910.
Leland, *Itin.*	*The Itinerary of John Leland in or About the Years 1535-1543.* Edited by Lucy Toulmin Smith. 5 vols. 1907-1910.
Monasticon	Dugdale, W. *Monasticon Anglicanum.* Edited by J. Caley, H. Ellis, and B. Bandinel. 6 vols. in 8. London, 1817-1830.
Pevsner, *BE*	Pevsner, Nikolaus. *The Buildings of England.* Harmondsworth, 1951-.
P.R.O.	Great Britain, Public Records Office.
RCHM	Great Britain, Royal Commission on Historical Monuments.
RSG	*The Society of the Friends of St. George's and the Descendants of the Knights of the Garter. Reports.*
SANH Proc.	*Somerset Archaeological and Natural History Society. Proceedings.*
VCH	The Victoria History of the Counties of England.

Bibliographical Note

The bibliography for this study consists almost entirely of works devoted to individual monuments. These works can be quickly found by consulting the appropriate catalogue entry. Only articles on fan vaults are mentioned here. The greater part of Chapter 2 was published in my *The Art Bulletin* article cited below.

Robert Willis, "On the Construction of the Vaults of the Middle Ages," *Transactions of the Royal Institute of British Architects,* I (1842), 1-69. Recently reprinted in Robert Willis, *Architectural History of Some English Cathedrals,* (2 vols., Chicheley: Paul Minet, 1972-3), II, Appendix.

F. E. Howard, "Fan Vaults," *Archaeological Journal,* LXVIII (1911), 1-42.

Jacques Heyman, "Spires and Fan Vaults," *International Journal of Solids Structures,* III (1967), 243-57.

Walter C. Leedy, Jr., "The design of the vaulting of Henry VII's Chapel, Westminster: a reappraisal," *Architectural History,* XVIII (1975), 5-11.

Walter C. Leedy, Jr., "Wells Cathedral and Sherborne Abbey: Workshop Connections in the Late Fifteenth Century," *Gesta,* XVI/1 (1977), 39-44.

Walter C. Leedy, Jr., "The Origins of Fan Vaulting," *The Art Bulletin,* LX, nr. 2 (1978), 207-13.

Index